Kay Kuzma · Brenda Walsh

BETWE
HELL
»»»»»»» and «««««««
HIGH WATER
[God Was There]

SURVIVAL STORIES FROM
HURRICANE KATRINA

Pacific Press® Publishing Association
Nampa, Idaho
Oshawa, Ontario, Canada
www.pacificpress.com

3ABN
3ABN BOOKS

P.O. Box 220, West Frankfort, Illinois
www.3ABN.org

Cover design by Mark Bond
Cover photo: iStockphoto.com
Inside photos by Sonya Reaves, Brenda Walsh, Kevin Komarniski, and Keli Forbeck.

Copyright © 2006 by
Kay Kuzma and Brenda Walsh

Printed in the United States of America by
Pacific Press® Publishing Association
All rights reserved

In a few cases, names have been changed to protect the privacy of individuals.

Library of Congress Cataloging-in-Publication Data

Kuzma, Kay.
Between hell and high water: survival stories from Hurricane Katrina—God was there/
Kay Kuzma, Brenda Walsh.
p. cm.
ISBN 13: 978-0-8163-2153-7
ISBN 10: 0-8163-2153-1
1. Hurricane Katrina, 2005. 2. Hurricanes—Louisiana—New Orleans. 3. Hurricanes—
Gulf Coast (U.S.) 4. Disaster victims—Louisiana—New Orleans. 5. Disaster victims—
Gulf Coast (U.S.) 6. Disaster relief—Louisiana—New Orleans. 7. Disaster relief—Gulf
Coast (U.S.) I. Walsh, Brenda, 1953- II. Title.

HV6362005.L8 K89 2006
976'.044—dc22   2006043299

3ABN Books is dedicated to bringing you the best in published materials consistent
with the mission of Three Angels Broadcasting Network. Our goal is to uplift Jesus
through books and audio and video materials by our family of 3ABN presenters. Our
in-depth Bible study guides, devotionals, biographies, and lifestyle materials promote
the whole person in health and the mending of broken people.

Additional copies of this book are available from two locations:
3ABN: Call 1-800-752-3226 or visit www.3abn.org
Adventist Book Centers: Call 1-800-765-6955
or visit www.adventistbookcenter.com

06 07 08 09 10 · 5 4 3 2 1

—DEDICATION—

To the volunteers who left their comfort zones
to serve Katrina's survivors.

You have demonstrated "pure and undefiled religion"
(James 1:27).
You have visited the homeless in their trouble,
fed the hungry,
given water to the thirsty,
cared for the sick,
provided clothing for the naked,
mucked out water-damaged homes,
cleared the rubble and fallen trees so others could come,
and mourned with those who lost everything.

Because of your unselfish, caring acts of service to those
who could not help themselves . . .
we dedicate this book to you.

—Acknowledgments—

We would like to express our gratitude to the many who have helped to make this book possible. To the volunteers who endured blistering hot, humid temperatures, putrid smells, and pestering insects to assist in the interviewing process: Sheri Dye, Kevin Komarniski, Andrea Mathews, Sonya Reaves, and Thea Stoia.

To the Gulf Coast Katrina survivors, residents, and others who gave their time to share their painful stories or the stories of others: Wayne Alley, Brenda Ashton, Ashley Bleidt, Sam Brothers, Alfred and Audrey Brown, Karen Burgess, Chelsea Checkan, James and Merry Jane Checkan, Jen Colter, Boyd Cook, Monique and Jamall Dayries, Sheryl and Joseph Donald, Mike Dowdy, Joe and Margaret Dubuisson, Reggie and LaChandra Duppard, Freida Feigel, John Gooding, Joshua Haley, Juni Halveston, Joseph Heckler, Sherry and Lloyd Helveston, Andy and Kim Jaworski, Gary and Carolyn Karl, Wilbur LaFleur, Barbara LaFontaine, Pat LaFontaine, Ken Micheff, George Mitchell, Pieter Nolden, Mary Noto, Michael and Lorri Quatroy, Lori and Martin Ryan, Kelvin and Emily Schulz, Dr. John Stearns, Dennis and Betty Strong, Bill Tudury, Charles Richard Uhlmann, Elmer Umbehagen, Mark Umbehagen, Alane Vix, Jack Welch, Ruby Wellons, Rhonda West, James "Red" Whicker, and Kevin and Olga Young.

To those tireless volunteers working with ACTS and to the staff of Bass Memorial Academy who went out of their way to host, advise, transport, share stories with and encourage us—especially Dianna and Dale Bass, David Canther, Rick and Debra Hutchinson, and George Seden.

A special thank you to those who worked tirelessly to obtain signed release forms making the publication of this book possible: Brenda

Marie Abbott and Denise Wolfe, who served as God's detectives, scouring the Internet to find "impossible" addresses and phone numbers of every person with a story in this book. And the project was completed in just one week with God's help and the assistance of the Morrell Foundation and people such as, Renee Aue-Weaver, Roy Cole, Lee Dimick, Nancy Fitzsimmons, Mike and Keli Forbeck, Tammy and Luke Gambill, Virginia Gustin, Elmer Havelin, Tommy Kidd, Barbara LaFontaine, Ken and Tammy Micheff, Shirley Poole, Bryan Rutkosky, Rita Sheel, Britt Steele, Joyce Stevenson, Spring Styer, Charles Taylor, Alane Vix, Rhonda West, James "Red" Whicker, Deanna Whitehouse, and all the Gulf Coast neighbors and acquaintances who were willing to go knocking on doors to find those who could be located in no other way. Some even went the extra mile and took photographs of people and places we had not been able to obtain previously.

And we don't want to forget our "prayer warriors" who prayed continuously during the search: Ethan Capener, Codi Musick, Shayne Musick, Levi Wolfe, Sarah Wolfe, and Tyrel Wolfe. All in all, this combined effort was nothing short of a miracle. (Be sure to read "The Rest of the Story" at the end of the book!) To all of you, we are deeply grateful.

And to our husbands, Jan W. Kuzma and Tim Walsh, who joyfully open doors of possibility for us to follow where God leads, even if they at times get left behind—we love you and thank you.

—CONTENTS—

—INTRODUCTION—

It wasn't on our agendas. On Monday, September 12, 2005 (just two weeks after Katrina), Danny Shelton, president of Three Angels Broadcasting Network, called from Waveland, Mississippi, where the network was taping material for broadcast. "There's an incredible story here," Danny told us. "Stories of God's power and protection and of the miracles that are continuing to happen as volunteers unselfishly meet the needs of survivors. A book needs to be written. Will you please come?"

We really didn't want to. Writing about hurricanes was outside our comfort zone. But feeling called, we cancelled trips and found a support system to take over our home duties, and three days later we were headed to the Gulf Coast.

As we neared the end of our nine-hour journey from Knoxville to Bass Memorial Academy at Lumberton, Mississippi, the headquarters of ACTS, a disaster relief organization, we prayed: "OK, God, we don't know how to go about this. You're going to have to open the way. Please lead us to the people who have stories You want told." We don't think the devil was very happy with this arrangement. Two hours after we arrived—and one hour into our first interview—a call came from

Kay's daughter. "Daddy has fallen and may have a hairline hip fracture. Mom, I think you should come home!" Two hours later, Kay was on her way home to care for her husband, leaving Brenda alone with recording equipment and cameras—and the putrid smells of muck and mold; the nasty love bugs, flies, and mosquitoes; and daytime temperatures of 104 degrees.

But God was still in charge and leading each step of the way. The injury that Kay's husband sustained was not as serious as first feared. And Brenda was led to one incredible story after another.

In the following pages you will read these gripping accounts of how people survived the worst hurricane in United States history—and the sorrowful stories of those who did not. You'll learn how God was working amazing miracles in the midst of the storm. You'll be held spellbound as you read how a former NFL football player tried desperately to keep alive his mother, who was trapped in

Kay was able to stay in Lumberton, Mississippi, only a few hours before having to leave to care for a family emergency.

a New Orleans hospital on life-support, and how he feared for his own life at the Superdome. Then there's the heart-wrenching account of being buried under water for thirty minutes with only a PVC pipe to breathe through, or the lady who couldn't swim who was swept away by the violent flood waters, frantically grabbing tree branches and all the time unable to shake off the rats who clung to her back! And through it all, between hell and high water, *God was there!*

Chapter 1

INTERSTATE 10: HIGHWAY TO HELL

"They're killing us!"
—Phyllis Delone

Interstate 10 is the southern-most east-west, coast-to-coast interstate highway in the United States. It stretches from California's Santa Monica beach, through Phoenix and on to Texas, linking El Paso, San Antonio, and Houston before it leaves the wide-open, dry, desertlike spaces of the West and plunges into the swamps, lakes, and bayous of the Deep South on its way to New Orleans. When it reaches the Big Easy, I-10 becomes *the longest series of viaducts passing over water* anywhere in the world as it races over Lake Pontchartrain to Slidell, Louisiana. Then it quickly exits the urban area for the forests that lie just north of Mississippi's Gulf Coast towns—Waveland, Bay St. Louis, Pass Christian, Gulfport, and Biloxi—that make up what some call the "Redneck Riviera" with their powdery white sand beaches and offshore casinos. After Mobile, Alabama, the highway runs through the woodlands that dominate the rest of its eastward journey, until 2,460 miles later, I-10 rolls into Jacksonville, Florida, and greets the Atlantic.

Why Interstate 10?

Why do we start our story with I-10? It isn't because this highway is a lifeline connection between major U.S. cities, although it is. But we begin here because I-10 is intimately connected to Katrina—the Category Four hurricane that slammed into the Gulf Coast in the early morning hours of Monday, August 29, 2005. Katrina was one of the worst natural disasters that has ever hit the United States, making useless debris out of high-end Gulf Coast resorts that are no more. Gone are the quaint little towns with their graceful antebellum homes, the mom and pop souvenir shops and seafood cafes along Highway 90; gone are the infrastructure, the businesses, the majority of people—and the children. Some people left by choice—they were the lucky ones. The others either survived miraculously—as you will see in the stories you're about to read—or they didn't. The sad fact is that hundreds didn't make it as the rising flood waters trapped them in their attics and slowly sucked the air from their lungs. Or the winds tore down their shelters and exposed the old, the young, the crippled, the sick, and the weak to the cruelest of the elements and then washed them away to their deaths.

Through the years, I-10 has meant safety for the Mississippi Gulf Coast residents. Regardless of a hurricane's strength, most residents knew that if they could get to the interstate, they'd be OK. It was built north of the coastal flood zone, so no one expected waves to wash over its asphalt. But then, no one expected Katrina's mammoth waves riding on thirty-foot storm surges, pushed by 175 mile-per-hour winds.

Thirty-six years ago Hurricane Camille ravaged the Gulf Coast. And a year before Katrina, Ivan licked at I-10, taking out a small part at the causeway over Escambia Bay near Pensacola, Florida. But apart from a few wash-outs, I-10 has stood proudly through the threatening tropical winds and rain that pelt the coast every year during the summer hurricane season. It stood, that is, until Katrina, when the headlines announced, "I-10 Twin Spans Across Lake Pontchartrain Collapse."

In addition to the demise of I-10 over the Louisiana waterways, major sections of the eastbound lanes in Mississippi, especially between Gulfport and Biloxi, were damaged and impassable because of storm debris. People expected the winds. They expected the trees to snap, making passage impossible until someone chain-sawed or bulldozed their way through. But no one expected the water! The storm surge left downtown Gulfport under ten feet of water. Not only were the coastal communities flooded, but streets and homes were under water as far as six miles inland! Residents around Diamondhead, Mississippi, now recognize I-10 as the boundary between the total wasteland on the south and partially standing, twisted buildings that might possibly be salvaged on the north.

Residents of New Orleans thought they were home safe; that they would sustain only wind damage. Then Monday afternoon the Seventeenth Street levee and the Industrial Canal levee began buckling and then broke under the relentless pounding and pressure of Katrina's storm surge, putting most of the city and the surrounding parishes under as much as twenty-six feet of toxic, polluted seawater and forcing thousands to flee from their homes and take refuge in places like the Superdome, the convention center, and the elevated portions of I-10.

The Horror of I-10's Asphalt Camp

And so we begin this journey between hell and high water in New Orleans, five days after the storm, atop a stretch of I-10 where an asphalt camp is inhabited by more than three hundred New Orleanians displaced by Katrina. Most thought that by climbing the exit ramps they could escape the hell they had lived through in the Superdome, where they rode out the

Included in the aftermath of Katrina were miles of wrecked and flooded automobiles, leaving the landscape looking like a battle zone.

Many survivors returned to find virtually nothing was left standing in their former neighborhoods—only rubble and destruction.

violence of the storm. Others had arrived at the Superdome too late to gain entrance. When they were turned away, they had sought refuge under the elevated portions of the interstate, where they were at the mercy of the elements. But after a day or two, they were driven from this shelter by the stench of decaying bodies that had been hurriedly placed there until the water receded enough for trucks to haul them to the morgue. The survivors had little choice but to climb the exit ramps, hoping for fresh air, food, water, and evacuation.

That was Day 2—or for some, Day 3. But the days passed, and no help came. Babies cried, the elderly moaned in pain, nerves jangled, throats parched, stomachs growled, skin burned. Then there were the sick—and the dying. They were running out of medicine, patience—and hope.

Others returned to homes that were still standing but uninhabitable due to flood damage by toxic, polluted seawater.

Day 4 came and went. Still no help. Where were the buses that had been promised to come and take them to a better land—anyplace that would offer food, water, and shelter from the oppressive heat? Now, insect infested, sweat soaked, starving, and dehydrated, they watched the lives of their family members ebb away under the scorching sun.

The scene looked like one from some third-world country: dirty barefoot children in sagging diapers, torn clothing, soiled blankets, the elderly in wheelchairs with swollen ankles, a rusty bicycle tipped on its side, trash littering the site, and one overflowing portable toilet. But this was not somewhere in the third world. This was America. This was New Orleans, the very harbor that in 1951 had offered sixteen-year-old Jan Kuzma and his family a safe place to enter a country that they were

Hurricane Katrina, one of the worst hurricanes in history, smashed into the Gulf Coast with winds up to 175 m.p.h., leaving countless scenes of destruction.

told "flowed with milk and honey." This was America the beautiful, a place to live in freedom and grow up with plenty after having suffered the deprivation and ravages of World War II in occupied Poland.

But the city that had opened her arms to the Kuzma family more than fifty years earlier was a far cry from the city that now could not even take care of her own.

How had three hundred New Orleans residents ended up trying to survive on an elevated portion of I-10? Forty-three-year-old Rickey Brock's story is similar to that of many who were told on Sunday—the day before the storm—to evacuate. "We couldn't evacuate," says Rickey. "I've got a truck, but it ain't runnin', and I don't have insurance." He and his family had no choice but to hunker down and hold on as they were hit by one of the worst hurricanes in history. They made it through the eye of the storm, but when the water started rising, they found a rowboat and paddled their way out of their neighborhood along Dorgenois Street. They headed to the Superdome but were too late, so for the first two nights they slept under the interstate.

Now, on top of I-10, Rickey and his fellow refugees tried to adjust to their new situation. Some slept under plastic tarps; others built makeshift shanties to protect them from the blazing Louisiana sun. Some draped sheets over stacks of the blue plastic containers that typically held five gallons of water. One group of more than a dozen stretched out in single file across I-10 to squeeze under the narrow band of shade from highway signs. They hung laundry—still soiled—over the concrete barriers. They smoked and paced and complained and stared into space and wondered if their loved ones were still alive. They recounted ghoulish tales of hearing trapped people pounding and yelling from the attics of their homes as the floodwaters slowly took their lives—and of the floating bodies, the terror, the stench of foul water, the cry of the relentless wind. And they pleaded with the occasional passerby to take the phone numbers of relatives and call for help.

"They're killing us!" said forty-six-year-old Phyllis Delone, voicing the lament of many who expected relief by the Red Cross and rescue by FEMA,[1] But on Day 5 there was still little hope to offer these people, other than the promise that buses were on the way.

Then they came—a steady stream of emergency vehicles, ambulances, police cruisers, and a ten-truck national guard convoy. But instead of stopping to help those camped on I-10, the vehicles navigated around them. "Overhead, helicopters roared," writes Ceci Connolly, a reporter for the *Washington Post,* "some landing between the Superdome and I-10. A giant Huey military transport helicopter hung above for fifteen minutes, its mission unclear. Then it finally moved on. Clouds of dust and debris swept over the crowd."[2]

As night came on, those that could slept fitfully; babies whimpered, the angry cursed, the devout prayed, the sick got sicker . . . and the weakest died.

When No One Seems to Care

It's not a pretty picture, is it! Surviving the terror of the storm and thinking you're safe, only to find yourself helplessly stranded on an elevated portion of I-10, dying a little bit each day because there's no one to bring you a morsel of food to quell your pains of hunger or a drink of pure water for your cracked lips and parched throat. No one to shield you from the burning rays of sun. No one to rescue you from your pain and misery. No one to quiet your fears of the unknown. No one to reassure you that your family and friends are safe and that your children are alive. And there's absolutely nothing you can do to save yourself.

The fact is, most of us think we're living "north of I-10." We're safe! We're not going to get caught in the storms of life. Bad things happen to other people, not to us. Other people suffer, other people get hurt, sick, lost, and abused. Other people have to endure pain, worry, anxiety, paranoia, fear, and frustration. Not us. We know a time of trouble—such as never before—is coming. But we somehow think ourselves magically immune. We read stories of other people who have found themselves trapped "between hell and high water," but not us. We're lukewarm; we have credit cards and pocket money, and although we may want lots of things, we're pretty much in need of nothing (see Revelation 3:16, 17).

FLASH! "I-10 Collapses!" "I-10 Is Underwater!" "Sections of I-10 Are Washed Away." Your comfortable world is suddenly turned upside down. How do you survive when you're flooded out of your comfort zone? How do you keep optimistic when your world seems to be a floating mass of debris? How do you go on when you are enduring such intense emotional and physical pain that all hope is lost?

The sad news is that most of the Katrina victims who put their faith in human beings were bitterly disappointed. But there need be no disappointment with God. No matter how dire your circumstances, He can rescue you. And even though help may seem far away, with God there is always hope.

Here's the good news:

O LORD, You are my God.
I will exalt You,
I will praise Your name,
For You have done wonderful things. . . .
For You have been a strength to the poor,
A strength to the needy in his distress,
A refuge from the storm,
A shade from the heat. . . .

He will swallow up death forever,
And the LORD God will wipe away tears from all faces. . . .

And it will be said in that day:
Behold, this is our God;
We have waited for Him, and He will save us.
This is the LORD;
We have waited for Him;
We will be glad and rejoice in His salvation
                    (Isaiah 25: 1, 4, 8, 9, NKJV).

---

1. FEMA (Federal Emergency Management Agency) is the agency of the United States government under the U.S. Department of Homeland Security whose mandate it is to provide disaster relief.

2. Ceci Connolly, "Frustration Grows In Days Stranded On Interstate 10," *Washington Post*, Sept. 3, 2005, A13.

-Chapter 2-
THE BIG ONE HITS

"and [they] knew not until the flood came, and took them all away."
—Matthew 24:39

Katrina: a name that will forever strike terror into the hearts of those who survived her fury.

She started out mild enough—a Category One hurricane when she hit land the first time just north of Miami on Thursday, August 25, 2005, and then weakened as she blew across Florida, becoming a mere tropical storm. But over water once again, Katrina intensified. By August 26 she became a Category Two hurricane, heading for Louisiana and Mississippi. On August 27 she was upgraded to a Category Three, and on Sunday, August 28, she hit Category Four status. Then, as if unleashing every last bit of venom, she rapidly intensified to a Category Five hurricane with winds of 175 miles per hour Once hitting land near Buras-Triumph, Louisiana, she dropped to an intense Category Four and bore down on New Orleans and the Gulf Coast of Mississippi and Alabama with sustained winds of 145 miles per hour and even higher gusts.

A hurricane is like a huge straw sucking up water, which creates a storm surge. When Katrina's surge hit the Gulf Coast, it was thirty feet high in some places—the highest ever recorded. At the height of the storm, she reached a minimum pressure of 26.64 inches or 902 millibars (the smaller the number, the bigger the storm), making her the fifth most intense Atlantic Basin hurricane on record and the third worst hurricane to ever hit the United States—surpassed only by hurricanes Rita and Wilma, which quickly followed Katrina. President Bush called Katrina "one of the worst natural disasters in our nation's history."

As Katrina pushed north across land, leaving in her wake flooding, tornadoes, and untold damage, federal disaster declarations blanketed ninety thousand square miles of the United States, an area almost as large as the United Kingdom of Great Britain, leaving five million people without power, which could take months, perhaps years, to restore. With damages estimated to exceed two hundred billion dollars, it was the costliest tropical cyclone of all time. But the real cost is not in dollars and cents; it is in lives—probably thousands—and the loss of personal keepsakes, hopes, and dreams—all priceless!

Living Through the Storm

Michael and Lorri Quatroy are just two of the half million people who in less than twelve hours had their life possessions ripped away from them, along with their hopes and their dreams. Michael says, "The day after the

hurricane, we came back to Waveland [Mississippi]. It was a mistake! Our home was gone—the whole subdivision was gone! When I asked my father about our trailer home, he pointed to the woods. There was the frame of our trailer, twisted like a pretzel, and there were looters back there stealing our stuff! That really got to me. It's like kicking a dog when it's down!"

Michael and Lorri Quatroy rode out the storm in their pickup truck, fearing for their lives as the wind tossed the truck around and trees fell around them.

Michael and Lorri painfully recall how they survived the storm. When the rain and wind first began, they knew they had to leave Waveland. But where should they go? Maybe Hattiesburg. But it was too late. They had no place to stay there—and the roads were crowded with others who had waited until the last minute to abandon everything that was dear to them.

By this time the Quatroy's only thought was to get to higher ground. They threw a few things in the back of their truck, put their two dogs in the cab with them, and headed north on Route 603. They crossed I-10. Around Kiln, the storm

After Katrina passed, the Quatroys returned home and found nothing left of their mobile home except a twisted frame.

grew more intense. With blasting rain and gusts of wind buffeting their truck, they drove to the home of their friend John Gesangles, knowing he would take them in. Too late! As they sat rocking and tossing around in their truck, they were stunned as they watched the roof of their friend's house blow off. They couldn't believe their eyes. Now their only hope was to ride out the storm in their truck. Michael turned off the ignition and gave in to the mercy of the wind. First the gusts lifted the back of the truck and then slammed it down. Then the whole truck would lurch sideways. During the storm, blasts of wind shoved and pushed the truck over three hundred yards from where they had originally parked!

When we asked Lorri if she prayed during this pounding, she said she never quit. She knew their lives were totally in God's hands. As the fierce gusts of wind continued to buffet them, Lorri became consumed with worry about all the oak trees falling around them. All she could think was what might happen if one little acorn—or one little pebble—were picked up and hurled at them with all the

The power of the storm is evident here as this large tree was ripped from the ground roots and all.

force of gusts of over 150 miles per hour At that speed, a pebble would be like a deadly missile, shattering their windshield and perhaps killing them. Or what if a massive piece of debris slammed into them? That *would* be the end!

When we asked Michael about praying, he admitted, "I have never prayed in my life. I don't even know how to pray. I was too paralyzed with fear! But God must have heard Lorri's prayers because, somehow, we survived!"

"What are you going to do now?" we asked.

Michael admitted, "We're at a loss. We're confused. There is no place for us to turn to. There may be a lot of help, but we don't know where to go. The good thing is, I bought two tents, but we've got nothing else. Nothing!"

Lorri added, "We are still alive, but what is life with *nothing?* All our lives we've lived to get things—and now it's all gone! We have *nothing!* We're in shock. We just have to start all over again. I don't even know if our daughter and my mother are still alive! Michael and I went through Hurricane Betsy as children, but now we're both on disability. Michael has epilepsy and high blood pressure. I can't get around. How do you start over? I'm confused. It's too much for us, and now look at the sores on our legs from being in that polluted water!"

The stories of survivors like Michael and Lorri Quatroy are heartbreaking. What do you do when you've lost everything? And, like Job, your body is covered with sores?

Perhaps the agony of it all was best expressed by Juni Halveston from Ocean Springs, Mississippi, when he said, "I'm forty-two years old and haven't cried in thirty-five years. When I saw the devastation of this place after Katrina, I broke down and wept. I've never seen anything like it in my life."

A Vietnam veteran put it this way: "It was a war zone. Total devastation. Worse than Vietnam!"

The Dying, the Bruised, and the Broken

Dr. John Stearns, a volunteer with an ACTS (Adventist Community Team Services) emergency medical clinic working from a parking lot in Waveland, Mississippi, said that the day after the storm a naked woman walked out of the woods carrying her dead baby. He cried when he heard her story of being swept away from her home by the surging flood waters. She desperately tried to save herself and her child by grabbing on to the branches of trees with one hand, while at the same time trying to hold her baby above the water with the other. Helplessly stranded, she was forced to watch her child's life ebb away from exposure to the wind and the cold polluted water that held them captive for over twelve hours. *How many other babies and young children were swept from their cribs or from the protective arms of their parents and buried under the debris?* We'll never

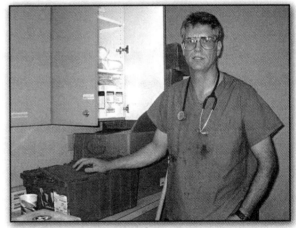

Dr. John Stearns, a volunteer with the Adventist Community Team Services (ACTS), tried to help survivors—like the young mother who appeared out of the woods carrying her dead baby.

know! And what about the depression and guilt of the parents who tried their best to save their children—but their best wasn't good enough?

This young mother was only one of a number of survivors who walked out of the woods that day. Most of them were naked, with not even shoes on their feet. The force of the wind and waves ripped the clothing from their bodies!

Almost all the patients being seen in the makeshift clinics that had been set up along the Gulf Coast needed medical care for injuries sustained from flying and floating debris—bruises, abrasions, lacerations, even broken bones. Walking on the debris scattered everywhere would pose a high risk for injury, even for anyone with shoes. But can you imagine having to walk barefoot for blocks—even for miles—on shattered glass, sharp twisted pieces of metal, splintered wood, rusty cans, exposed nails, broken furniture, and garbage as if you were walking over a giant landfill, searching desperately for help?

And even if the survivors—like the Quatroys—were fortunate enough to escape with shoes on their feet, they still needed medical care for the sores and burning rashes that resulted from their skin being subjected to the toxic, contaminated, sewage-filled water! For three to five days following the hurricane, everyone suffered from the absence of safe water. Not just to quench their thirst; there was no water to even rinse the filth off their bodies—much less any possibility of bathing. Some didn't even realize the extent of their injuries until they were able to wash away the toxic mud.

Adding insult to injury, daytime temperatures in the gulf region in the weeks following Katrina soared upward to 104 degrees Fahrenheit, making an already miserable existence, aggravated with mosquitoes, flies, and bugs, even more unbearable. It's no wonder people succumbed to the elements, dying from heat stroke, asthma attacks, heart failure, seizures, and a host of other medical conditions.

Then there were those critical and chronically ill patients who were abruptly cut off from sources of medications and life-saving treatments—those, for example, needing daily dialysis or those with heart disease whose lives depended on blood thinners to keep their blood from clotting and causing strokes and certain death. Those with congestive heart failure needed diuretics to keep themselves from drowning in the fluid that built up in their lungs. And the thousands needing blood pressure medications, antibiotics, and antiseizure medications.

What about cancer patients whose chemotherapy was interrupted? That's life-threatening in itself, not to mention the extreme suffering caused by lack of narcotics to ease their excruciating pain. How many diabetics, without insulin to control their blood sugar levels, succumbed to diabetic comas?

Did you know that those suffering from Parkinson's disease sometimes must take five to ten medications a day? The time for taking their medications is so crucial that being even thirty minutes late could throw them into crisis, causing them to lose body functions—speech, bowel control, and memory—and triggering seizures resulting in death.

Emphysema patients died immediately without their oxygen. Those suffering from liver cirrhosis may not only be

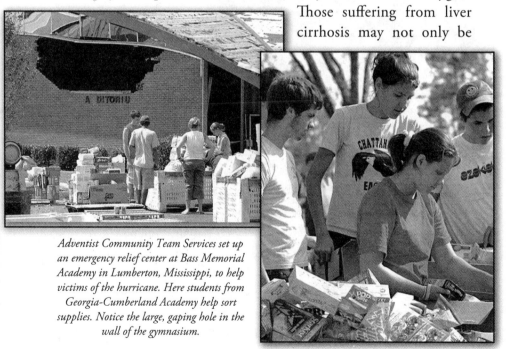

Adventist Community Team Services set up an emergency relief center at Bass Memorial Academy in Lumberton, Mississippi, to help victims of the hurricane. Here students from Georgia-Cumberland Academy help sort supplies. Notice the large, gaping hole in the wall of the gymnasium.

dependent on vital medications but also need blood and platelet transfusions. Most neurology patients are dependent on medications to prevent seizures and, even more importantly, steroids to prevent swelling in their brains, causing coma and death.

Years ago many of these patients would have been in a hospital during a natural disaster such as Katrina, thus increasing their chances of being evacuated or airlifted to safety. But today, because of the prevalence of the HMO system in America, critically ill patients increasingly are being treated at home, thus raising the potential risk for dying. Add to this the fact that Katrina destroyed hundreds of thousands of medical records!

What about those who lost their glasses in the storm and couldn't see to escape? Or the disabled in wheelchairs and the elderly who couldn't walk, much less swim, to safety? Some struggled and fought for their last breath, while others gave up—resigned to their fate. And we haven't even begun to discuss the medical needs of the babies and the children—and the mothers whose labor pains began on the morning of August 29. Or the women with sanitary needs and no supplies, no restrooms, no privacy.

A search-and-rescue team looking for bodies. Each home had to be searched because so many people died as a result of being trapped in their attics.

We were shocked with reports of the human violence after the storm—the looting, the robberies, the rapes, the threats, the shootings—but few have stopped to consider how much of that violence might have been caused by individuals with psychiatric disorders who weren't able to get their medications!

For many, surviving the actual storm was only the beginning of their reign of terror. Now they must face the threat of gastrointestinal illnesses caused by sewage-polluted, contaminated water. Add to that the increased risk of West Nile virus from the plague of mosquitoes that were feasting on these stagnant pools. Fifty-two cases of West Nile fever were already recorded in Louisiana in the summer months prior to Katrina, and forty of those involved encephalitis or meningitis, so this risk was very real.

Then there was the possibility of dying from food poisoning or outbreaks of such dreaded communicable diseases as typhoid, yellow fever, cholera, pandemic influenza—and who knows what else—in a population in which sanitary conditions were impossible and few were up-to-date with protective immunizations.

In addition, almost all were hit with the reality that some of their family members, neighbors, or friends hadn't made it and that their bodies would be found in their attics where they were trapped or someplace among the debris. Rhonda West lost a number of her family members in the floodwaters of New Orleans—five died in their living room. They had been under water for six days before their bodies were found and Rhonda was called to identify them. Rhonda recalled the horror in these words, "As a paramedic, I've seen people who were decapitated—and everything else. But nothing can prepare you to see your seven-year-old cousin with her face filled with maggots. For two days I couldn't sleep. Every time I closed my eyes, that's all I saw."

Months after Katrina, Reggie Duppard's forty-six-year-old brother, Jonas Jr., who was living in New Orleans, was still missing. The Duppard family feared the worst but hoped for the best. Their prayers were answered when on December 8 Reggie learned his brother's name had finally appeared on a FEMA list from Texas! Not all were this fortunate. In December, rotting bodies were still being found in the rubble!

Why Did They Stay?

For many the question was, Why did these people stay behind? Why were so many caught ill-prepared?

They knew Katrina was coming.

Meteorologists predicted her intensity.

They charted her course.

Two days before Katrina made landfall, President George W. Bush declared a state of emergency in Louisiana, Alabama, and Mississippi. Mandatory evacuations were ordered for New Orleans and other Louisiana parishes in Katrina's path, as well as coastline counties in Mississippi and Alabama, although they came too late for many people to mobilize.

It wasn't as if Katrina came upon New Orleans and the Mississippi/Alabama Gulf Coast as a thief in the night. If people had heeded the first warnings, most would have had plenty of time to get out of her path.

Why didn't they go? The lament heard from those who stayed and miraculously lived to tell about it was, "I just didn't think it would be this bad!"

Many measured predictions about the force and fury of Katrina against what they had experienced with Hurricane Camille, thirty-six years earlier. That was a widespread problem. They expected the wind—but not the water. And because of this, when Katrina blew into town, they were *not* prepared!

History should have alerted them to the danger. Flooding as a result of tropical storms and hurricanes has threatened the Gulf Coast since it was first settled. You might understand those early settlers building on the higher land of coastal Mississippi or Alabama, but in the marshland of New Orleans? Why would anyone build a city below sea level— and even below the water level of Lake Pontchartrain, which borders one side, and the Mississippi River that flows on the other? The historical answer is found a one-syllable word: *greed!*

Looking Back at the Beginning of New Orleans

The threat of hurricanes and flood didn't stop the scheming Scotsman John Law from deciding in 1718 that it would be more financially profitable for him if he could conduct his trading business from a town built within easy access to both Lake Pontchartrain and the Mississippi River. Why let the threat of flooding stop him if there was money to be made? So what if it meant building below sea level, as long as he could bilk money from French investors for settlement rights and reap the profits from the lucrative river trade?

That first year, when the brutal sweltering heat and the rising and falling waters of the Mississippi made building almost impossible, the settlers should have abandoned the site. But greed won over wisdom, and instead of choosing a safer, less lucrative location, they constructed levees to keep out the floodwaters. Thus was born *La Nouvelle Orleans.* Environmentally, it also began the demise of the New Orleans that Katrina hit, driving over 250,000 New Orleanians into exile throughout the nation. But we're getting ahead of the story.

New Orleans was never a place for the weak. In addition to the hurricanes and spring flooding that usually poured about two feet of muddy river water and debris into the city, those early settlers were plagued with mosquitoes, rats, and poisonous snakes. Disease ran rampant. The city was hit so often with the ravages of cholera, yellow fever, and other tropical epidemics that it was labeled a "damp grave" for those foolish enough to live there—especially during the oppressive hot, humid months from June to October. Yet, in spite of this, New Orleans grew. Flooded land was reclaimed merely by building more levees. Today, 70 percent of the city sits below sea level.

Since 1871, on average, one hurricane every three years has made landfall in the Louisiana/Mississippi Gulf Coast region. In 1893, the Louisiana Hurricane hit with what was probably Category Four strength, killing more than two thousand people when its storm surge of fifteen feet or more hit New Orleans. In a list of the ten deadliest U.S. natural disasters, it's listed as number four.

Then there were the hurricanes of the 1960s. Hurricane Betsy hit New Orleans with a storm surge of ten feet in 1965, causing the worst flooding the city had seen in decades, but the response was merely to raise the levees twelve feet. Then just four years later,

Camille, a Category Five storm with a surge of at least twenty feet and with winds that topped 200 miles per hour, destroyed over five thousand homes when it made a direct hit to Mississippi's Gulf Coast. This storm of the century left residents thinking, "If I survived Camille, I can survive anything."

About a week after Katrina hit the Gulf Coast, the comment was made, "Camille killed a lot of people last week."

"You mean Katrina, don't you?" the listener corrected.

"No," the person countered, explaining that almost all the people who stayed behind to face Katrina made that decision based on Camille. They thought nothing could be worse than Camille! What they failed to consider was that Camille, although a Category Five hurricane, was a fast moving, tightly compacted storm that came in at low tide. Hurricane Katrina, although just a Category Four after hitting land, came in at high tide, covered a huge expanse—more than three hundred miles—and took her time moving northward! This combination produced a gigantic storm surge as high as thirty feet in some places, which caused from three to six miles of inland flooding. And why were the Mississippi Gulf Coast towns of Waveland, Bay St. Louis, and Pass Christian hit so severely? Because hurricanes blow in a circular fashion around the eye of the storm—and they were in the path of what is often referred to as the "dirty," or most deadly, side of the storm.

Predicting the Big One!

Since 1969 when Hurricane Camille hit, scientists have been predicting the next *big* one—with the warning that the levee system wouldn't hold. Over the years, hundreds of miles of earthen levees, concrete floodwalls, and pumping stations had been built to keep the water out of the New Orleans area, but everyone knew the levees had been built to withstand only a Category Three hurricane. In addition, the whole system of levees was sinking and needed immediate repair. To make conditions worse, New Orleans's natural defenses against hurricane flooding—the surrounding marshland and the barrier islands—were dwindling.

It wasn't as if the city wasn't warned that danger was imminent. Here are but a few of the predictions that were published less than five years before the *big* one hit! Note how accurate they were!

> A major hurricane could swamp New Orleans under twenty feet of water, killing thousands. Human activities along the Mississippi River have dramatically increased the risk, and now only massive reengineering of southeastern Louisiana can save the city. . . . New Orleans is a disaster waiting to happen. (*Scientific American,* October 2001).

"Keeping Its Head Above Water: New Orleans Faces Doomsday Scenario," was a headline in the *Houston Chronicle* in December 2001. The article went on to predict that a severe hurricane striking New Orleans "would strand 250,000 people or more, and probably kill one of ten left behind as the city drowned under twenty feet of water. Thousands of refugees could land in Houston."

In June 2002, John McQuaid and Mark Schleifstein wrote a five-part series, Washing Away, for the *New Orleans Times-Picayune*. In part, they said,

> It's only a matter of time before South Louisiana takes a direct hit from a major hurricane. Billions have been spent to protect us, but we grow more vulnerable every day. . . . If a Category 5 hurricane hit the city from the south, hundreds of thousands would be left homeless, and it would take months to dry out the area and begin to make it livable. But there wouldn't be much for residents to come home to. The local economy would be in ruins.

In September 2002 Walter Williams did a serious short feature called "New Orleans: The Natural History," in which an expert said that a direct hit by a hurricane could damage the city for six months. It was noted that the New Orleans ecosystem was incredibly fragile and volatile and warned that if no action was taken, the city could be wiped out in the next hurricane.

The design of the original levees, which dates to the 1960s, was based on rudimentary storm modeling that, it is now realizing, might underestimate the threat of a potential hurricane. Even if the modeling was adequate, however, the levees were designed to withstand only forces associated with a fast-moving hurricane that, according to the National Weather Service's Saffir-Simpson scale, would be placed in category 3. If a lingering category 3 storm—or a stronger storm, say, category 4 or 5—were to hit the city, much of New Orleans could find itself under more than 20 ft (6 m) of water. ("The Creeping Storm," *Civil Engineering Magazine*, June 2003).

The potential for such extensive flooding and the resulting damage is the result of a levee system that is unable to keep up with the increasing flood threats from a rapidly eroding coastline and thus unable to protect the ever-subsiding landscape. ("What if Hurricane Ivan Had Not Missed New Orleans?" *Natural Hazards Observer*, November 2004).

An article in the *American Prospect*, "Thinking Big About Hurricanes," described the aftermath of a major storm surge:

Soon the geographical "bowl" of the Crescent City would fill up with waters of the lake, leaving those unable to evacuate with little option but to cluster on rooftops—terrain they would have to share with hungry rats, fire ants, nutria [water rodents], snakes, and perhaps alligators. The water itself would become a festering stew of sewage, gasoline, refinery chemicals, and debris (May 2005).

In June 2005, the FX docudrama *Oil Storm* depicted a Category Four hurricane hitting New Orleans and forcing residents to evacuate and hide out in the Superdome.

Facts That Most New Orleanians Didn't Know

Some of the devastation of Katrina can be traced to the levees that have protected New Orleans from flooding since the nineteenth century. These old levees, as well as the newer levee system put in place by the Army Corps of Engineers nearly forty years ago, cut off the region's main source of sediment, the raw material for building wetlands in the delta. More recently, the weight of large buildings and infrastructure and the leaching of water, oil, and gas from beneath the surface across the region have also contributed to the problem. The consequence is that the coastal wetlands of Louisiana have been washing away over the years, and the city is sinking deeper—while the sea level is rising. In the last one hundred years this process has added several feet to all storm surges—causing higher flooding from weaker storms.

Add to this the problem caused by the intrusion of salt water in the canals that have been dug by oil companies and private individuals in the surrounding marshland. This erosion of the wetlands not only has caused Louisiana to lose twenty-four square miles of land each year—1,900 square miles of land since the 1930s—but also has destroyed Louisiana's first line of defense against hurricanes that draw their strength from the sea but quickly weaken over land. *Wetlands have the capacity to absorb storm surges at the rate of one foot for every 2.7 miles of wetlands.* As a result, hurricanes moving over the fragmenting marshes toward the New Orleans area now retain more strength.

The basic fact is, the engineering of the river has brought the Gulf of Mexico right to the doorstep of New Orleans, making it more vulnerable to hurricanes!

And Then Katrina Hit

And so Katrina blew her way over the compromised marshlands surrounding the Louisiana coastline and made landfall as a Category Four hurricane with sustained winds of 145 miles per hour at 6:10 A.M. CDT (Central Daylight Time) near Buras-Triumph, south of New Orleans. She worked her way up the eastern Louisiana coastline, almost completely obliterating Plaquemines and St. Bernard parishes, grazing eastern New Orleans and crossing the eastern section of Lake Pontchartrain, blasting Slidell in St. Tammany parish. A few hours after she first hit the Louisiana coastline, she made landfall for the third time, smashing into the Mississippi and Alabama Gulf Coast and sending a ten- to thirty-foot storm surge across two hundred miles of pristine white sandy beaches. A thirty-foot storm surge was recorded at Biloxi, Mississippi—the highest ever observed in America. The storm surge in Mobile, Alabama, was the highest in that location since 1917, besting the surge created by Category Three Hurricane Frederic, which hit the city directly in 1979.

At first, it seemed that the New Orleans area had survived with only massive wind damage. *Then the levees broke—and the worst nightmare in New Orleans history began.* Foul, putrid, oil-contaminated water flooded 80 percent of the lowest lying parishes. The death, the devastation, the terror, and the agony was so great that it has been referred to as the inner ring of Hell!

After hitting the Gulf Coast, Katrina raged on for hours, slowly moving north, spawning killer tornadoes in the southern states and causing flooding as far north as Cookeville, Tennessee. The last public advisory on Katrina was at 11 P.M. EDT (Eastern Daylight Time) on Wednesday, August 31, right before she died in southeastern Canada.

Katrina may have died, but the effect of the destruction she left behind will live for years—and maybe forever.

Something to Consider

Are you ready for the storm ahead? Are you ready for the end of the world? Are you ready for Jesus to come? It's not as if we haven't been warned!

> "Watch therefore, for you do not know what hour your Lord is coming. But know this, that if the master of the house had known what hour the thief would come, he would have watched and not allowed his house to be broken into. Therefore you also be ready, for the Son of Man is coming at an hour when you do not expect Him" (Matthew 24:42–44, NKJV).

We've been told that when people say, " 'Peace and safety!' then sudden destruction comes upon them, as labor pains upon a pregnant woman. And they shall not escape" (1 Thessalonians 5:3, NKJV). Obviously, a pregnant woman knows there is no escaping her labor pains. To ignore the signs—a world pregnant with sin, strife, disease, disasters, and all manner of evil, selfishness, and greed—is to put one's head in the sand. The end will come, and it will be soon.

When Jesus' disciples asked Him, "And what will be the sign of Your coming, and of the end of the age?" (see Matthew 24), here is the list Christ gave them:

1. People (Satan) masquerading as Christ (verse 5).
2. Wars and rumors of wars (verse 6).
3. Famines, pestilence, and earthquakes (verse 7).
4. A time of major trouble (tribulation) when Christians will be hated and killed (verses 9, 15–23).
5. False prophets will deceive many (verse 11).
6. Lawlessness (verse 12).
7. The sun and the moon will be darkened, and the stars will fall (verse 29).

Note how many of these signs have been fulfilled. Some may say all have been fulfilled except the great tribulation when we will have to flee for our lives. But wait a minute. Just think of the number of people throughout history who have had to flee because of their faith! And even though you may not be on the run at this minute, there are others in this world who are! Obviously, it would be foolish to say, "I'm going to wait for the great tribulation before getting ready." That just might be too late!

Finally, Jesus says that at the time of His coming, people, even though warned, will be pursuing their own pleasures just as in Noah's day.

> "But as the days of Noah were, so also will the coming of the Son of Man be. For as in the days before the flood, they were eating and drinking, marrying and giving in marriage, until the day that Noah entered the ark, and did not know until the flood came and took them all away, so also will the coming of the Son of Man be" (verses 37–39, NKJV).

Here's a modern day paraphrase: "And as they [the people of New Orleans and the Gulf Coast] did not know until the flood came and took them all away, so also will the coming of the Son of Man be."

-Chapter 3-
A JOURNEY THROUGH HELL

"If I died and went to hell, I'd have it on the devil,
because I've already been there."
—*Kelvin Schulz*

Kelvin and Emily Schulz and their three younger children—Allison, twenty-one, Buddy, seventeen, and Suzanne, ten—used to live at 600 South Beach Boulevard in the tiny coastal town of Bay St. Louis, Mississippi. But only sections of their home are left; the rest is a pile of rubble. The story of their escape is nothing less than a miracle of courage and quick wit, which they attribute to the Lord. Here's their story.

Emily works for the veteran's hospital in Biloxi as a home-based primary care nurse, taking care of veterans in their homes. The Sunday morning before Katrina hit, her boss called, requesting that she come to work because she was the only nurse on her team that could be reached. Emily felt obligated to go, even though her ten-year-old pleaded, "Mama, please don't go. I want you to stay here with us."

"You'll be fine, Sweetheart," Emily reassured her daughter. "Daddy will be here to take care of you. Our house has been around since 1847. It made it through the hurricane of 1947, and it withstood Camille. It's a very strong building, so you don't have to worry."

There was no doubt in Emily's mind that what she said was true. If any house could withstand a hurricane in Bay St. Louis, it should be their house. That's why her brother called to say he thought it was a good idea to have their eighty-year-old mother ride out the storm at Emily's place instead of at his home in Waveland. Emily agreed. So without any concern or feeling of foreboding, she left for work.

Kelvin and Emily Schulz following their ordeal with Katrina. Kelvin and the children floated for hours, but managed to survive. Sadly, Emily's mother died in the storm.

Kelvin, Emily's husband, is a general contractor and a licensed real estate broker; he also owned a refrigeration and air conditioning business that he ran out of their home. Kelvin, too, had no doubt their residence could weather any storm. It had been an old theater building with a basement that should be a safe harbor for the family against the wind. The first story was a solid warehouse filled with his equipment. The second floor contained his office, their four-bedroom residence, and a balcony.

Sunday night, in preparation for the storm, Kelvin moved a water pump into place, just in case the basement flooded. He also had a generator and extra fuel so the family would have electricity when the power went out. He and his son, Buddy, screwed boards over the doors and windows and sandbagged the doors to prevent floodwater from getting inside. Then he moved the vehicles out of the path of the storm. They were ready for anything—or so he thought! After watching TV for a while, the family went to bed, knowing Katrina would hit sometime between six and eight o'clock the next morning.

When Kelvin awoke about 4 A.M., the electricity was out, and the wind was tugging against the doors and the boards over the windows. As the hours passed, the wind became more intense. Rain pelted the house, but there was still nothing to worry about. Most of the family was up by then and in the basement to wait out the storm. Then the water started to rise, so everyone moved to the first floor. Kelvin checked his watch. When he saw it was seven-fifteen, he thought the hurricane must be about over. He woke up Buddy and yelled, "Help me get the pump started!" Buddy jumped out of bed, put on his tennis shoes, and ran to help his dad. They started the pump, and Kelvin went to check on the front of the house.

Suddenly, the boards protecting one of the doors blew off—"Just like flicking a fly off your arm," Kelvin says. "It was that easy." He remembers thinking, *That's impossible!* Eight heavy screws were holding the plywood in place! Alarm registered in the pit of his stomach. Then, just as suddenly, the door cracked, and water began to stream in. He frantically tried to put up something to block the door, but the situation just got worse. Kelvin gave up and headed over to the other door to save it. But before he could do anything, the protective plywood covering flipped off that door, the glass broke, and water and debris came gushing in, flooding the first floor. The equipment he had stored on the first floor began to be pushed around by the churning water. "Get upstairs!" Kelvin screamed to his family. By now the water was three feet deep, and they had to struggle to make it to the stairs. His heart was pounding, but he kept telling himself, *Surely, we'll be safe here. The worst of the storm must be over.*

Kelvin raced up the stairs to the second story and looked out the window. Just like you'd peel an apple, the wind was peeling the siding off the building next to his neighbor's house. Debris was flying everywhere. Kelvin glanced at his watch: 8 A.M. He squinted, trying to see the neighbor's house through the torrents of rain. He couldn't make it out, but he thought it was because of the sheets of rain being blown by the ferocious blasts of wind. Later he realized the reason he couldn't see the house was because it was no longer there!

The water just kept coming up and up. All at once, Kelvin saw a commercial refrigeration unit floating in the water. He recognized that it had come from a sealed storage building located on their property.

There was no way it could be floating in their yard! Then he saw the roof of the storage building itself—floating away. As the water kept rising, he watched with total unbelief as, one by one, the other buildings on their property disappeared under the water. That's when reality hit, and he cried out, "God, what have I gotten my family into?"

And the water just kept rising!

Just then Buddy yelled above the shrieking of the wind, "Dad, the side door is blowing in!" Kelvin and his son grabbed a board to try to brace the door, but the next thing they knew the whole door just blew off its hinges, and water started coming up the side steps. By this time the water was up to their waists!

Various objects floated in the water around them and below them, knocking into the walls and second-story floor; the bumping and thumping sounds were unreal. Then a part of the second-story floor collapsed. Desperate to find his hunting vests, which could serve as life preservers, Kelvin yelled to Buddy above the roar of the wind, "Grab the guns from the gun cabinet. Maybe the vests are in there!" Searching the cabinet, Buddy frantically threw the guns on the bed behind him.

"The vests aren't here," Buddy yelled to his dad.

"Forget the vests!" his dad ordered. "Just get out of there."

Suddenly Buddy felt the floor moving underneath his feet and could see the walls visibly buckling in front of him. Panic gripped his heart as he made a mad dash out of the room with only seconds to spare as that section of the house collapsed behind him.

Then it got progressively worse. It was like a wild ride at Universal Studios or Disneyland—but this was for real. The floor was jumping and popping; objects were knocking around; and more walls were threatening to fall.

"Kids," Kelvin yelled, "Get up on the balcony part of the house. It's stronger because of the way it's braced." The kids climbed up, but the floor kept jumping around. It seemed like the whole building was about to collapse. Kelvin looked around in desperation. The house would have to be abandoned. He called to his mother-in-law, who was sitting in a nearby recliner.

"Let's go, Jane! Come on. Get ready. We've got to go. We've got to go *now*. Hurry!" But Jane just sat there with her head down, shook it slowly, and said, "Kelvin, I'm too old for this. I'm not going to leave." The children had already been pleading with their grandmother, but her resolve was set in steel. "I'll never make it," she lamented. She would ride out the storm where she was and would accept her fate— come hell or high water!

Kelvin didn't try to argue with her any further; there wasn't time if he were to save his own children. Jane had lived through Camille, had asthma and other serious medical problems, and was ready to face death. Kelvin turned away and screamed to his children above the wind, "Look for the life preservers. Maybe they're in the attic." Allison found one that fit Suzanne and an air ring that she quickly put around her own waist. Buddy and Kelvin each grabbed an air mattress. Spontaneously, Kelvin grabbed two flashlights. It was 9:35 A.M. There was no time to think of anything else. The only thing on their minds was getting out alive.

Logically, the best way to get out of the building would be through the bedroom window. But, instead, Kelvin ran to the side door and directed his children to follow him. All at once, the wall with the window, where they had just been standing seconds before, collapsed. Had they been there, trying to leave through the window, their fate would have been sealed. Something—or Someone—seemed to beckon Kelvin to that side door. Again, between hell and high water . . . God was there!

As the wall collapsed and the floor started to fall, Buddy and Suzanne fell into the water. Quickly, before they were sucked under, Kelvin grabbed them with strength he didn't know he had, pulling them to safety. Above the wind, Kelvin scolded, "Why did you jump into the water?" Then he realized they hadn't jumped; the force of the storm had knocked them off their feet!

When the roof collapsed, it started to float. Kelvin seized on this as their only chance for escape. There could be no hesitation. He grabbed his ten-year-old. "Suzanne, you first," he ordered, as he shoved his little girl onto the floating roof. But as he was trying to push Allison onto the roof, her legs became tangled in some telephone cable attached to it. He pulled. She kicked. He tugged. But her legs wouldn't budge. There was too much debris in the way. He screamed for help. Buddy quickly pulled on the debris that was floating by, while Kelvin once again tried to free her legs. Her life depended on getting loose. And Kelvin had no intention of leaving her there to die. Then, as if God heard their panicked cries, the wires gave way. Her legs were scraped and cut—but she was free!

Next Buddy joined his sisters, and then Kelvin managed to crawl up beside them. By now the air ring around Allison and the two air mattresses had been punctured. The family clung to the roof as the cold rain pelted them like dried peas from a sling shot. The wind blasted. They shivered from the exposure, but at least they were floating *above* the churning, smelly, water polluted with brine and sewage, rather than having to swim though it.

Just then their dogs ran to the doorway, hesitated and looked at the family as if to say, "Don't leave us here!" Kelvin, touched with concern for their beloved pets, pulled the trembling dogs from the doorway, across the watery gulf, and onto their floating roof "raft," just as they watched the backside of their house blow away—piece by piece.

Kelvin and the children hunkered down on the roof as best they could and floated and floated. Would this nightmare ever end? The rain was blistering. It felt like they were being sandblasted. As debris came by, they grabbed pieces and tried to hide beneath them in order to protect themselves from the rain and from being hit by flying objects. Large pieces of plywood and metal sheeting were flying around them like someone was throwing stones. Allison put her arms over her head, while Suzanne lay in a fetal position. Buddy and Kelvin were trying their best to protect themselves and the girls with a sheet of hard plastic they had picked up from among the floating debris. At one point, Kelvin saw half of a house still standing. He debated whether they should try to jump to it, but decided not to. It was a wise move, because a few minutes later the house collapsed and disappeared under the water.

They floated on and on—and the hours ticked by. They were hungry, but the craving for a drink was even more overwhelming. Kelvin felt as though he were going to die of thirst. His eyes were smarting from the saltwater blowing into them. He could only imagine how his children were suffering. His heart ached for them. Fatigue was setting in, and his whole body was screaming for sleep, but this was not the time to let down his guard. He had to keep a constant lookout for flying debris. At one point as he was looking around, Kelvin couldn't believe his eyes. He realized that there wasn't a building left standing in their whole neighborhood. Everything had disappeared under twenty-five feet of water! Was there no house strong enough, or no tree tall enough, to withstand the wrath of this angry storm?

Suddenly, something massive and heavy hit their hard plastic shield causing it to bang against Kelvin's head. If it had not been for that piece of plastic, he would have been knocked out or, even worse, decapitated. Then the wind caught their piece of plastic and ripped it from their grasp. There was so much debris in the water by this time that they fished out some other pieces to hold over themselves.

The dogs shivered and put their noses between their paws. But the safety of their "raft" was not to be for much longer. By now six or seven hours had gone by since they made their escape onto the floating roof— and still the wind was so intense that it blew the rain horizontally—not just diagonally! The roof began to tilt to one side and take on more water. "We're sinking," the children screamed. They had to make a move or they would be left helpless in the swirling angry water. Kelvin spotted a boat about seventy-five or eighty feet away. It was lodged against the side of a house; what appeared to be a "highway" of debris lay between them and the boat. If they could only reach it, it would provide some protection from flying debris—and it would float!

Kelvin spotted this boat lodged against the side of a house. He and the children managed to crawl inside where they survived the storm.

Kelvin caught a glimpse of his own boat on the other side of the house, but quickly decided against trying to reach it because it was directly in the line of the wind and flying objects. The other boat was shielded by the house. "Kids," he called as he pointed, "we're going to go for that boat. Don't stand up! We'll have to crawl over the debris to get there. If you stand up and fall through, there is no way of coming up through this mess. It would be like falling through ice. But if we crawl like crabs, spreading our arms and legs wide, I think we can make it! You've got to follow me. It's our only hope!"

Fear gripped him as he gingerly began crawling over the debris. The rain and wind were still pounding them. Any slip could be deadly. Slowly he moved forward. The children were terror-stricken as well, but they had faith in their father. One by one, they followed, and like a mother cat leading her kittens to safety, Kelvin led his children over one piece of floating debris to another until they reached the boat. Then came the dogs. Even they must have sensed their salvation was in following their master.[1]

By the time everyone was safely in the boat, their eyes were burning from the saltwater and they were shivering from the cold, but they were safe. They rummaged through the boat and found life preservers, pillows, and other objects that they used to protect themselves from the weather as much as possible. Kelvin could tell that his youngest daughter, Suzanne, was getting hypothermia, so he cradled her in his arms, letting the heat of his body warm her. A couple times he yelled at Allison as she stuck her head above the edge of the boat to see what was happening. "Keep your head down! You're going to get hit with debris," he warned. It was not until they were safe in the boat that Kelvin realized that although his girls were dressed, his son had gotten out of bed so quickly that morning that he had on only underpants and tennis shoes—not even socks!

It was now midafternoon. Their lips were cracked; their bodies were scratched and bleeding; and their throats were parched. Kelvin kept thinking, *This has to end soon.* But the storm dragged on and on. And there in the rocking boat, surrounded by his children, their three dogs and their two cats which had somehow found them, he fell asleep, exhausted!

They stayed in the boat a couple hours until the water receded enough for them to climb out and go inside the house against which the boat was lodged. The house had been knocked off its foundation, but it was still standing. They had no idea whose house it was, but after the hell they had been through, it was like heaven to them to be inside. And amazingly, as they made their way up to the second floor, they found beds that were still made—and dry. Apparently the beds had floated with the rising water! They began to search the house for something to keep them alive and found two precious bottles of water that were still sealed. It was like finding treasure!

They stayed in the house for a while until the water receded further, but when they tried to go outside, they found debris still flying in the wind, so they went back in the house until the wind died down a bit more. When they finally decided to leave the safety of the house, it was almost dusk. They stepped out into a world of utter chaos and ruin, wading knee deep in muddy, souplike water that stank of gas, chemicals, feces, raw sewage—and death. Dangerous debris was everywhere: exposed nails, broken glass, splintered boards, broken equipment, tree branches, and fallen timber. Gingerly, they picked their way through the obstacles for five hundred feet or more just to get to the road. They had to crawl over logs and fallen trees—and watch every step to make sure it was safe. Days later, when Kelvin was able to wash off the mud caked on his legs, he discovered he had scrapes, cuts, and open sores. Allison's legs had scrapes and cuts from trying to get loose from the telephone cable, but the other two children had survived with only a few scratches!

The four-block journey to what was left of their home was a sad one, because they knew their grandma hadn't made it. Later, a body was found about fifteen or twenty feet from where they had been floating. DNA samples were taken, but weeks later they still hadn't received confirmation. But in their hearts they thought it was probably their grandma.

Now, trudging "home," Kelvin's thoughts turned to his wife. He and the children began wondering, *Was she alive? Had their mother survived the storm?*

That night they stayed in what was left of their house. The next day Allison's boyfriend came and took them to stay on a tugboat in Gulfport until they could find somewhere to live.

Meanwhile Emily Shulz was literally locked in the VA hospital in Biloxi, because authorities wouldn't let any employees leave until they had somewhere safe to go. Unable to communicate, she had no way of knowing whether her family had survived. All she could do was hope and wait.

She made it through the storm without incident. From the hospital floor where she was working, all she could see were the trees being blown by the wind. She knew the back bay had come up because there was debris floating in the water—but she had no idea how much the water had risen—and she had no time to worry. The nursing staff was frantically trying to get the patients out of their rooms to the safety of the hallways, far away from the windows that could come crashing in. It was chaotic trying to find oxygen outlets for those whose lives depended on it. The patients had no idea what was going on, and some were angry. It was stressful but, thankfully, God spared them during those hours from knowing just how bad it was outside the hospital walls—and what their families were going through at the time.

The veteran's hospital in Biloxi is an old facility; it has been there since 1900, and the thick solid walls kept out even the sound of the storm. The buildings sustained very little damage. The north wing had some windows blown out, and there were some leaks in the ceiling, but the hospital never lost electricity. Everyone was thankful that new generators had been installed just three months before.

When Emily got off her shift at seven o'clock that night, she went downstairs to the lobby where there was a TV showing pictures of the surrounding area. She saw that the local Red Lobster restaurant was gone, Edgewater Village was gone, and the casino that was floating off-shore was now in the middle of the road—three blocks inland from the ocean. Her first thought was, *Oh no! My family is gone!* She was para-lyzed with fear. But there were no working phone lines to get informa-tion. Not even cell phones were making connections. There was no news at all from Hancock County, and only a little was being reported from neighboring Harrison County. This gave Emily a sinking feeling in the pit of her stomach. But there was nothing she could do. For her, the most difficult part of surviving Hurricane Katrina was not knowing if her family was dead or alive.

Hours later, from the fifth story of the hospital, she was able to use her cell phone to get through to her oldest daughter, who wisely had evacuated to Jacksonville, Florida, with her young children just days before! "Alisha," Emily demanded anxiously, "have you heard any-thing?"

"Oh, Mama," Alisha answered, her voice breaking, "Nothing's left over there."

Emily took a deep breath. "Honey, your daddy's a survivor. He's a boy scout master. He's got good sense and good skills. I feel like he would take care of his family. If anyone could, by the grace of God, it's your daddy!"

The next day Emily was frantic to find out something about her family, but for her own safety, the hospital authorities wouldn't let her out of the VA hospital without an escort. Finally, she got the associate director of Building 2 to take her in a government car. They got as far as Fire Station 2 in Bay St. Louis, Mississippi, where the car got a flat tire. In desperation, she went into the fire station and asked, "Has anyone seen any members of my family?"

Relief swept over her when she heard the words, "We saw your husband and your son over by Valentine."

"What about the rest of them?"

"Oh," they responded, "we're sure they're OK."

So with hope welling in her heart, Emily made it to Valentine, where a neighbor across the street broke the bittersweet news to her, "Everyone's OK, except your mother."

It was heart wrenching to learn that her mother had not survived the storm. But she knew her mother was a wonderful, church-going, praying person and that she would not have been able to endure the devastation that Emily was seeing at this moment: All the beautiful, quaint coastal towns were gone. She also knew that her mom wasn't in good health and had not expected to live past seventy. God had granted her ten extra years; her mother was ready to die. For that Emily was thankful.

Once Emily had news that her family had survived, her fears calmed. She still, however, had no idea where they were. All she knew was that someone picked them up in a truck. "Please don't take me back to the VA hospital," she begged her driver. But she had nowhere else to stay; she had no choice but to go back to the safety of the hospital. As they drove through debris and fallen trees on the way to Biloxi, everywhere she looked she saw total devastation!

Back safely at the VA hospital, scenes from that day flooded her mind. She couldn't turn off the utter horror of it all. She tossed and turned all night. All she could do was pray, "Lord, please let me find my family." The next morning, she finally got in touch with her daughter's boyfriend.

"Mom," he shouted into the phone, "are you OK? We were so scared."

"Yes, I'm OK."

"Where are you?"

"They won't release me from the VA hospital until I have a safe place to go."

He told her that they were all together, staying on a tugboat, and he would come for her as soon as he could. She was finally able to leave at eleven o'clock. What rejoicing there was when the family was at last in each other's arms. "Thank You, thank You, God," Emily cried. "Thank You for helping Kelvin have the strength and wisdom to save our children."

Their worry then turned to Kelvin's ninety-five-year-old mother, who had stayed in New Orleans with her other son during the storm. They didn't know what might have happened to her. Miraculously, after the storm, she waded out of the house in water that was up to her chest! Finally, a national guard boat picked her up and took her to the Superdome, where she stayed for two days. By that time, she was so severely dehydrated that she had to be airlifted to medical care. She was supposed to go to Atlanta, Georgia, but she ended up in a hospital in Nashville, Tennessee. All this time Kelvin had no idea if his mother had met the same fate as Emily's mother. So many of the elderly didn't make it! You can imagine the rejoicing when the family got the news that Grandma Schulz was alive.

After telling their story, Emily added, "I can't thank God enough for opening so many doors for my family in order to get them through the storm. I know He has a plan for us. When I retire—and maybe before—I want to have the opportunity to become a volunteer and help others, like they have helped us. The volunteers have come from out of town—from far away places—and have given their time and energy to provide food, clothing, and other vital services for us. That's what I want to do. I may have lost my mother, but I praise God for saving the rest of my family. We will go on from here, and we won't look back. We're going to live a very simple life. We don't need much—as long as we have each other."

During the storm, Kelvin had to be brave for his children's sake. But reliving this terrifying ordeal was emotionally draining. He was visibly shaken. His chest was heaving. He didn't show this emotion in front of his wife. He wanted to protect her from knowing just how bad it was. His last comment, however, said it all. "I don't ever want to walk on the edge of death again. I can't do it."

Is God Calling You to Follow?

Consider Emily's comments for a moment. She feels God has a plan for her to step out and be a good Samaritan for others; to volunteer to help others who can't help themselves. Did you know that God has a plan for your life too? Is God calling you to leave your comfort zone and follow Him? Is He calling you to a new work, to a different location, perhaps? Is He calling you to step out without the security of a salary or retirement benefits? Is He asking you to do something you've never done before?

What if Kelvin's kids hadn't trusted their father enough to leave their childhood home and crawl out of its crumbling shelter onto a floating roof as he asked them to do? What if they refused to snuggle together under the shelter that he provided when they were being battered by the flying debris at the height of the storm's fury? And when their roof-raft began to sink, what if the kids had been too frightened to follow their dad as he crawled out over the debris to the safety of the boat?

Today, your heavenly Father is calling you to leave your place of comfort and do a special work for Him—just as He called fishermen two thousand years ago to leave their boats—and as He called the apostle Paul to leave his prestigious life as Pharisee par excellence!

It may not be easy to follow! Do you think it was easy for Paul to follow when Christ called him? His journey of obedience led to some pretty painful places. Here's what Paul says about it:

I have worked harder, been put in jail more often, been whipped times without number, and faced death again and again. Five different times the Jews gave me thirty-nine lashes. Three times I was beaten with rods. Once I was stoned. Three times I was shipwrecked. Once I spent a whole night and day adrift at sea. I have traveled many weary miles. I have faced danger from flooded rivers and from robbers. I have faced danger from my own people, the Jews, as well as from the Gentiles. I have faced danger in the cities, in the deserts, and on the stormy seas. And I have faced danger from men who claim to be Christians but are not. I have lived with weariness and pain and sleepless nights. Often I have been hungry and thirsty and have gone without food. Often I have shivered with cold, without enough clothing to keep me warm (2 Corinthians 11:23–27, NLT).

By recalling all these things, Paul isn't complaining. He's boasting about what an honor it is to serve God even during the toughest of times. In these last days of earth's history, Satan is fighting God's people with a fury that's stronger and more forceful than Katrina, Rita, and Wilma—and all the rest of the 2005 hurricanes—wrapped into one!

And into the midst of the storm, God is calling His people to follow Him into some pretty scary situations for His glory. *He's calling you.*

The question is, Will you trust your heavenly Father enough to follow Him into the storm and across the debris to the safety of His boat? He doesn't promise riches and fame, nor does He promise no pain! But He does promise that He'll rescue you if you get into trouble—if you just trust Him. Here's what He says: "Trust me in your times of trouble, and I will rescue you, and you will give me glory" (Psalm 50:15, NLT).

The exhilaration of following Christ—and giving Him the glory—cannot be equaled by any adrenaline rush man can devise. Step out and follow Him, and you'll exclaim as did Paul, "Since I know it is all for Christ's good, I am quite content with my weaknesses and with insults, hardships, persecutions, and calamities. For when I am weak, then I am strong" (2 Corinthians 12:10, NLT). *Why?* Christ made it clear to Paul—and He's saying the same thing to you: "My gracious favor is all you need. My power works best in your weakness" (2 Corinthians 12:9, NLT).

---

1. A home video of Kelvin leading his children over the debris to the boat was taken by a neighbor's son, Andrew McDonald, and was shown on CBS News on September 6, 2005, under the title, "A Journey Through Hell."

Chapter 4

DON'T LET ME DIE

"Therefore whoever hears these sayings of Mine, and does them,
I will liken him to a wise man who built his house on the rock . . ."
—Matthew 7:24, NKJV

D'Iberville, wedged up against St. Martin's Bayou and across the bay from Biloxi, Mississippi, had survived numerous hurricanes, including Camille, with some flooding from the bayou—but seldom from the bay. That's why Katrina's thirty-foot storm surge, which rushed through the bay past Biloxi and hit D'Iberville, was such a shock. But the giant surge was worse here than elsewhere along the Gulf Coast due to the tons of debris that it picked up from Biloxi and brought with it. The storm literally decimated D'Iberville with debris-filled killer waves. Months after the storm there were still piles, ten to fifteen feet high, of uprooted trees, broken furniture,

Brenda Walsh interviews Wayne Alley who told her about his next-door neighbor who survived Katrina on the roof of his house!

Wayne surveys the storm damage as the task of cleaning up and rebuilding begins.

rusted appliances, and mangled metal and wood—not only from D'Iberville, but also from the homes and businesses in Biloxi that had been swept away and deposited there.

Saved by Shingles

By ten o'clock on that fateful morning of August 29, most of the homes along Racetrack Road in D'Iberville had water up to their roofs and tons of debris knocking at the windows and walls. One by one, they were pushed off their foundations. Most floated momentarily and then broke up as the wind, water, and debris continued to batter them. The Breasher family was just one of many who were forced into the upper stories of their homes by the rising water of the first surge. Then, as following surges hit and the attics filled with water, people were either trapped and drowned or forced to escape into the unknown dangers of the storm. Connie and Sharon Breasher and their adult son chose the second option! With panic in their hearts, they realized their

Connie and Sharon Breasher were not able to climb to safety on the roof of their own house (the white house in the background) but managed to ride out the storm on the roof of Wayne Alley's house next door.

only hope of living through the storm was to leave the shelter of their water-filled attic. Racing to the window, they yelled at each other, "We have to get on the roof and pray the house will stand. Grab the dogs. Let's go!"

The shock of the cold water took their breath away. The current was swift. They had to get on the roof—their lives depended on it. They swam around the house to the lowest part of the roof and clung to the sharp metal edge as best they could, dodging debris in the water and being blown about by the wind. Their two dogs frantically tried to keep their heads above water. The Breashers tried to climb onto the roof, but it was too steep and slippery. Over and over again, they tried, before finally giving up the impossible task. Frantically, they looked for something else to cling to. The only other house left standing on their block was the brick house with its shingle roof, belonging to their neighbor, Wayne Alley. Could they make it? They shoved away from their own house and began the desperate and dangerous fifty-yard swim. At last they reached the Alleys' house, grabbed the edge of the roof, and found a handhold on the shingles. As the water continued to rise, they were finally able to pull themselves up on the roof—and then to pull their struggling dogs to safety as well.

All this time, Wayne and Brenda Alley were riding out the storm at the local hospital where Wayne worked. Until they returned home the next day and discovered twenty feet of debris piled behind their home and their neighborhood destroyed, they had no idea of the full extent of the agony their neighbors had endured. Who would have thought that life or death might someday be determined by the type of roof on your house!

Saved by Exceeding the Building Codes

After Camille hit Waveland in 1969, Chuck Reed decided to build his house better and stronger than the construction code required. He poured extra concrete for the foundation and built with two-by-sixes rather than with two-by-fours. Then he anchored the roof and tiled it rather than using metal or shingles that could be blown off with hurricane force winds.

For over thirty years his home had withstood the summer's tropical coastal storms. Then came Katrina! When the first surge of water hit, flooding the ground floor, Chuck climbed to the second story. When the water kept rising, he knew better than to climb into his attic because there were no windows there from which to escape. So he anxiously waited by a second story window, hoping the water wouldn't reach that high and he'd be safe. But it did.

When he realized that his escape route would soon be cut off, he made the decision to swim out the window into the briny mass of water and cling to the side of his house. As the water rose, he continued to find handholds higher and higher on the house.

At one point a telephone wire, still attached to a nearby pole, washed close to him. Chuck grabbed it and quickly tied it around his waist, thinking that if he lost his hold on his house, at least he wouldn't be swept away by the current.

By the time the water reached the base of the roof, adrenaline was pumping through Chuck's veins. Getting up on that tiled roof was his only hope. He tried to grab a tile and pull himself up, but his hand slipped. He tried again and again until the tips of his fingers were rubbed raw and bloodied by the rough tiles. At last, as the water kept coming up, he was able to wedge his fingers between two tiles and pull himself out of the water. Now clinging to the roof for his life, Chuck heard screams above the roar of the wind and, for the first time, became aware that bodies were floating by. Some were beyond his reach, others were desperately trying to get onto his roof. He had to do something.

Bracing himself, Chuck reached down, trying to grab the hands of a desperate woman. Her pleading eyes were filled with panic and fear. "Don't let me die! Don't let me die!" she begged. He reached as far as he could, trying frantically to make contact with her outstretched fingers, when suddenly a huge refrigerator floated by, knocked into her, and forced her under water. When she surfaced, she was far beyond reach. Guilt swept over him—he had tried so hard to save her and had failed. It seemed hopeless. Chuck grew bolder, leaning out further for the next person who floated by, knowing that if he slipped he was still tied to the pole, so he wouldn't be washed away like the others. He began grabbing anything he could—an arm or leg, clothing—even hair. Sometimes a huge piece of furniture, a door, or a log would push the people away from him—and each time the panicked look on their faces as they were washed away struck terror and guilt into his own tortured heart. But not all were lost. He began to pull people to the safety of his roof, one after the other.

At one point, Chuck spotted his own brother thrashing in the water, desperately swimming against the current. The brothers lived only two blocks apart, so when his house succumbed to the storm, Chuck's brother decided to swim to Chuck's house. He knew his brother's house was built stronger than most in the area, and he desperately hoped that Chuck was still alive. Chuck was able to grab him just before a gust of wind would have surely swept him past the safety of the roof and most certainly to his death.

In the next couple hours, Chuck pulled twenty-one people from what would have been a watery grave. As soon as he got them safely on the roof, they inched their way up to the peak, where they found handholds and lay low, hoping they wouldn't be blown off by the wind or hit by a flying piece of debris—and praying earnestly that the water would crest before it reached the top of the roof. There were no trees in sight, no other roofs above water. If wind or water tore them from their perch, there was no other place for them to go.

Miraculously, just when they all thought they were doomed, just as the water reached the peak of the house, it crested—and slowly began to recede. Chuck now did a very strange thing. Afraid the telephone wire tied around his waist might entangle someone and cause them to be thrown into the water, he untied himself from the very thing that had given him the courage he needed to save the people floating by. Only seconds later, a huge piece of metal hit the telephone pole, ripping it out of the ground. Horrified, Chuck watched it as the wind and the current swept it away. If he had still been tied to the pole, he would have most certainly been yanked off the roof and probably swept to his death!

Twenty-two people were saved because of the heavy tile roof—and the excellent construction of Chuck's house, which allowed it to stand in the midst of one of the worst disasters in America's history.

Reflecting on the experience, Chuck was so filled with emotion that his voice quivered and cracked. "Why me?" he exclaimed. "Why all those people on the roof? Why were we saved—and the others swept to their deaths?"

"God must have had special plans for your life and the lives of those you saved," someone told him.

"But didn't God have a plan for those who didn't make it?" Chuck asked.

Yes, God has a plan for each of His children, but God does not ask us to understand Him or His ways. He asks only that we trust Him! Although floodwaters may come near us, we can still trust Him. We can still hold on to Psalm 32:6, 7.

For this cause everyone who is godly shall pray to You
In a time when You may be found;
Surely in a flood of great waters
They shall not come near him.
You are my hiding place;
You shall preserve me from trouble;
You shall surround me with songs of deliverance (NKJV).

Saved by Three Extra Feet

Dennis Strong and his family were saved not by their choice of roofing material, but by building their entire home above what the building code required—specifically, their decision to add three feet to the foundation.

When Dennis's mother-in-law gave him and his wife, Betty, the lot at 3086 Racetrack Road in D'Iberville, he was somewhat concerned about building so near the coast. But the land was on a thirteen-foot rise, making it slightly higher than other homes in the area. He asked his good friend who lived behind them how much water had covered the property during Camille. "Not more than a foot," his friend replied. So Dennis, thinking no storm could be worse than Camille, made the decision to go ahead and build on the lot. But just to be on the safe side, he decided to build his house on a foundation three feet higher than normal.

Betty Strong stands in the living room of her home—now open to the outside since most of the walls have disappeared.

Most contractors cut corners to save money, but Dennis's cousin was the builder, and he suggested building the entire house above what the building code required. Instead of two-by-fours on sixteen-inch centers, he used two-by-sixes on twelve-inch centers. Instead of a hurricane clip on every other rafter, he put one on every rafter. In addition, he ran what's called a strong back down the side and used three-fourth-inch plywood instead of the half-inch that was required by law. All those things, his cousin

Dennis and Betty Strong in front of their house, surrounded by belongings they have been able to salvage.

Like so many Gulf Coast residents, Dennis and Betty Strong were grateful simply to be alive following Katrina. Signs such as these sprouted up—partly to inform and partly as a symbol of determination.

told Dennis, would make the best hurricane-proof house ever seen. Eighteen years later, this decision to overbuild literally saved the life of Dennis and his family.

During the years, the Strong family had survived a number of hurricanes from the safety of their home. That's why they ignored the mandatory evacuation notice. "Nothing could be worse than Camille," they reasoned. But they were wrong! When Katrina hit, not only were Dennis and Betty and their two children (seventeen-year-old Kyle and fourteen-year-old Gracie) in their home, but also Betty's eighty-three-year-old mother, her brother and his wife, and her cousin, Terry.

Debris scattered across the floor of Dennis and Betty Strong's house.

About seven-thirty the morning of August 29, most of the family were still sleeping as Dennis and Kyle were walking around the inside of the house, watching the trees bend horizontally with the gusts of wind. Suddenly, Kyle yelled to his dad, "Papa, look! There's water in the backyard."

"It's coming from the bayou side," Dennis told him, "so we don't have to worry. There won't be more than a foot." Minutes later, the water had reached the patio. Dennis called to Betty, "Go wake up everyone in the house and get them into the living room, just in case." Kyle then went to the front door, "Papa," he yelled. "Look out the front!" Water was already coming up the steps—and this water was from the bay!

Just then the phone rang. It was their neighbor, Ronnie. "Dennis, I have four feet of water in my house. (It was lower than the Strongs'.) Can I come over?"

"Sure," Dennis said, "come on." A few minutes later, Ronnie jumped out of his truck and waded through the water to get into the house. By this time water was covering the steps of Dennis's house. The men started putting down towels by the doorways to keep the water out of the house, but water seeped in under the glass storm doors and filled the space between the doors like a fish bowl. As the floor flooded, Dennis pulled down the folding attic stairs and ordered everyone to climb up.

Dennis and Ronnie stayed behind to monitor the progress of the storm. Suddenly, the doors to the house burst open, and the living room flooded with four feet of water, sending the men scrambling to the attic stairs. They resisted the urge to pull up the stairs, which would close the opening, knowing it was far more important for them to keep an eye on what was happening below. They told the others to get away from the attic opening, and then they watched with mounting anxiety as the water continued to rise. The women yelled, "What's happening down there? Is the water going down?" Dennis didn't want to worry them, so he calmly replied, "Yes, it's going down."

Finally the water got so high that it pushed the steps into their folded position and slammed the attic door shut with a deafening thud. The women jumped in fear and demanded, "Why did you close the door?"

The men, trying to hide the terror that began to grip them, replied, "We got tired of looking down."

Even though they could no longer see what was happening below, they could hear the walls creaking and the furniture swirling as if in a giant mixer as objects hit the ceiling. They heard the sounds of glass shattering as windows exploded. The house shook as the water slammed against it and the wind shrieked in its fury.

Betty briefly considered that what was happening around them had to be worse than her husband was telling her. But to control her own panic and that of the others, she couldn't let her mind go there. She forced herself to believe that it wasn't as bad as it sounded. Certainly, everything would be OK.

Suddenly, without warning, one whole wall of the attic blew out, exposing them to stark reality. It was as if they were in front row seats of an I-Max theater witnessing the uncontrollable wrath of a storm of such magnitude that their minds could not comprehend it. How could it be possible that just a few minutes before they were secure, believing there was no danger—and now they were facing the worst possible fate? They were paralyzed with fear.

Dennis screamed above the roar of the storm, "Get back! Get back!" Hit by the urgency of his demand, they fled from the opening and cowered together against the other side of the attic, not knowing which wall would go next.

No longer could Dennis pretend that things were going to be OK! Now for the first time, he was forced to consider the unthinkable; they might have to abandon their house. His mind raced over the options they still had. They could break the window on the side of the attic where the wind was not so intense and perhaps reach the roof. Or would it be better to break a hole in the roof and climb through that? Which would be safer?

Just as Dennis went over to the side of the attic to check if they could escape through the window, water began coming in that side. Not wanting anyone to know, he calmly returned to his family and nonchalantly made the comment, "worst case scenario, we're all going to have to swim somewhere."

Dennis and Ronnie then began looking for possible places where they could swim to if the water reached the top of the attic doors. But there was nothing close enough for Betty's elderly mother to swim to safely. And the stench of the sewage-polluted water was so disgusting, that the thought of having to swim through it was incomprehensible. So they waited there in the attic with water lapping at their feet, anticipating the worst—and they prayed!

The hours ticked by. Four hours. Five hours. But, praise the Lord, the water never came any higher. Finally, the water had gone down a foot. Then another three feet. Through the gaping hole in their attic wall they kept watching Ronnie's house to determine the progress of the receding water. Just as Dennis whispered under his breath, "It's over," the wind switched directions and began blowing straight out of the south at 130 or 140 miles per hour, ripping shingles off the roof. When Dennis looked up, he could see large spots of daylight overhead where the shingles should have been. *Oh no,* he thought, *the roof's going to go!* There was nothing they could do but hunker down in the closets of the attic and pray like they had never prayed before in their lives.

Around four in the afternoon the wind died down to around 30 or 40 miles per hour, and the water had receded enough to safely walk outside. As Dennis surveyed the damage, reality hit. They had lost everything! He began to cry.

Three weeks after the storm, Dennis commented, "Since we've lived here, we've been through a few really bad hurricanes, and we always said, 'Nothing could be worse than Camille.' So we stayed. Now we know. This one was worse. We've never seen water come from both the bayou and the bay. It makes you realize that the next one could be even more deadly! That's why Betty doesn't want to rebuild here. We were one of the lucky ones who had flood and wind damage insurance. They'll just end up bulldozing this place down. It was a fine house, but there's nothing left! And if it hadn't been for the extra three feet we built on—and the super heavy construction of the roof—we would never have made it! God was good to save us this time. We're not going to push our luck—or presume He'll do it again."

Building on the Rock

All the people in these stories were saved by something—a roof made of shingles or tile instead of metal, construction that exceeded the building codes, or a higher foundation. They were all saved by something that had been done years before in anticipation of a potential storm. They were saved by the way their homes were built! In a way, you could say, these were wise people. And when the big one hit, they were prepared. These are modern-day illustrations of the truth in Christ's parable about the wise man who built his house on the rock. It stood in the storm! While the foolish man's house—built on the sand—was washed away.

As important as it is to build for a potential hurricane, it's far more important to spiritually prepare for the storms of life, which is what Christ's parable was really about. If you want to make it through tough times with peace in your heart instead of anxiety and fear, you've got to build on a foundation of Jesus Christ. He is the "Rock of our salvation" (Psalm 95:1); He alone has the power to calm the storm. Only a close personal relationship with Him will bring contentment in whatever circumstance you may find yourself. There is no storm of human or satanic wrath that can disturb the calm that can be yours if you have constant communication with God. Jesus said it best with these words, "Peace I leave with you, My peace I give to you; not as the world gives do I give to you. Let not your heart be troubled, neither let it be afraid" (John 14:27, NKJV).

-Chapter 5-
A HARDHEADED WOMAN AND THREE FOOLISH MEN

"I haven't seen anything like Katrina.
The storm blew the sweetness right out of gingerbread."
—Louis Lassabe

A Hardheaded Woman

She was hardheaded. Everyone said so. Connie Heckler LaFleur—a fifty-three-year-old redhead from Missouri, living in the community of Lakeshore in Bay St. Louis, Mississippi. "You couldn't tell her anything," Wilbur, her husband of twenty-five years, lamented. "She had a mind of her own. She always did."

When Connie first heard Katrina was heading toward the Mississippi Gulf Coast and officials were recommending evacuation, she stubbornly announced, "I'm not leaving my home!"

Wilbur tried to reason with her. He pleaded with her, "Please, leave with me."

She refused to listen. "It takes too long to get out of this area. I'm not going to waste my time driving two hundred miles at ten miles an hour."

The day before the storm, her son Joseph Heckler called all the way from Iraq, where he was a civilian contractor. He tried everything to convince her to leave. "Mom, you've got to go. There's plenty of time to get out of there. They say this storm is going to be a big one. Please, Mom, go with Wilbur."

Wilbur stands beside the car in which Connie tried to escape. Notice the large rut by the tires where she spun her wheels in the rising water. Connie then ran up these stairs to the attic—where she lost her life.

But she wouldn't listen. She countered, "It won't be that bad. It's going toward New Orleans. Quit worrying, Joe, I've made it through hurricanes before, and I'll make it this time!"

Even that last night, just hours before the storm hit, her best friends came by the house and tried to get her to leave with them. "It's not too late to get out of here," they urged, but she wouldn't go! "Come on, Connie, don't be so stubborn." But her mind was made up!

She thought the house could withstand the hurricane. The foundation was thirteen-and-a-half feet above sea level and built according to the building inspector's specifications. Plus, it was all bolted and screwed with storm protectors on the windows and doors. She also knew that even though Camille had left a water line at a height of eight feet on the brick wall of the house, the

Brenda stands between Wilbur LaFleur and his stepson Joseph Heckler.

building had withstood the fury of that storm. The house would stand again. She would be safe. What Connie wasn't counting on was that Katrina would dump a thirty-foot swell of sea water into Bay St. Louis!

Early Sunday morning, after pleading with his wife once more, Wilbur packed his truck, gave her a farewell kiss, and hugged her just a little longer than usual. Then he climbed into his truck. He turned back once again hoping she would change her mind, but she stood firm. They waved, and her last words to him were, "Good luck."

He took Highway 190 west toward his mother's house near Lafayette in southwest Louisiana. It was slow going. It took him almost twelve hours, *but he made it!*

Connie didn't.

The next day when Wilbur saw the news stories about Katrina, he knew!

Apparently Connie also realized her danger when the water started to rise early that Monday morning. At one point she tried to leave. She started the car, but the water was too deep. The wheels merely spun, digging a hole in the ground twelve to eighteen inches deep. When she realized escape by automobile was impossible, she ran back into the house, and as the water continued to rise, she moved as high as she could into the attic—where there was no escape. At this point she called her granddaughter, Kassie Lee Johnson. Her last words were, "It's too late. I can't get out of here, and the water is coming up. This is it!"

A few days later, Wilbur found her body about a block away near a pond. She was surrounded by a mass of bricks, trailer bodies, and her dishes—she had a different set of dishes for every holiday—and a big collection of pots and pans. The house at 6015 Lakeshore Road that had seemed to her so invincible was completely destroyed—washed away, as were all the other buildings on the block.

Connie left behind five children and eleven grandchildren—all of whom tried to convince her to leave.

Her son Joseph was frantic when he viewed Katrina's destruction on TV in Iraq. But the only news reports were of New Orleans and Biloxi. There was nothing about Bay St. Louis or Hancock County. Presuming the worst, he was able to get a message delivered to the Red Cross that he was needed back home. Released from his contract, he arrived in Bay St. Louis just in time to identify his mother's body. "It's the hardest thing anyone can ever be asked to do," he said with tears in his eyes. "It's heart wrenching to see your mother all puffy and bloated—when it didn't have to be this way."

It was a very sad, difficult time for all the family and friends who tried so hard to change the mind of this hardheaded woman!

"I made it through Hurricane Betsy, and I made it through Camille, and before Katrina, I thought I could make it through any storm," Wilbur commented. "But I don't feel that way any more. If you made it through this one, you're just plain lucky. But I guarantee, you won't hang around for the next!"

Died for a Pot-Bellied Pig

It was right before Katrina hit. The mandatory evacuation order had been given. Now the FEMA representative was going through the streets of the towns along the Gulf Coast of Mississippi, trying to convince the reluctant to leave. He spent quite a bit of time in Waveland with one particular man. "The storm is coming. It's going to be a direct hit to this area. We can only imagine the devastation it's going to cause. It's not safe to stay. Please come with me." Finally, it seemed as if the man was convinced. "I've got to get something first," he said and turned to go back into his house. A few minutes later he appeared with a pot-bellied pig in his arms.

"I'm sorry," the FEMA official said. "We have orders to take only people."

The man sighed and shrugged his shoulders, "If you can't take my pig, then I'm not going either."

Once again the man from FEMA pleaded with him. "I'm offering you a free ride. If the storm is as bad as they say, at least you'll be safe. If it isn't, the pig will survive, and you'll be back home within a day to feed it." But nothing the official said would convince the man to leave without his pig. His decision was firm. "I've weathered all the other storms; I can weather this one, too."

Reluctantly, the FEMA official got back into his truck and drove away without him.

As Monday morning dawned, wind-driven torrents of rain, growing ever more ferocious, whipped the ocean into a fury and began building up the greatest storm surge in the history of the Gulf Coast. Leaping over the beach and Highway 90 that bordered it, the wave slammed into the homes along the coast. Sturdy houses that had withstood years of being beaten by hurricanes were suddenly reduced to splintered debris, as if they were made of straw. The man and his pot-bellied pig were in one of those houses.

Three days later, the FEMA official returned. When he saw the devastation, a wave of nausea swept over him as he thought about the man who had refused to leave. The official's instinct told him that no one living as close to the beach as this man did could have survived. Now it was his job to search for the missing. Lifting a large piece of debris, his heart sank as he discovered the bodies of the foolish man and his pot-bellied pig. Tears came to his eyes. Then he broke down and sobbed, "It didn't need to end this way. It didn't need to be!"

Can you imagine how our heavenly Father must feel if, after sending His Son to this earth to save us, we refuse His invitation for a free ride to safety?

The Atheist in Mississippi Is No More

When the winds of Katrina started, Pieter Nolden was an atheist. He was a sailor and knew the ways of the wind and the storms of the

Pieter Nolden, the atheist who prayed for God to save him from the storm!

sea. He had traveled the world for thirty-six years— the Netherlands, Australia, New Zealand, Papua New Guinea, you name it—and never really felt the need of God. He could take care of himself. But Katrina changed all that. Never before had he feared for his life as he did during the nine hours that Katrina's rage ravaged Mississippi's Gulf Coast and held him and his friends captive in their attic. It seemed like an eternity.

Pieter was the only one awake in his home in Bayside when he saw the wave coming. He screamed to the others, "Get up! We're gonna get hit!" By the time he got everyone into the attic, they were surrounded by thirty feet of water. The water was crashing into the house; the unrelenting wind hit the roof above them, ripping off the metal roofing and plywood, sheet by sheet. Torrents of cold biting rain found the exposed places in what had been the roof and left those huddled in the attic drenched and shivering. And the sounds—the banging of debris and the incessant whine of the wind—made it feel as though they would be thrown to the fury of the storm and the waves at any moment.

That's when Pieter prayed. He later said, "I don't know who I was praying to, but I was talkin' to somebody." Then he reflected, "And He must have been listening, 'cause I'm here! I'm here! But I'm not sticking around for the next one." He shook his head emphatically. "No way. I'm gettin' out of here and goin' back to the Netherlands, where I grew up."

Saved by a Jug and a Fallen Tree

His neighbors called him "Cappy." For years Charles Richard Uhlmann had been the captain of a boat. He was familiar with the sea, and he thought he knew all about storms. That is, until Katrina.

So at nine o'clock that Monday morning, there was Charles, sitting in his camper home thinking he'd be fine. He wasn't even worried when the trees began popping and banging around him and the strong gusts of wind began lifting his camper

Charles Richard Uhlmann standing in front of his destroyed home.

off the ground, raising it up a foot or two and then slamming it to the earth. His only fear was that a tree might fall on it. He had lived in Bayside, Mississippi, for fifteen years and had safely survived six hurricanes without any major damage. Why should he be concerned now?

Suddenly, what he feared most happened. A tree cracked. It hit another tree, breaking its fall, and then hit a third. It cracked again and landed with a loud thud on the roof of Charles's camper. If the tree had fallen straight down on his camper, hitting it with full force, he would have been dead. Amazingly, although his camper top was bashed in on one side, the ceiling held where he was sitting, and he wasn't hurt! But he knew that outside the safety of his camper a pretty big storm was raging.

Then he heard the roar of the water. The water came so fast that it flooded his camper before he could get out. He had to push hard to get the door open—knowing that was his only way of escape should the water rise any more. It was coming up about a foot a minute. Before he could think clearly of what to do, the water was four feet high. He weighed his options: He could stay in his camper and take a chance of being trapped inside and drowning or get out, brave the elements, and have a chance to live.

Quickly, he put a strong leather belt through the handle of an empty six-gallon water jug and tied it to himself before swimming toward the open door. He waited until the last minute to leave the protection of his camper. He held on to the door frame until the water was only ten inches from the top, then forced his way out. The jug popped him to the surface, and immediately he began to feel himself being swept away with the current. He frantically kicked with all his strength to get to the tree that was leaning on his camper. Finally reaching it, he climbed as high as he could into its branches and held on for dear life.

From his perch, he watched in horror as pieces of people's lives washed past him—broken furniture, floating washing machines, roofing, and tons of debris. Cars were knocked over like matchbox toys, then pushed away by the current. Six cows floated by; five were dead, but the sixth was putting up a futile fight for its life. A van floated into his yard and then disappeared beneath the surface. And all the time the wind screamed, and his tree was popping and bending, threatening to break and throw him into the disgusting river of smelly raw sewage and floating junk.

For eight fear-packed hours he clung to the tree repeating again and again, "Don't break, Baby. Don't break!" And telling himself, "Hang on, Baby. Hang on!"

After the water started going down, he could see that his neighbors, Pieter and three others who had also foolishly stayed behind, had survived from their exposed attic. With a jubilant shout, he called to them. "I'm OK! I'm OK!" About this time, a neighbor climbed down from his roof and found a little skiff. He came by and offered Charles a lift, but he couldn't get the boat close enough to rescue him. So Charles waited until the filthy water got down to about four feet before he jumped out of the tree.

Charles lost everything but a few items he had in his van, which at the height of the storm, had been covered by five feet of water. Two weeks after Katrina, Charles was working hard trying to get the van to start. He'd drained the oil, changed the transmission fluid, and cleaned the carburetor, and now he was going through the ignition system. His only comment was, "I was saved by a water jug and a tree. I'm lucky— very lucky! When the next one hits, I'll be long gone!"

If Charles were a Bible-quoting man, he's probably admit that he was a good example of the truth of Proverbs 14:12: "There is a way which seems right to a man, but its end is the way of death" (NKJV). Or if he were trying to convince someone to evacuate before the next hurricane, and the person were resisting, he might quote Proverbs 12:15: "The way of a fool is right in his own eyes, but he who heeds counsel is wise" (NKJV).

There's a Little Bit of Foolishness in All of Us

All of us make mistakes that we regret. We've done thoughtless things that have come back to haunt us. We've made foolish decisions that have ended up hurting us and others. But the most foolish mistake of all is thinking we can save ourselves, thinking we're self-sufficient and don't need anything or anyone. Thinking that if we just keep doing what's right, we'll be safe.

That's what the five foolish virgins thought in the story Jesus told about preparing for His coming. They thought they had enough oil in their lamps to make it. But when they really needed it, their lamps had run dry. And they had no extra.

You remember the story. It's in Matthew 25, verses 1 through 13. Here's how the New Living Translation tells it:

"The Kingdom of Heaven can be illustrated by the story of ten bridesmaids who took their lamps and went to meet the bridegroom. Five of them were foolish, and five were wise. The five who were foolish took no oil for their lamps, but the other five were wise enough to take along extra oil. When the bridegroom was delayed, they all lay down and slept. At midnight they were roused by the shout, 'Look, the bridegroom is coming! Come out and welcome him!'

"All the bridesmaids got up and prepared their lamps. Then the five foolish ones asked the others, 'Please give us some of your oil because our lamps are going out.' But the others replied, 'We don't have enough for all of us. Go to a shop and buy some for yourselves.'

"But while they were gone to buy oil, the bridegroom came, and those who were ready went in with him to the marriage feast, and the door was locked. Later, when the other five bridesmaids returned, they stood outside, calling, 'Sir, open the door for us!' But he called back, 'I don't know you.'

"So stay awake and be prepared, because you do not know the day or hour of my return."

Here's the lesson: When it comes to salvation, we can't do it by ourselves. Just being good isn't enough. As smart as we think we are, we can't save ourselves. We've got to have the "oil" of the Holy Spirit within to convict us of sin. (Sin is basically doing things our way instead of Christ's way.) We've got to be willing to listen to the instruction that the Holy Spirit gives us—and act on it. We've got to be so filled with Christ's Spirit that His will becomes ours. Only then will we have faith enough to let go of the pot-bellied pigs in our lives that keep us from totally surrendering to Christ and accepting His gift of salvation.

If you've been thinking you should surrender all to Christ, but you're still foolishly holding on to some selfish habit or desire, don't wait until it's too late. Don't risk missing the greatest event in the history of the universe—the coming of Jesus—because of your own selfish agenda. Instead, be like the three wise men two thousand years ago, who, when they saw His star, left everything behind to find Him!

Jesus is calling you. He's saying, "My child, listen to me and treasure my instructions. Tune your ears to wisdom, and concentrate on understanding. . . .

"Then you will understand what is right, just, and fair, and you will know how to find the right course of action every time. For wisdom will enter your heart, and knowledge will fill you with joy. Wise planning will watch over you. Understanding will keep you safe" (Proverbs 2:1, 2, 9–11, NLT).

-Chapter 6-

It Had to Be
a Miracle

"Weeping may endure for a night,
But joy comes in the morning."
—Psalm 30:5, NKJV

Whether or not people survived Katrina had a lot to do with where they were the moment the powerful surge of sea water hit them. For the Mississippi Gulf Coast residents, the closer to the beach they were, the more they were at risk for being hit by the almost thirty-foot wave that broke over the shoreline. For those in New Orleans and the surrounding parishes, their survival depended on where they were when the levees broke.

The following are stories of those who survived—even though they were in the wrong place at the wrong time! These are stories of how God intervened and changed the course of history for so many who were caught in Katrina's path: How some were saved—when so many around them were lost.

Trapped in the Attic

The only thing Sheryl and Joey Donald feared about hurricanes was the tornadoes they spawned. Why should they worry? They lived in a no-flood zone in Biloxi, Mississippi, two blocks from the river. When the water started coming into their house, Sheryl really wasn't concerned. She told her seven-year-old granddaughter, Kaitlin, "Go get Pops and tell him we need a mop."

"A mop?" her husband shouted above the wind. "Look out the front door!" She couldn't believe her eyes. Within minutes their car sank under seven feet of water from the storm surge hitting the river. They had just enough time to pull down the attic door, grab Kaitlin and her twelve-week-old cocker spaniel puppy, and race up the stairs. It all happened so fast they didn't even think to bring food or water. They had no idea at the time that they would be trapped in the attic for twenty-six long, agonizing hours.

Once in the attic, Sheryl was in a fog. She couldn't think straight. Thank goodness her cell phone was in her pocket. It never even occurred to her to call 911, but realizing that she needed to let someone in her family know what was happening to them, she called her sister, Tereena Gary, in Lafayette, Louisiana. Once Sheryl told her that they were trapped, Tereena called 911. She couldn't believe the reply from the emergency operator. "Good luck," he said. "There are 180 people in Biloxi trapped in their attics!"

The storm was so violent, Sheryl feared that any minute the roof would blow off. The whole house shook. The furniture below was being tossed around like dollhouse toys. When the objects bumped against the ceiling making loud banging noises, Kaitlin would run to Sheryl for comfort. The child was terrified.

As the water began seeping through the attic door, Sheryl's heart filled with fear and foreboding. She didn't know how to swim! She looked at her husband and then back to Kaitlin. Water was now covering their feet. How much longer would they be able to survive? Would this become their watery grave?

Joey got up and looked out the window at the trees being whipped by the wind. "There's a tree over there," he said, "about a hundred yards away. If worse comes to worse, I think we could make it to the tree."

Sheryl, resigned to her fate, shook her head, "No, Honey, you know I can't swim. I'd never make it. But if it becomes a matter of life or death, promise me that you'll take Kaitlin. You must save her."

"Honey," he replied, "I'm not leaving here without you." But by the look in his eyes, she could tell he knew she was right. He couldn't possibly save both of them. And if a choice would need to be made, he would have to save his grandchild.

Joey came over and held his wife, and with an extra squeeze said, "I love you, Honey." Then turned his face to the window. Not wanting to alarm Kaitlin, Sheryl held back the tears that so desperately wanted to flow. And she prayed!

Sheryl Donald and her granddaughter Kaitlin.

Just as Joey was trying to remove the window to be ready in case they had to make a quick escape, he noticed the water was no longer coming up. "Look!" His voice expressed excitement. "Look! I don't think the water is rising any more. Let's wait just a minute."

Sure enough, the water receded a bit more.

A sense of relief flooded Sheryl's soul. She threw herself into her husband's arms. "Honey, I think we're going to be OK." They spent the rest of those long, long hours trying to keep Kaitlin's mind off the food and water for which she kept pleading. She was so thirsty—and very, very hungry. The puppy turned out to be a blessing, as it kept Kaitlin entertained. When the water drained out of the attic, they were physically and emotionally spent. Exhausted, they slept fitfully on the damp attic floor with their arms around each other.

Finally, when the water receded enough that they could leave the attic, they could not believe the devastation. The town where the Donalds had lived for twenty-two years was completely destroyed. Everything was floating. Windows were broken. Trees and power lines were down. Cars were upside down. Their house was torn apart.

Since the car they had parked beside their house was destroyed, Joey wanted to walk to his business about five miles down the road to see if their Toyota truck had survived the storm. "I'll be back in just a little bit," he promised. But Sheryl didn't want him to leave her. After he reassured her that everything would be OK, she reluctantly agreed that he should go. A short time later he returned, and that little truck looked like a limousine. Having saved only the clothes on their backs, she and Kaitlin and the puppy joined Pops in the front seat. Later, as Sheryl was recalling the moment, she commented, "As we started to drive off, we didn't know where we were going. But we were going somewhere."

Trapped in the Carport

Mary Noto, a grandmother—and a great-grandmother—lived with her daughter, Barbara LaFontaine, in Bay St. Louis. When she first saw the wave of water coming toward their home, adrenaline shot through her veins. "Get off the phone," she screamed at Barbara, pointing to the street. "Look!" Barbara had been keeping relatives apprised

of how she and her mom and the others were weathering the gales of wind-driven rain. They had thought that Hurricane Katrina was about over—and now this!

Hours before, when Katrina's wind and rain first started, Barbara's son, Tommy, and his wife, Pat, as well as their seven-year-old daughter, Tonya, Pat's six-year-old

Mary Noto, along with her daughter and brother, survived Katrina by standing on her car and clinging to the roof of her carport.

79

niece, Lauren, and Pat's parents, Kevin and Monica, were all together in Mary and Barbara's home—along with Mary's brother. When Mary suddenly yelled, "Look!" they all stopped what they were doing and stood paralyzed with fear as they watched the cars in the street being swallowed up by the raging water.

Within seconds it was at their doorstep, then flooding the floor. If it didn't stop soon, they would all be trapped. Suddenly chaos broke loose. Tommy sprinted out the door—with Pat, her parents, and the girls following. They frantically slogged through the water to get to their boat that was beside the carport. Too late! The onslaught of rushing water had already filled and sunk the boat. The only

Barbara LaFontaine helped pull her mother back on the car when her strength was failing.

thing still floating was two life preservers. Tommy grabbed them and rushed back to the little girls, buckling them into the preservers just as the waves were about to sweep them all away. Frantically, Tonya grabbed on to Tommy's back, while Lauren clung to Kevin.

"Don't worry about us," Barbara screamed into the wind. "Save yourselves!" They were able to swim over to a house that had people on the roof who lifted them to safety—all except Tommy. When the people reached back to get him, he was gone. In that split second, the current wrenched Tommy away from the house and pushed him back toward the woods.

At the mercy of the wind and rush of rising water, Mary, her brother, and Barbara helplessly watched the agonizing drama before them. The last thing they saw of Pat before she was washed out of sight was her arms wrapped around an inner-tube. Could this be happening? One minute they were a big happy family, together in what they had considered a hurricane-safe house—the next, they were torn away from each other and thrown into the unknown. Would they survive?

Now Mary and Barbara's attention turned to saving themselves. Their house had no attic and no tall furniture on which to climb. Besides, their physical condition made climbing almost impossible. Surviving the wind was bad enough, as it whipped around at over a hundred miles per hour with terrifying gusts that literally pushed people around. But the water—the putrid, foul smelling water and the debris that it was bringing in its wake—this was an unknown. They feared for their lives.

Mary especially felt responsible for her brother, who was suffering from advanced stages of cancer. Since it was difficult for him to take care of himself, she had pleaded with him to weather the storm at her place. After all, her house had never flooded and had withstood the winds of past hurricanes. It would be a safe place. Now her wishful thinking had just been washed away. What she was experiencing was like a terrifying nightmare in which you see the danger coming, but you can't get your feet in gear to outrun it. What should they do? None of them were what you'd call spring chickens!

"We've got to get out of the house or we'll be trapped," Mary yelled above the wind. The alternative—weathering the storm from outside its protective walls—didn't sound like much of an option since they had just witnessed what had happened to Tommy and Pat. But it was the only option they had. They waited until the water was swirling about their waists and then reluctantly waded into the carport.

The car was the only thing that might be high enough to save them—if only they could get on top of it. By now the hood was submerged, and the water was still rising. Somehow, at ten minutes to ten o'clock (Barbara remembers looking at her watch), all three of them managed to crawl up on top of the car. Then they began praying for deliverance as they had never prayed before in their lives.

The wind was howling through the open carport, threatening to blow them away; trees were falling; and the stench of the water was nauseating. But they held on for dear life. Survival for them meant one giant balancing act! Mary wedged her toes into the crevice between the windshield and the wipers to try to keep herself on top of the car, until her toes were bruised and bloody and her legs began to cramp. Barbara held tight to the top of the carport and spread her feet wide to keep as balanced as possible. Mary's brother held on to both of the women.

At one point a strange dog swam into the carport and started scratching at them to get on top of the car. His actions threatened to knock them off their already precarious perch, and although Mary hated to do it, she had to keep pushing him away until he gave up and was washed away. It seemed a cruel thing to do, but they were fighting for their lives.

Hour after slow, miserable hour, they stood on the car. Mary's legs began to cramp up in the cold water. In agony, she bent down to rub them, lost her grip and was swept from her perch to what she knew would be a watery grave. At that moment, she had neither the strength or the determination to fight on. She was about to give up when her brother grabbed her by the hair and yanked her head above water. At the same time Barbara grabbed her pant leg. Together they pulled her back onto the car. They had come this far together, and they weren't going to give up now!

As the water kept rising, their heads were forced higher and higher toward the top of the carport, until only their faces were out of the water. Just when they were thinking they would certainly drown, the water crested and slowly began receding. They had looked death in the face, cried to God to save them, and at what seemed like the last moment—when they were utterly helpless—God came through.

By three twenty-five that afternoon, when they slid off the car into waist-deep water, they were so stiff and sore and water-logged they could hardly walk. But that didn't matter—they had survived Katrina! A few hours later they learned that Tommy, Pat, and the other family members had also miraculously survived. Mary and her family can testify to the truth of Psalm 34:17: "The LORD hears his people when they call to him for help. He rescues them from all their troubles" (NLT). (You'll find Pat's incredible story in the next chapter.)

Praying for a Puff of Wind

While everyone else was running from the coming storm, Jack Welch and two of his friends, Ron and Nellie, came back to Bay St. Louis just before Katrina hit to make sure his rental trailers and houses were secure. As the wind started howling and the rain began to fall in sheets, he watched the roof on the trailer across the street blow off. Then the porch went.

Jack decided to get in his big truck and check on the rest of his rentals. Finding everything in order, he was thinking that he should check on his buddy, Tony Page, who lived over on Elm Street, when he saw the water coming. Jack backed up, whipped around, and started toward his friend's place with the water lapping at his wheels. He laid on his horn to get everyone's attention.

Before he knew it, the murky water was up to his chest. If he was going to get into their house, he was going to have to swim for it. Later he commented, "And let me tell you that water was comin' in so fast that I didn't think I was gonna make it."

Jack's friends had to literally pull him into the house. Inside, they all sat on top of the floating refrigerator and washing machine to keep above the floodwaters. But soon their heads were bumping against the ceiling. They had to go higher. Their only option seemed the attic. After everyone scrambled up the attic steps, it soon became obvious that they were sitting in a death trap. There were no windows in the attic—no way to escape should the water come any higher. And swimming back down through the house would have been suicide with all the appliances, furniture, and household items being churned around as if in a giant cement mixer.

That's when Jack began praying, "Good Lord, You know we're in a big heap of trouble. We don't have any way out of this attic—no ax to

Jack Welch stands by his big truck. His friends thought his prayers were almost too effective!

chop a hole in the roof. So Lord, if you could just cause a puff of wind to take one piece of plywood off the roof, I'd be mighty thankful. That's all I'm asking for. Just one puff of wind. Just one piece of plywood."

Suddenly the house was hit by a huge gust of wind, and right before their eyes, Jack and his friends watched a section of plywood lift off the roof, making a big hole. The rain and daylight flooded in, making it possible for them to climb out onto the roof.

From their rooftop perch, Jack and his friends watched as trees bent and broke and all types of things were blown or floated past. It was an absolute nightmare. They were especially concerned about the dogs being washed past them—and began saving as many as they could. During the next seven hours, as they feared for their own lives, they rescued seventeen dogs. Every kind of critter you can imagine was up there on the roof with them!

At one point a large shed from a couple blocks away came floating down the road toward them. Jack was afraid if the house were hit by something that large, it might cause severe structural damage. So he said to himself—but loud enough for the others to hear—"Shed, please go away." They all laughed when it looked as though the shed took him seriously. Instead of hitting them, it was swept away from the house and went on down the road and into the woods.

That night, after the water receded, leaving a filthy paste of muck on everything, Jack and his friends were jubilant that they were still alive.

That alone was a miracle. It was so hot and humid that he and his friends decided to sleep outside. There were eleven of them, all lying out on mattresses, and all hot and sticky. That's when Jack muttered, "Good Lord, give me a puff of wind."

Everybody started screaming, "Don't you ask for no wind!"

Jack said, "Suddenly here comes a puff of wind, and it cooled everybody off! God worked a lot of miracles for us that day. That first puff of wind saved our lives, but that second puff sure made us a lot more comfortable. You can't tell me that the Lord God doesn't care about us. He sure came through for us with those two puffs of wind. I couldn't ask for nothin' more!"

A "Seeing Eye" Dog

Eighty-year-old George Mitchell lived in Biloxi on the other side of Back Bay from Dennis and Betty Strong. Here is the story Dennis told us about his friend:

George was out in the ferocious wind walking his dog on a leash and checking on his neighbor's house when the tidal wave hit. The force of the water washed him back into his house! The water was so high, he couldn't get his feet on the floor, so he started swimming. But he never let go of the dog that had been his constant companion for eighteen years.

He and his pet "dog-paddled" for an hour or so before George came upon a mattress that was floating in the mass of debris. His first thought was for the safety of his pet, so he pushed and shoved until he got the dog up on the mattress. By that time, he didn't have energy enough to drag himself up, so he just held on to the mattress as best he could. He was exhausted! When George would momentarily fall asleep and lose his grip, his dog sensed it and would begin licking his face to wake him up.

All the while there were water moccasins swimming around that George had to keep pushing away. The water must have disturbed their nest somewhere nearby. He knew the snakes were deadly, but he also knew they could not strike while swimming. That knowledge, however, did little to calm his rapidly pounding heart. Unless you're Steve Irwin, the crocodile hunter, swimming with snakes can be somewhat unnerving!

When George and his dog were finally rescued and taken to the hospital, George was told the dog couldn't come inside. "Oh yes he can!" George said emphatically. "He's my seeing eye dog. He is the one who kept me alive."

The dog is blind. George is not!

Doubting Thomas Lane

The storm was particularly brutal to the very young—and the old. Woody is a seventy-two-year-old man who survived the onslaught of Katrina even though a part of his roof was pulled off. The next day, when medical officials heard that he had survived, they sent the emergency ambulance service to check on him. Amazingly, he was up on a ladder carrying a four-by-eight piece of plywood to mend his roof. The medics ended up helping him get the plywood on the roof and then prayed with him. As they left he called to them, "I'll meet you on Doubting Thomas Lane in heaven."

Apparently he used to be a real skeptic when it came to the reality of God and His saving power, but a few years back when Woody was sick, he said that an angel showed up by his bedside. He's been a believer ever since and credits his faith in God for keeping him safe through the deadly forces unleashed by Katrina.

Mama, Don't Leave Me

The intensity of the storm surprised Brenda Ashton and her husband, Tom. They had been warned by their son's girlfriend, Ginger, to get out of their Biloxi, Mississippi, home, but they hadn't taken the warning seriously. As the wind began battering their house, Brenda was beginning to think, "Maybe Ginger was right." But it wasn't until she walked out onto the sun porch and looked at the ocean that she knew how the people in the 2004 southern Asia tsunami must have felt. The waves were huge—and building. She screamed, "Ginger *was* right! We need to get out of here!"

She and her husband ran out the door, jumped into their car, and went tearing down the street trying to put as much space as they could between themselves and the ocean. The next day, after Katrina's fury was spent, they went back to check on things. Where their house used to be, nothing was left except a cement slab. Brenda commented, "My neighbors told me that ten minutes after we went flying down the street, my house was coming behind me saying, 'Mama, don't leave me!' All the precious things we were going to pass on to our children are gone. Instead they have Pop and me—and a few mementoes we've salvaged that they can put in a Hurricane Katrina curio cabinet."

Brenda went on, "Our neighbors on both sides of us didn't do so well. We tried to get our elderly aunt and uncle to leave, but Pete had emphysema and refused to go to the hospital, and Martha wouldn't leave him. A lady that usually helps our other neighbor chose to stay with Pete and Martha that night just in case they needed her. The night before the storm we could see Pete and Martha drinking coffee in the kitchen. Then they turned off the light and went to bed. It makes me shudder to think how they must have been shocked awake by the cold wave of water that filled their house and then swept them to their deaths.

"The day after the storm, we found the body of Myrtle, the lady who went to stay with them. Then we found Martha and Pete a few blocks away. It makes me very sad to think about all the people who didn't make it. It was a miracle we survived; I only wish the others could have been as fortunate."

Was It Really a Miracle?

Why did Brenda just happen to look out her window at that very moment and see the waves coming? Why were she and Tom able to outrun the deadly waves while their neighbor's homes and lives were swept away?

Why did miracles apparently happen to one and not to another? People who were hanging on to trees, being tossed back and forth by Katrina's powerful gusts of wind, with twenty or thirty feet of water swirling below them and trees snapping and falling all around them, said it was a miracle that the trees they were on didn't snap. Was it?

What about the boat that was floating without a plug? People could look right down the hole and see the water below, yet it didn't leak. That boat made the difference between life or death for five people. Why didn't it fill up with water and sink? The people say an angel must have plugged the hole. It had to be a miracle. Was it?

Or what about the mother who, when her house was completely covered with water, put her baby in an Igloo cooler and then swam along beside it holding on for dear life? In desperation she cried out to God, and a boat suddenly appeared out of nowhere. Hands reached down and picked up the cooler. Then she found herself in the boat. She first checked to see if her baby was all right. Then she turned to thank the man who had pulled them to safety—and there was no one in the boat! She said it had to be an angel who saved her and her child. Was it?

Kathy Pinn's home and business in Waveland were toppled by Hurricane Katrina's onslaught. She fled to Florida, but in the days after the storm she kept in touch with her friend Jim Brewer from Diamondhead. In one of their conversations she told Jim how much she wished she had taken with her an antique cake mold that her grandmother had given her. Jim searched through the rubble of her house for two hours. Finally he said, "God, if you want me to find it, then put it in front of me." Jim looked down—and there was the cake mold.[1] Was that a miracle?

Gary Karl lost everything. The week before Katrina, he had finished a ten-thousand-dollar remodeling project on his home in Waveland, Mississippi. Not only was the house completely flooded, but a tree fell on it. He was told by the insurance agent that they couldn't check the house for insurance purposes until the tree was removed. Trying to get the tree off the house, he fell off the roof and ended up in the hospital. Two days later, he had a heart attack and had to have two stents put into his arteries. Why didn't he get a miracle?

The truth is that God *is* in the miracle business. He loves his children so much that He wants to help them in every possible way. He has the power to do remarkable things—like keep trees from snapping and boats from sinking. And when He perceives in His all-knowing omnipotence that a young mother is going to need a boat and someone to lift her and her baby out of the life-threatening water—He can commission one of His angels to do the job. On August 29, probably every angel in heaven was on standby, ready to go into active duty! Even if the task was as insignificant as moving a cake mold into plain sight!

But even though God has the power to do all these miraculous things, it's kind of like the way we handle things as parents. Do good parents do everything for their children that their children want—or demand? Of course not. They first determine if their help will ultimately be good for the child. If a lesson can be learned better by withholding help, parents, in love, withhold it.

Now, if you're the child, you may not like that very much. You would rather live in a magical world in which you get everything you want and the people around you anticipate your needs and provide before you ask. But should that happen, you would never learn the life-lessons that you need to learn in order to be strong and mature.

And so it is with God. He's not only in the miracle business, but He's also in the faith-building business. His objective for His children is to take them from baby faith to grown-up mature faith. He wants you to be strong and mature spiritually. And He knows that at times faith is learned best when His kids have to do without for a season—and exercise their faith. Just as muscles grow strong when exercised, so does faith!

How do you know how far along you are on your "faith" journey? How do you measure how advanced you are in any subject? You take a test.

Gary Karl (above) was hit by a series of tragedies: His house was flooded; a tree fell on it; he fell off the roof trying to remove the tree; and then he had a heart attack! Right: Rick de Fluiter and Pastor Ken Micheff help clear debris from Gary's home.

Faith is best tested in times of trouble. Here's a truism: the bigger the trouble you're in, the more faith you need to know that God has everything under control. Then when He does choose to intervene, it will have a greater impact on you.

It's impossible, standing this side of eternity, to know the mind of our heavenly Parent and why He works a miracle for one and not for another. We just have to believe that He (in his Godly "parent" wisdom) knows what's best for us. We have to believe that Romans 8:28 is true, that all things do work out for the best for His children. It may take a while—it may take years—or we may never know until we're walking those streets of gold how something was being worked out for our good. His way of doing things, obviously, isn't our way. But we can take courage in the fact that "His way is perfect" (2 Samuel 22:31).

Just as children don't always understand why their parents do the things they do, our job is not to understand our heavenly Parent. Rather, it is to have such a close relationship with Him that we'll know without a shadow of a doubt that we are loved supremely. For we are saved by grace—His love gift on Calvary—through faith. (See Ephesians 2:8.)

God's ultimate objective for our lives is greater than our momentary happiness, prosperity, or freedom from pain. It's even greater than life itself. His ultimate objective for our lives is to save us for eternity. Sometimes that means He works a miracle for us—and sometimes it means that He doesn't.

And by the way, if you're still wondering why Gary didn't get a miracle when he was falling off his roof and having a heart attack, rest your mind. He did! It came in the form of a dedicated group of volunteers from the Ithaca Seventh-day Adventist Church in Michigan, under the direction of Pastor Ken Micheff, living out the gospel commission to serve others, doing what Christ did two thousand years ago—caring for those who were in need!

When Gary was at his very lowest point, when he didn't think he could finish cleaning up his house or yard, when he thought he would never get that fallen tree off his roof—because scalpers in the area were charging over a thousand dollars to remove a tree and he just didn't have the money—help came! They did all the things he couldn't do, and they did it without charge. *That was a miracle!*

---

[1]Thirteenth in a series: *Portraits of Katrina: Jim Brewer, Diamondhead,* by Ryan LaFontaine, Biloxi *Sun Herald,* September 16, 2005.

Chapter 7

A CAT, A FROG, AND A POODLE

*"If I would have died in the storm, I wouldn't have drowned.
I'd have died of a heart attack first."*
— Ruby Wellons

A Cat in the Freezer

When Ashley Bleidt heard that there was a mandatory evacuation order for Pass Christian, Mississippi, she grabbed the most precious thing in her life—her cat Tom-Tom—and drove to the temporary shelter that had been set up for evacuees.

"Sorry," she was told when she tried to check in, "animals are not allowed."

"But I've had Tom-Tom for a long time. He's my family. I just can't leave him behind to drown!" She had always felt as if she were the black sheep of her family. An outcast! Tom-Tom made her feel like she belonged to someone. He loved her just the way she was, and he meant everything to her. He made her feel important. No way would she leave him to face the coming storm on his own. So she got into her car and, having no place else to go, drove back to her home on Railroad Street, where she figured the two of them could brave the storm together. The problem was, she didn't have any idea how bad Katrina would be! Twenty-four hours later, seventy percent of Pass Christian was leveled and the rest severely damaged! But that's getting ahead of the story.

For the first five hours of the hurricane, Ashley and Tom-Tom hid in the linen closet in her bathroom until the water started coming in under the door. She tried to stuff towels and dirty clothes under the door to keep the water out, but it just kept coming in faster and faster. That's when Tom-Tom started freaking out and began clawing, trying to escape the rising water.

Ashley, began to panic as she realized the water wasn't going down. She pushed the closet door open, waded out of the bathroom, and looked out the bedroom window. Water was up to the window sill and quickly flooding her home. She started throwing furniture out the window, thinking that if something would float, she would put Tom-Tom on it, grab on herself, and escape her flooding house. Everything sank in the churning water.

Next Ashley made her way to the bedroom door and tried to open it so she and Tom-Tom could escape through the house. The pressure of the water on the door was too much, however. It wouldn't open. She pulled and yanked until she finally managed to open it enough to squeeze through—still holding on to her precious Tom-Tom, who by this time was going crazy and clawing at her.

Ashley waded through waist-deep water to her kitchen counter and climbed up. But soon that, too, was flooded. She watched in horror as first one piece of furniture and then another began bobbing around. Suddenly, there was a tremendous splash as the refrigerator toppled over on its back and floated in the water. Thinking quickly, she jumped up on the refrigerator as it floated by and pulled Tom-Tom up next to her. The wind was so strong and things were bumping into her so hard that she was terrified Tom-Tom would fall into the water and drown.

The room was churning like a giant washing machine. Ashley was having a hard enough time staying on the refrigerator herself; how could she save her cat? By now he was frantic! Realizing she had no other options, she quickly jerked open the freezer door and shoved him inside, leaving the door open only enough for him to be able to breathe.

The water continued to churn. The refrigerator was no longer in the kitchen; water pressure had pushed it to the living room. As the raging flood shoved Ashley against the ceiling, she realized that any minute she could be crushed. But there was no place to go. Without warning, a strong surge of water ripped the front door away, and she felt herself being sucked through the doorway. She tried desperately to hold on to the door frame, but the current was too strong, and the refrigerator slid out from under her. Ashley screamed for Tom-Tom. Her heart wanted to go after her dear cat, who was rapidly being carried away from her, but she realized it was no use. Ashley watched in disbelief as the refrigerator was sucked under and disappeared from sight.

Her efforts now turned to saving herself. The only thing standing above water that she could see when she looked across her yard was a tall tree. With adrenaline pumping and driven by fear, she managed to swim to that tree and cling to it for dear life.

Before Ashley knew it, the water was coming up higher and higher, forcing her to climb higher in the tree. But there was so much space between the next higher branch that she couldn't reach it and still hold on to the branch she was clinging to. Ashley was terrified that she would be swept away if she let go. Finally, the water was so high that she had no choice. She had to let go, but she managed to float just enough higher to grab that next branch.

Climbing as high as she possibly could, Ashley wedged herself between the trunk and a large limb, praying that it would hold as the wind stripped away the leaves. The strong gusts tossed her from side to side, and her skin scraped on the rough bark, rubbing it raw. Looking down, she watched all kinds of debris float by in the putrid, foul-smelling water—furniture, cars, metal, animals. It was terrible, just terrible! Suddenly, Ashley shuddered! Something was crawling up her leg; she tried to brush it off. A few minutes later, she felt a crawling sensation on her back, then across her arm. Black spiders. Huge black spiders. She was terrified of spiders. In any other circumstance, she would have screamed and fled for her life. Now she could do nothing. The twenty-seven feet of water swirling below was far more terrifying. She forced her eyes shut and tried to think of other things.

Then without warning, she was violently jerked, lifted from the limb, and forcefully thrust back against the trunk. The pain was excruciating, but Ashley held on. A funnel of water rose beside her. Looking down, she could see a circle in the water all the way to the ground. Other funnels were spinning around her. She was being hit by tornadoes—which were far more terrifying than the hurricane force winds with the razor sharp pricks of blowing rain that pelted her already cut and bleeding body. Ashley began to panic. She thought she was going to be shaken

Ashley Bleidt is sitting by her tent in the front yard of an elementary school that has been turned into a Red Cross relief center just outside Waveland, Mississippi.

out of the tree. She began to bawl like a baby. Reality hit. I'm not going to make it! I'm going to die, she thought. Ashley began to shiver. She was freezing cold.

Then Ashley's skin began to burn from the chemicals in the polluted water. It felt like needles stinging her. The water smelled so bad, she thought she was going to throw up. But she had no other place to go. Then a calm came over her. Maybe she would make it. She took courage and held on as she continued to be buffeted by the wind. Time ticked on—and so did the storm. Ashley clung to that branch for eight hours. At one point she looked around and was surprised to find she was not alone. There on another branch was a possum, clinging to the tree. Together—unafraid of each other—they waited out the fury of the storm.

When the water went down, two men came close enough to hear her screams and waded through the muck to her tree. She tried to lift herself, but her legs wouldn't move because they were numb from lack of circulation and the pain in her back was too severe. The men were not tall enough to reach her. Spotting a trash can floating in the water, they grabbed it and tried to stand on it, but under their weight, it sank into the mud. "We can't reach you! You're going to have to slide down yourself."

Straining, Ashley managed to grab an overhead branch. She lifted herself just enough to get her legs off the limb where they had been wedged and then slid down the trunk, scraping her body against the rough bark. The men caught her, breaking her fall, and held her up until her legs were strong enough to hold her. Putting their arms around her to give her support, they walked with her, almost a mile, to Long Beach, where they found a police officer, who directed them to a clinic.

Although her body was bruised and bleeding and her back was killing her, it was the pain in her ear that was driving her crazy. It was as if something were hammering on her eardrum. A nurse poured alcohol down her ear, and a big black spider crawled out! Ashley almost fainted! She had spider bites, bruises, and scratches all over! Later, she learned that her pelvis was broken, probably by the tornado that lifted her out of the tree and thrust her back against the trunk.

When Ashley went back to look at what was left of her house, she just cried. It was completely destroyed. Pilings from the beach were on her porch, and someone else's deck was on the other side. All the houses on her street were gone; the apartments next to her were completely destroyed. She shuddered, because she knew many people had stayed behind, thinking they would be safe. Later, she learned her girlfriend who lived in the apartment building next to her house had broken a hole into the attic and had saved seven people, but the rest were missing and presumed dead.

When asked what she planned to do next, Ashley shrugged her shoulders. "I have no place to go—and the Red Cross will soon be kicking us out of this shelter. I've got nothing left, nothing! But maybe I'll get a cat for Christmas. Male or female, I think I'll call it Tom-Tom."

A Frog and Other Unwelcome Guests

If you're thinking that holding on for dear life to a tree in the middle of a hurricane with big black spiders crawling on you is pretty bad, then read on, because it can be worse!

Jen Colter, like Ashley Bleidt and so many others, decided to ride out the storm from her home. After all, her house in Bay St. Louis had never before flooded. But when the wind and the waves hit, her house started breaking up. As one entire side collapsed, Jen was swept away in the current. She clung to the closest board and frantically started kicking toward her neighbor's house, which was still standing. But the current kept taking her farther and farther away, until she found herself among the trees in the woods about two blocks from her home. The incredible thing is that she made it that far without knowing how to swim. Jen kept herself above water by holding on to floating debris. But once caught in the mass of trees, the only thing she had to hold on to were the branches.

It would have been safer to hold on to the lower, stronger branches. The problem was, the water was so high that she found herself in the tops of the trees, trying desperately to keep her head above the surface by holding on to the tiny branches, which snapped off easily. To make matters worse,

Jen Colter spent a terrifying night battling water moccasins and even a large bullfrog that landed on her head and refused to budge!

other creatures were trying to survive as well—and they weren't your typical family pets!

Water moccasins! Jen is petrified of snakes. When she saw the first snake dart past her, Jen nearly had a heart attack. Her heart began racing so fast, she thought she would die. Her breathing was so rapid she began hyperventilating and almost passed out. If only she could climb higher in the tree to get away from those horrible reptiles—but there was no place to go! All Jen had was a precarious hold on a few tiny branches in the upper most part of a tree.

As Jen struggled to hold her nose above water, something big plopped on her head. She screamed! Without thinking, Jen almost let go of the branch she was holding as she tried to brush the creature away. When that didn't work, she began violently shaking her head to get it off. But the harder she shook, the more the creature dug into her hair. All Jen could think of were snakes, alligators, lizards. What was it?

Then above the roar of the wind, she heard a loud, raspy croak right next to her ear! A frog! A huge bullfrog was sitting on top of her head! Jen shuddered. *How can this be happening to me?* she wondered.

As if this weren't bad enough, the water moccasins started swimming closer to her. Could it be they were attracted to the frog—or were they merely curious? Every time one swam within arm's reach, Jen would hold on to the branch a little tighter with one hand and swat the snake away with the other. The effort was just enough to cause the snakes to be caught up in the current and be dragged in the other direction. All day long Jen battled the snakes, thankful this was happening in the daylight so that she could see the snakes coming. The only way Jen survived was thinking about her family, her friends, and her life—which she knew would never be the same again. Throughout it all, she prayed, shouting to God above the wind. "God, help me! God, You ain't done with me yet. I'm not goin' down like this. God, You've got to help me."

At one point during the storm she saw a deer a short distance away, trying desperately to swim and hold its head above water. For a brief second, they stared at each other, and Jen could see the terror in its eyes. The sight will haunt her for the rest of her life. Minutes later she watched the deer disappear beneath the surface.

For six hours, Jen clung to the tree. As the water receded, she grasped the next lowest branch, inching her way down until her feet touched the ground. The water was still above her waist. But now, with both hands free, she was finally able to fling the frog from her head.

When she walked out of the woods and told her story, Jen ended by saying, "I can't believe I made it through the hell of that storm. I am just so thankful to be alive." Then she paused and added, "I guess the frog was too."

"What's in My Pants and on My Back?"

Remember Pat LaFontaine's story from the last chapter? She and her husband, Tommy, had run outside the safety of the house and were washed away in opposite directions by the powerful storm surge that hit Bay St. Louis, Mississippi. Tommy was washed by the current into the wooded area behind their home. Like so many others, he survived by finding a secure perch in the top of a tree and praying the limb wouldn't break off, the tree wouldn't be up-rooted, and he wouldn't be hit by flying debris. But wouldn't you know it, the tree he latched on to was filled with red ants! For six hours Tommy endured the driving rain, the furious gusts of wind—and ants in his pants!

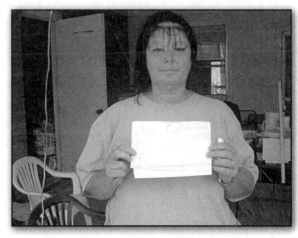

While Pat LaFontaine was trying to survive by clinging to the branches of a tree to keep from drowning, rats were clinging to her back to stay out of the water themselves! Nothing she could do would dislodge them!

And what happened to Pat? She, too, was washed into the woods—quite a distance from Tommy. Since Pat couldn't swim, her survival depended on the inner tube she was clinging to for dear life. Sharp debris, however, punctured the tube, and it began to leak. Her "life preserver" was disappearing! Pat desperately grabbed for the branches of trees. At last she found one that seemed strong enough to support her. But it was quickly submerged by the next surge of water, and she had to climb higher.

The water was murky and cold; the rain was pelting her skin; and there was a putrid smell everywhere!

Suddenly Pat felt something on her shoulder. The creature's claws penetrated her thin tee shirt and dug into her skin. Holding to a branch with one hand, she struggled to get whatever it was off her. She was horrified when she realized that the animal clinging to her was a rat. But her efforts to knock the rat off her back caused the branch to break, and her head plunged below the surface of the filthy water.

Pat thrashed and sputtered as she unsuccessfully struggled to force her head through the debris and above water again. Thankfully, a gust of wind cleared the surface of the water around her, and she was able to grab for another branch and then another, trying to stabilize herself—holding on as tight as she could, choking and sputtering. Minutes later, the rat found her again, and its claws dug into her once more. This time, Pat didn't risk batting it away for fear she would go under again. She chose to submit to the unwelcome guest on her back, rather than lose her life. Then she felt another rat latch on!

To add to her torture, strange dogs kept trying to get on top of her in order to save their lives. She might have been able to cope with one or two. But five? Pat knew how vicious dogs could be when pack instinct took over. Her splashing kept them at a distance, but they continued to bark and growl. She couldn't figure out if they were barking and growling at her or the rats. She hoped the dogs would scare the rats away, but nothing was going to dislodge those rats! Every time the dogs came close enough to threaten the rats, the rodents just dug their claws deeper into Pat's skin, leaving bloody marks around her shoulders and back. At last the dogs tired, and one by one, they gave in to the current that swept them deeper into the wooded area.

Throughout this whole ordeal, Pat thought she would go crazy. At last the water began receding. How thankful she was when it was low enough for her to finally knock those rats off her back! As Pat finished relating the story of her terrifying experience, she shuddered. "It was the worse thing I could ever imagine happening to me." Nothing on reality television could have been any worse than what Pat experienced on August 29, 2005! And you can be sure, she'll be long gone the next time a hurricane threatens the Gulf Coast!

Saved by a Poodle

It was August 27, and warnings were predicting a direct hit for Slidell, Louisiana, where Ruby Wellons and her sister, Elouise Knight, lived. When their brother called from Seattle, urging them to go to the Superdome, Elouise said, "Ruby, if you want to go, I'll understand. But they don't allow animals, and I can't leave Snowball. She's like my child."

"We promised to stay together," Ruby replied, "and that's just what we're going to do." That decision, because of a poodle, saved much heartache and pain—and perhaps their lives.

Since Slidell was under mandatory evacuation orders, the sisters decided to ride out the storm in Elouise's daughter's empty house that was just seven miles away in a remote area in Pearl River, Louisiana. They felt safe going there because the house was in a no-flood zone.

Ruby Wellons and her sister survived for three days following Katrina on two small bottles of water, a can of tamales, and a can of creamed corn.

En route, they passed a number of markets and never once thought about getting any food. When they passed the Shell station, Ruby glanced at the gas gage. It registered a quarter tank. "Should we stop and fill up?" she asked.

"No," replied Elouise, anxious to get to where they were going. "We can do it tomorrow after the storm." They were used to hurricanes. They came quickly, blew furiously, dumped heavy rain, and after a few hours, moved on. They were both sure that they'd be home in less than twenty-four hours.

Katrina, however, was different. Katrina hung around, slowly wreaking the most harsh and widespread damage of any storm ever to hit the Gulf Coast.

Ruby and Elouise slept fitfully in the Pearl River house and woke early to the roar of the wind and the beating of the rain on the roof. Almost immediately, they lost power. That's when they remembered that they couldn't get water from the well without electricity! Why hadn't they thought to fill up the bathtub and every empty container in the house before the storm hit? Horrified, they watched the giant oak and pine trees as they bent almost horizontally, yielding to the force of the wind, then cracking and falling around them, blocking the entrance to the property. They were trapped. Why hadn't they stopped for groceries? The roar of the wind was so loud it sounded like a giant freight train coming through the house. Terrified, they prayed, "Lord, maybe we made a mistake by not going to the Superdome. If You don't choose to save us, we accept our fate." And all the time, Snowball huddled under the bed, whimpering with fear.

Twelve hours later, when the wind died down, the sisters were overjoyed that their lives had been spared. What they didn't know was that their suffering had just begun. So many conveniences, which they took for granted, required electricity. There was no water to drink, to bathe in, or to flush a toilet. Having no other option, they found a bucket and placed it out under a tree. They unscrewed the toilet lid from inside the bathroom and put it on the bucket. For ten days, that served as their toilet.

For three days, they survived on two small bottles of water, a can of tamales, and a can of creamed corn. The heat was unbearable. They heard helicopters flying over and waved frantically, hoping the pilot would see them and drop some food, but it didn't happen!

On the third day, the roads were cleared enough for them to get back to Slidell. They found their homes were under water. Power lines were down. They waited seven hours in line to get gas, only to be told, when there were just twenty cars in front of them, that there was no more gas. How frustrating! They were hot, sticky, smelly, and dehydrated. They drove to a friend's house and were thrilled to find that the outdoor faucet still worked. They filled their jugs, even though they knew they shouldn't drink the water without boiling it. *But how are we supposed to boil it without electricity?* they wondered. Then Ruby took a shower right out in the front yard. Soaped herself up, clothes and all, and squirted the ice cold water down her shorts and blouse. What an incredibly wonderful, refreshing feeling! Then, having no place to stay in Slidell, they crept back to Pearl River with the gas gage nearly on empty, grieving the loss of their homes.

On the fifth day—having survived without food or pure water—they learned that FEMA was handing out MREs (meals ready to eat) and bottled water in Hickory, a few miles away. They prayed they'd have enough gas to get there and back. There must have been three hundred cars ahead of them. Hours later, with a case of food and some bottled water, they returned to Pearl River.

That night Ruby and Elouise sat on the floor like two children under the Christmas tree, opening their MREs. They were literally starving. Food their grandchildren would have gagged on tasted like it had been prepared by a gourmet chief—meatloaf and potatoes, lasagna, a plain cookie, and a sugary grape drink. Ruby had always hated grape drinks, but she drank every drop. It was delicious! They were glad to be alive! But Snowball, who was already suffering from Cushing's disease, didn't fair as well. Two weeks after the storm, not being able to get proper food and medication, she died. Life would go on—but as miserable as conditions were at Pearl River—they would never forget the role that little poodle played in sparing them from the greater misery of the Superdome.

Later, Ruby and her eleven-year-old granddaughter, Courtney Tanner, were cleaning up the debris at her place in Slidell. "Look Mama," Courtney said pointing to the fallen pine tree, "that's where Daddy found the refrigerator." They laughed as they remembered how funny it looked in the branches of the tree. How it got there they would never know. It just showed them the tremendous force of the wind and surge of water that had hit Slidell. But amazingly, when her son got the refrigerator out of the tree, took it home, cleaned it up, sanitized it, and plugged it in, it ran perfectly.

"How ironic," she said, "that almost as quick as you could snap your finger, Katrina took everything we had, and in return brought us a brand new refrigerator! We like to think of it as a gift from God."

You Can Survive More Than You Think

What does it take to be a survivor? As you consider the fear factors endured by the Katrina survivors, you're probably agreeing with Ruby Wellons when she said that if she had been thrown to the terror of the waves and had to endure spiders, rats, frogs, and water moccasins, she would probably have died of a heart attack before she would have drowned. But the truth is, you can survive more than you think.

You can't choose the trials that are going to come to you. You may think you couldn't survive the death of a spouse—or a child. You may think you couldn't survive the throbbing pain of broken bones and internal injuries caused by a terrible accident or the advancing stages of cancer or knowing you were slowly dying of Lou Gehrig's disease or of progressive nuclear palsy, or knowing you were going to have to live your whole life paralyzed, blind, or deaf. And you may think you wouldn't have survived Katrina if exposed to some of the terrors the Katrina victims had to face, but here's the good news: You can do everything with the help of Christ who gives you the strength you need (paraphrased from Philippians 4:13, NLT).

Just as Ruby considered the refrigerator the storm brought as God's gift to her, you might consider this superhuman strength that God promises as His gift that the storms of life bring to you!

Only God knows what lies ahead, and in mercy He chooses not to reveal the future. If He did, and you knew what you were going to have to endure, you would spend your life worrying about it, wouldn't you? Jesus came to give you an abundant life. (See John 10:10.) And it's almost impossible to experience that kind of life when you're having anxiety attacks! But when tough times come, what an incredible sense of calm and security you can have if you believe that God will never ask you to go through something you're not able to handle. (See 1 Corinthians 10:13.)

One of the most reassuring pictures of Christ in Scripture is of Him sleeping through a violent storm. (See Matthew 8:23, 24.) How could He do it? Because He trusted completely in His heavenly Father. You can have this same faith. If you believe that God is in charge of your life, and you don't want to do anything but God's will for you, then you don't need to be concerned when you find yourself facing a storm. He obviously knows much better than you do the experiences that will build your character and the trials that will mold you into the person He wants you to be.

The next most reassuring picture of Christ in the Bible is what He did when His fearful disciples woke Him up. (See Matthew 8:25–27.) He stood in that violently rocking boat and told the wind and the waves to settle down—and they did!

Are you questioning why He didn't do the same for the Katrina victims? Jesus *is* in the business of calming storms. He has power over physical storms, but He doesn't always choose to change the course of nature. However, you can be assured that if you ask Him, He will always calm the storms in your heart. He can take away your fear. He can settle your nerves. He can place peace in your raging spirit. With Jesus, you can always say as Paul did, "I have learned in whatever state I am, to be content" (Philippians 4:11, NKJV).

-Chapter 8-
PRAYING FROM THE POT AND OTHER UNUSUAL PLACES

*"I didn't know if I should try to act as if it were no big deal,
or if I should start crying and repenting!"*
—Chelsea Checkan

Although the Checkans live in Slidell, Louisiana, Merry Jane was terrified that the giant oak and pine trees in their yard might hit the house when the storm came. They had always stayed during previous hurricanes, but this time she was adamant that they leave. After talking to their extended family, everyone decided that the safest place to go was the old post office building in Bay St. Louis, Mississippi. Their daughter, Kim, and her husband, Andy Jaworski, had converted the building into a lady's boutique. It was a sturdy structure with a large finished basement that would provide excellent protection from the wind. So when the storm hit, eleven family members were there—including the Checkan's sixteen-year-old granddaughter, Chelsea.

It wasn't long, however, before water started seeping into the basement. "Grab your stuff and get to the main floor!" Then panic struck when that floor, too, began flooding. How could this be happening? The building was thirty-one feet above sea level! By now they could hardly hear each other over the shrieking of the wind. It was worse than a horror movie! Chelsea grabbed her things and ran upstairs. A few minutes later, she tried to return to help the others and found herself wading in water up to her calves. They all began screaming, "We're going to die. The roof's going to blow off." And the water just kept coming up.

Before long everyone was huddled in the bathroom of the third floor loft. By this time Chelsea was almost out of her mind with fear—crying and shaking and praying. She called her aunt on

James, Merry Jane, and Chelsea Checkan hid from the storm in a third-floor bathroom along with other family members. Everything around them was destroyed—but they emerged alive!

her cell phone, but she was so scared all she could say was, "Aunt Angie, Aunt Angie," over and over again.

"Chelsea!" her aunt said, trying to get her attention. "Chelsea! Are you OK?"

Chelsea's response was simply, "Pray for us. Pray for us!" Then the connection was broken.

Later Chelsea admitted, "I didn't know if I should try to act as if it were no big deal or if I should start crying and repenting! I was freaking out! I thought I was going to die."

Her grandmother tried to distract her. "Let's sing something," she suggested trying to sound cheerful. "Maybe 'Take Me Out to the Ball Game,' or 'Row, Row, Row Your Boat.'"

At that, they all started laughing. "No, not that one!" they yelled above the wind. Rowing a boat was the last thing in the world they wanted to think about.

Chelsea continues her story, "So, there I am, sitting on the pot, hanging on to this big pipe for dear life so that if the roof goes, I won't get blown away. And my grandma is talking about singing songs, and

I'm feeling like I'm gonna throw up! Half the time I'm having an anxiety attack because I don't know what is going to happen, and half of the time I'm praying. I remember saying, 'God, if I'm going to die, let me die quick.' "

At one point her dad came up to her with tears in his eyes and said, "It's going to be all right." She looked at him and said, "I can tell by the way you look and the way you're talking to me that it's not!" What was happening around them was so frightening that not even her father could mask his fear!

When the water receded and the wind died down and the sun came out, Chelsea finally let go of the pipe and came out of the bathroom! They celebrated the fact that they were all alive, even though everything around them was destroyed. Smelly sludge and debris were everywhere! Trees were down. If you wanted to go someplace, you had to chainsaw your way through. The beach and the first block of buildings had disappeared completely. How thankful they were that the old post office building was on the second street from the beach and not the first! Bay St. Louis looked like a war zone!

That night was so hot that eight of the family members decided to take sleeping bags out on the loading dock and sleep there. They were awakened by a huge coast guard helicopter hovering overhead, shining a spotlight on them. The men in the helicopter must have been thinking that there were eight dead bodies lined up on the dock. Finally, they lowered one of the rescue workers down on a wire. He was equipped with night vision. Randy Checkan went over to reassure him that they were all, thankfully, very much alive.

Six weeks after the storm, the water in the basement had started to thicken into black, muddy goop. The smell was enough to make a person gag. Andy and Kim were very discouraged. How would they possibly ever get this mess cleaned up?

What a shock Kim had when she drove up to the old post office one afternoon to see a flurry of activity in the building. A large number of men had formed what looked like an assembly line and were hauling mud and debris out of the basement. When Kim asked what was happening, the men explained that they were Baptists from Las Vegas who had hired a bus and come down to help. They had asked the pastor of the Baptist church next door if he knew someone in need. He replied, "As a matter of fact, the fellow next door needs help."

It just so happened that they had with them the right equipment and the right number of people to complete the job of cleaning out the biggest room in just one day. Andy shook his head in disbelief at the kindness of these people who didn't even know him but were willing to donate their time to help. It would have probably taken Andy a couple months to do this job by himself. And as if this weren't enough, several days later, five women came to scrub and clean the first story of the building.

In commenting about how thankful the family was for this unexpected help, Merry Jane said, "The Baptist church next door may have lost their steeple, but not their kindness."

Snorkeling Through the Attic Roof

One of the most unusual stories of survival and answered prayer was related by Pastor Ken Micheff, who took a group of Ithaca, Michigan, church members down to Waveland, Mississippi, for a week during November 2005 to help people clear out their houses and clean their yards. Later, we were able to find Bill Tudury and hear his story first-hand.

When the first giant wave of water hit Bill's house, he knew he was in trouble. The flooding was immediate. He had to get out, or he would be trapped. He tried to open the door. It wouldn't budge. He watched frantically as water crashed against the front windows, but they didn't break. He tried to open a window so he could swim through, but he couldn't get any of them open. He was frantic. He had to escape, but how?

The water was rising so rapidly that he had no choice. He swam to the crawl space of the attic, which was the highest possible place in his house, hoping that it would be higher than the water. But the water just kept coming up. Now there was *no* way to escape. If he didn't do something quickly, he'd be completely entombed. There was no window in the attic, and he had no ax or hammer to chop a hole in the roof. The only thing in the attic was a six-foot piece of PVC pipe left over from the installation of a horizontal heating/air-conditioning unit.

Bill cried in desperation, "God, help me!" Then an idea came to him. There was one hole in the attic roof—the hole for the sewer vent pipe. It was not big enough to crawl through, but maybe he could breathe through it! With all the strength of a man frantically fighting for his life, he kicked at the vent pipe and finally broke a hole in it and inserted the PVC pipe. Could it be used as a snorkel?

Just as the water was threatening to bury him alive, he put the other end of the pipe in his mouth and began to breathe through it as the water covered him completely.

Now Bill began to pray as he had never prayed before. "Lord, don't let the water go over the top of the PVC pipe that's sticking out of the roof." He knew he needed to remain as calm as possible or his mouth might lose contact around the pipe. If that happened, he would certainly choke, and that would be the end. How can you be calm when you're slowly being buried with gray sea water, thick with sludge, sewage, and toxic chemicals? Bill clenched his mouth around the pipe so hard—trying to avoid taking in water—that he broke two teeth!

Bill Tudury holds the six-foot piece of PVC pipe through which he breathed for approximately half an hour while trapped under water in his attic!

Bill had no way to know just how long he was submerged. It seemed like eternity, but he estimated it had to about twenty or thirty minutes. After the second tidal surge, the water started receding until at last he was able to breathe on his own. At that point he was weak and dizzy.

When he finally made it down the attic stairs, he stumbled over to his friend's house and passed out. Later, he realized that by breathing through six feet of PVC pipe for that long, he had to be getting a strong dose of carbon dioxide poisoning from his own exhaling. The amazing thing was that he didn't lose consciousness until the water had receded and he was safe!

Bill credits God for his survival. He asked God not to let the water cover the top of his breathing pipe that was sticking out the attic roof. He knew it must have come close, but it was as if God said, "Stop, no further!" and the water backed off!

Launching Joe's "Ark"

It was two and a half weeks after the flood. Joe Dubuisson was in his garage on Markham Drive in Slidell, Louisiana, looking forlorn. He had a large industrial fan blowing toward him to try to beat the heat as he dumped his precious possessions—antique furniture, clocks, computer equipment, books, clothing, and everything else that had been in his house—in a heap next to the curb of his house. Treasures turned to junk! The valuable stuff of his life was now water-logged, mold-infested, and rusty.

When Katrina hit, Joe and his adult daughter, Janice, were the only ones at home. His wife, Margaret, was working at the hospital. They lived in a no-flood zone in a sturdy house. He wasn't worried because he knew that although hurricanes blow in with a mighty force, they quickly move on. What he didn't know was that just like in the days of Noah, his whole world would soon be under water!

On the day of the hurricane, the fierce wind had already been blowing for a couple hours when Joe got his first indication that Katrina was not going to be like other hurricanes. He heard the roar of the water coming. He ran to his door, and there was a wall of gray, debris-filled water surging down the street. In seconds, it leaped the curb, filled his yard, and was running through his house. He screamed, "Oh, no! Janice, we're in trouble! We're in deep trouble. Get out to the garage! Hurry! We've got to get you in the boat. It's our only hope!" Then he urgently called to their faithful black cocker spaniel, "Come on, Roscoe! Hurry! *Come!*"

They had only seconds to react. Quickly Joe helped his daughter into the boat that was attached to the boat trailer in the garage. By this time Roscoe was going nuts. Finally Joe got him settled in the boat. Now all he had to do was get the boat unlatched from the trailer, and hopefully they could ride out the storm in it. But it was fastened tightly; Joe fumbled with the latch, trying to release it. Why wouldn't it let go?

Lori Ryan and Joe Dubuisson stand outside what is left of Joe's home. Lori credits Joe with saving the life of her and her husband, Martin.

By now the water was waist deep. The wind was howling so loudly he couldn't hear himself think. He knew their lives depended on getting the boat off the trailer and out of the garage before the water rose too high and trapped the boat inside. He took a deep breath, because by this time, he had to dive under the filthy water to reach the release button. It remained stuck.

Joe started to panic. He could feel the trailer itself floating now, making it even more difficult to get the boat out of the garage. There wasn't that much space between the roof of the garage and the opening! He had time for only one more try or it would be too late. With fear gripping his heart, he took a deep breathe and dove once more, thinking, "We're goners! We're goners!" As his fingers reached the latch, he tried to turn it just as he'd done every time he had launched his boat in the past. As he did so, he prayed, "God, don't let us die." At that moment the latch released, and the boat floated away from the trailer. With a "Thank You, Jesus," Joe shoved the boat toward the garage door. Janice ducked as the boat scraped against the top frame of the door, but as Joe shoved again, the boat floated free just seconds before the water reached the top of the garage door! Praise the Lord!

Still fighting for his life and struggling with all his might, Joe managed to climb into the boat. At that moment, he was feeling a little like Noah must have felt! That's when he saw his neighbors, Lori and Martin Ryan, waving frantically through the window of their home. Not even taking time to start the motor, Joe grabbed the paddles and rowed in that direction. Then—just as if the Lord knew he needed one more miracle—the wind shifted. Instead of having to struggle against a head-wind, Joe was now being blown in the direction of his neighbor's house. By the time he got there, water had reached their armpits—and was still rising!

A month before, Martin had been in an automobile accident and had been hospitalized for three weeks. He had broken not only his arm but also two cervical vertebrae and two lumbar vertebrae. When Katrina hit, he had been home from the hospital for only a few days. He was weak and couldn't swim since his arm was in a sling and he was still wearing a cervical collar. Had it not been for Joe and the safety of Joe's "ark," Martin most certainly would have died in the rising water.

The only thing Lori grabbed as she and Martin fled from their house was her husband's bottle of pain pills. It wasn't easy getting Martin into the boat because of his cast and cervical collar, but somehow—with Joe pulling and Lori pushing—Martin made it.

Then Lori waded back into the house to gather up their pets. *Where were they?* She found the dogs on top of the washer and dryer in the laundry room. The water was so high the dryer had tipped over, and Pup-Pup had disappeared. Lori found him under some floating newspapers, grabbed him up in her arms, and sloshed back to the boat. Then she grabbed Fella, their beagle, and lifted him into the boat.

If you think it was difficult to get the dogs into the boat, the cats, Lili and Tharpe, were even less cooperative. In the commotion, they had climbed to the top of a baker's rack. They were terrified of the water and were scratching and hissing and freaking out. At last Lori got their harnesses and leashes on them, wrapped them each tightly in a towel, and handed them over to Joe, who put them in the bottom of the boat on a pile of life preservers. All this with the wind gusting at over one hundred miles per hour and the debris-filled water knocking against the boat, threatening to capsize it and making it almost impossible for Lori to pull herself into the boat.

Joe's only thought now was to get to the hospital to check on his wife, Margaret. He started the motor, and they began moving down the middle of the street past toppled cars, floating refrigerators and other appliances, fallen trees, and houses with their roofs blown away. They dodged flying debris and underwater hazards such as mailboxes and signs. *What if the boat hits something that rips a hole in the bottom? What if the motor quits?* It was like going through a wasteland with the rain beating down on them and the wind whipping them around. If they could just get to the hospital, which had been built on higher ground, hopefully, they would be safe.

Halfway there—as the ground rose and the water level dropped, they came upon a handicapped woman in a wheelchair in the doorway of her home. She was literally being swallowed alive by the flood waters and could do nothing about it. Her eyes were wild with fear and her face was drained of color. She never spoke; she just sat clutching the little coverlet around her shoulders. When they got to her, she was sitting as if in a stupor in about three feet of water. They never learned why she was there alone. Maybe someone got her to the doorway and ran to get help. Or maybe she had just been abandoned.

Somehow Joe and Lori managed to get her into the boat—along with the wheelchair—and on they went toward the hospital. A small boat filled with five people, three dogs, two cats, and a wheelchair amid the shrieking wind and flying debris—it must have been quite a sight!

When they arrived at the hospital, Joe was thankful to find that Margaret was safe. The hospital had survived without major damage, and Joe unloaded his "patients."

Tears overflowed Lori's eyes. "Joe," she said with heartfelt thanks, "without you and your boat, we most certainly would have died. There was no way my husband could swim, and I wouldn't have left him. We owe our lives to you."

"No," Joe corrected, "we all owe our lives to God."

Lori smiled. "Yes, you're right about that."

Joe added, "It's obvious to me that divine intervention released that latch on the boat trailer just when it did or we all would have been lost."

As Joe finished his story, standing next to the ever-growing junk pile where he was systematically dumping his life possessions, someone said, "It must be heartbreaking for you to lose all your antiques and valuable equipment!"

Joe looked at the pile and shook his head. "We're alive," he said. Then he pointed to the pile. "That's just stuff. I once thought it was important, *but it's just stuff.*"

God Turned the Twisters

When Katrina's wind began rattling the windows and then ripped the door off, Audrey Brown and her eighteen-year-old son, Lloyd Johnson Jr., realized that they would never survive this storm in their single-wide trailer, so they ran down the road to the house of her ex-husband, Alfred. It was a good thing they did, because just a few hours later the trailer was washed across the road, turned sideways, and dumped in a ditch.

Alfred's house was well-built and had withstood previous hurricanes, so a number of guys thought they would ride out the storm there. In addition to Alfred, there was Larry Everett, his sixteen-year-old son, Thomas, and a neighbor down the street, Sebastian—nicknamed Boo—whom Audrey had never met before. But Katrina's wind and water was too much even for Alfred's place, and it wasn't long before the floodwaters forced Audrey and the five men to swim out of the house.

Audrey had never been so scared in all her life. She was petrified of water. But now the fear of losing her life intensified as she struggled to keep her head above the surface. The men, being taller and stronger, had already made it to the rooftop, but Audrey, not even five feet tall, was too short.

Was she to die in that nasty water? Were all of them going to die?

She made first one attempt and then another, but to no avail. The men, sensing her danger, were screaming instructions at her. They tried to reach her

Above: Katrina caused Audrey Brown and her ex-husband, Alfred, to band together in order to survive and help rescue others. As a result, Audrey and Alfred are considering remarriage! Left: Volunteers from the Ithaca, Michigan, Seventh-day Adventist Church helped the Browns clear their land of debris and provided them with supplies.

116

hand to pull her up. Nothing worked. Her strength was starting to give way. She panicked and began to thrash in the water.

Boo took action. He dived off the roof into the churning water. Coming to the surface, he surveyed the situation, took a deep breath, and once more dived down into the murky water. He was able to swim beneath Audrey's legs. Then he got her balanced on his shoulders and shoved her up just as high as he could. The others reached down, caught her hands, and pulled her to the rooftop just as Boo was about to run out of breath.

Once she was on the roof, Audrey's fear only escalated. Now she became terrified either that the water would cover the roof—as it was almost to their feet already—or that they were going to be blown off. She was also afraid that her Chihuahua, Taco, and her cat, Kee-Kee, would be ripped out of her arms by the strong winds. She clung to them all the tighter.

Then the worst possible fear materialized right in front of them. They could see four tornado funnels coming at them! Objects were whirling in the air. Trees were snapping like toothpicks. It sounded like a freight train bearing down on them. That's when this little group of survivors grabbed each others' hands and began praying like they'd never prayed before.

They had no protection; just one little twister could have snatched the whole lot of them and dropped their broken bodies miles away in some ditch. But they were faced with not one, not two, but four tornadoes! Only God could protect them now. Then the unbelievable happened. Just as the tornadoes had almost reached their house, the funnels parted and went around on either side of them! It was a direct answer to prayer. It's not often in life that one witnesses such a miracle, but this incident was too dramatic to be anything other than a divine hand guiding the wind.

The Lord, however, wasn't through helping them. The men noticed a fifteen-foot antique sail boat chained up some distance away. They made a swim for it—which wasn't easy through the cold, churning water. Once they reached the boat, it was even more difficult to get it back to where Audrey was stranded on the roof. Paddling with a two-by-four and pulling themselves along with downed power lines, it took an hour or more to reach her. On the way, they rescued two cats and tried to get a dog. Then they discovered the boat had a hole in it. Someone grabbed a giant seed from a tree as it floated by and shoved it down into the hole! It worked!

A sense of relief flooded over Audrey as she was finally able to slide down the roof and into the safety of the boat. And she also managed to get her two pets into the boat too.

What was that? Voices above the howl of the wind? Thinking it might be people yelling for help, they headed in that direction. Sure enough, people were stranded on their rooftops. Maneuvering the bulky old boat around, they were able to rescue a few. Other people were also stranded, but the boat could hold only so many, and it turned out to be not be all that safe—at least not for those standing up in the boat, trying to pull it along with downed power lines! At first sixteen-year-old Thomas fell out; then a line became wrapped around Boo, and he went out into the water. Each time, due to the wind and current whipping them about, it seemed to take forever—maybe an hour or more—to get back to those who had been knocked overboard. Audrey said she did more praying that day then ever before in her life!

That's when they began hearing a noise that was different from the roaring of the wind. To their amazement, they saw a jet ski coming toward them. Apparently, one of the people stranded on a rooftop saw it floating by, swam to it, and was able to get it started. Now they had maneuverability. Those in the sailboat told the fellow on the jet ski where other people were stranded. He would go get them and bring them back to the boat.

At last the water started receding. They waited a while and decided that if they could get to Highway 90, surely help would be available. So they started to paddle in that direction. After eight long, agonizing hours, they crawled out of the boat into waist deep water and tied it to a stop sign.

They started walking from Lakeshore toward the Waveland police station, thinking they'd find help there. But it was destroyed. They didn't know what else to do but to keep walking down Lower Bay Road toward the Chevron station. Police officers eventually took them to the high school for the night.

Even though Audrey and her ex-husband lost all of their material possessions, they didn't lose everything. Instead, they rediscovered the love that they thought was lost forever. They're now talking about remarriage. Miracles do happen!

Prayer Is More Than a Life Preserver

Most people tend to use prayer as a life preserver. When the sun's shining and the sky's blue, they leave it in the closet of their lives. But when the clouds gather, the lightning flashes, the thunder booms, and the wind and the waves threaten their very existence, out it comes!

That's what Katrina did for people. On August 28, 2005, many Gulf Coast residents had very few cares in the world. Most didn't even give God the time of day, let alone think about really communicating with Him. Yet, twenty-four hours later, those same individuals were probably pleading with God for their lives.

How must God feel about His earthly children and their prayer habits—or lack of prayer habits? Aren't you thankful that God's divine intervention in human destiny is not dependent on the consistency, length, or content of our prayers? A simple, "Help me, Jesus," is all the permission God needs to tell Satan to back off so that His army of guardian angels can protect and save.

What is prayer? It's talking to God as if you were talking to a friend. And it's also the key to experiencing an unnatural calm and contentment when the storms of life hit. It puts you in tune with divine wisdom to work out everything for good. So often people don't pray because the outlook seems hopeless. But nothing is impossible with God. (See Mark 10:27.) Nothing is so messed up that it cannot be fixed up, no relationship too strained for God to bring about reconciliation and understanding, no habit so deep rooted that it cannot be uprooted, no one so weak that he cannot be strong, no child so willful that she cannot be obedient, and no storm so life-threatening that it cannot be calmed. Whatever your need may be, trust God to supply it. When challenges, anxieties, and problems come, stop pushing the worry button of your mind. Instead, give your troubles to God and trust Him for a miracle.

Jonah prayed from the belly of a whale. Daniel prayed from a den of hungry lions. Peter prayed from prison. Chelsea prayed from the pot. Bill prayed from under water. And Joe prayed from a fast-flooding garage. It's not where you are or when you pray that makes the difference. It's the fact that you have a close enough relationship with the God of the universe that you are willing to call upon Him and believe that He has the power to save you—no matter where you are or in what circumstances you find yourself!

The prayer line to heaven is never busy! King David used it often. Here's just one of his many recorded prayers:

"Hear my prayer, O LORD;
    listen to my plea! . . . .
I am losing all hope;
    I am paralyzed with fear. . . .
Come quickly, LORD, and answer me,
    for my depression deepens. Don't turn away from me,
    or I will die.
Let me hear of your unfailing love to me in the morning,
    for I am trusting you.
Show me where to walk,
    for I have come to you in prayer"
                    (Psalm 143:1, 4, 7, 8, NLT).

-Chapter 9-
TWIST OF FATE

"New Orleans . . . a sand castle set on a sponge nine feet below sea level,
where people made music from heartache, named their drinks for hurricanes,
and joked that one day you'd be able to tour the city by gondola."
—Nancy Gibbs

Kevin Young, a six-foot, five-inch, 285-pound ex-NFL football player, was born and raised in New Orleans. The city had been good to him. He was a high school All-American football player at George Washington Carver Senior High School and then awarded a four-year athletic scholarship to Tulane University. In 1987, he was a defensive end with the New Orleans Saints. It was their best year ever, losing to Minnesota in the first round of the NFL playoffs.

Now, almost twenty years later, Kevin owned a real estate business in Dallas, where he and his sister Roxanne had relocated. For the last year or so, they had been sharing the responsibility of going back to New Orleans every other weekend to help their sister, Barbara, care for their elderly mother, Myrtle. She had congestive heart failure and didn't always take her medications or follow her physician's orders. It was not uncommon for Kevin to get a call from Barbara telling him that their mother had been taken to the hospital as a result of not following doctor's orders. Kevin would then rush to New Orleans to assist in caring for her. During his visit, he would also complete different tasks—running errands or fixing up her home. On December 28, 2004, his mom had a massive stroke. A tumor was discovered—and later removed from her brain. She was placed on a ventilator and admitted to Ferncrest Manor Nursing Home for rehabilitation from the stroke.

Then came the fateful weekend in August when Katrina was building in the Atlantic. Kevin's older sister, Barbara, who lived in New Orleans, was on vacation in Texas for two weeks, so it was Kevin's turn to be with his mother. You might call it a twist of fate—or a "God thing"—that Kevin, instead of his sister, was in New Orleans when Katrina hit. Only the bold cunning of this giant of a man allowed him to go against hospital protocol, demand mayoral intervention for his mom to be admitted to a "safe" hospital, and purchase a canoe in an attempt to escape the violence of the Superdome . . . but once again, we're getting ahead of the story.

In happier days prior to Katrina, Kevin Young, with sisters, Roxanne Young (front) and Barbara Grigley (left), pose for a picture with their mother, Myrtle Jackson.

As you read on, you'll agree that God chose the right person to be with Myrtle through the worst living nightmare anyone could imagine. And by the way, Kevin was supposed to have gone to New Orleans the Monday before, which means he would have been back in Dallas when the storm came, and his mother would have been left alone. Instead, Kevin was delayed and didn't make it to New Orleans until Saturday—just about thirty hours before Katrina's fury began. It's as if God had it all arranged that he would be there to give his mother comfort and reassurance and to help nursing staff and officials with the evacuations.

As Kevin packed for his trip, he knew a hurricane was coming but thought nothing of it. After all, he had grown up in New Orleans.

Hurricanes were common. Authorities were always warning, "We advise evacuation." Some residents would leave the city—those with easy transportation and someplace to go—but most just hunkered down until the storm blew over. From a 2004 poll, 30 percent of the city, or a half-million people, stated they would not leave for mandatory evacuation. That was the mindset of the people, and Kevin was no different. He never once thought that this one would be the *big* one!

On Saturday night, he was having dinner with his mom in the nursing home when the orders came to get tracheotomy patients to higher facilities. It hit him like a jolt of lightning. *Higher facilities?* It sounded serious. "I'll be glad to help when you're ready," Kevin volunteered.

At six-thirty the next morning they began transferring patients to a deserted building that, until seven years ago, had been a hospital. There was a beehive of activity as the staff tried to make an abandoned hospital functional. It was like the *ER* television program. People were racing against time to get everyone cared for. Every situation was an emergency.

Can you imagine patients on ventilators that required electricity or battery backup, or needed someone to pump air into their lungs with an Ambu bag? It was chaos. Kevin's heart went out to the children and the elderly who had no family members to reassure them or care for them when the nursing staff was needed elsewhere. His mother was in a group of twenty-eight patients—all on ventilators—and he was the only person, other than an occasional staff member, helping them. What about the other patients who had no one? God put it in his heart to help wherever he could.

The medical staff was needed in a hundred different places at once. Everyone had a life-threatening demand. Things that we take for granted in a well-equipped hospital, where everyone knows where everything is, were major events here. How do you feed this many patients? How do you care for their personal needs? How do you reassure them that everything is going to be all right when your own heart is beating in fear?

At one point, as Kevin's mother was comfortable in a room on the fourth floor with her ventilator plugged in and working properly, he felt the urgency to check the exits. All four were blocked, and the elevator didn't work. He raced through the seven-story building to get an idea of where things were and how to get out if needed. He met the building engineer and began firing questions: Was the building safe? Would it stand? Were they in a flood zone?

He was told, "It withstood Betsy. We've got everything under control."

Kevin asked about evacuation, should it be necessary, and offered his assistance. He also noticed that police officers were going up and down the stairs. The police had moved into another section of the building.

There were so many needs to take care of during the night that Kevin got only a few minutes sleep. Children were calling for their mommies and daddies. Patients were hungry. They needed a drink. They were cold. They were in pain. They were asking, "What's happening? Is the building safe?" Kevin was going from one to another, trying to meet their needs, and if he couldn't, he would find medical staff that could.

About four or five o'clock in the morning, the wind started picking up, and the rain began coming down in torrents. Kevin could see the telephone poles shaking and then bending in the wind. "What's happening?" his mother asked. He didn't want to frighten her. How could he explain the fury he was seeing out the window? Wind was pushing cars around, their horns were blowing, trunks were popping open, and rising water was covering their wheels. "What's going on?" she asked again.

"It's pretty bad," he told her.

"We're going to be all right," she assured him. "God's got us in His hand." If she only knew the fear that was building in every cell of Kevin's body. This wasn't just a hurricane. This was a monster storm! He was beginning to wonder, *Will we survive?*

Then, just as Kevin thought it couldn't get any worse, the power began to fail. Circuits were overloaded. What they had endured during the last twenty-four hours was nothing compared to this. You couldn't see anything. Lights flickered again and then went out completely. Now there was a mad scramble to find some kind of power and make sure back-up batteries on the ventilators were working.

Although it was morning, the density of the clouds and rain allowed little light to filter in through the windows. Children were panicked! Adults were moaning and crying. The meager staff raced from bed to bed. *How long will the back-up batteries last?* They had to get more generators. But when Kevin tried to find the building superintendent, he was no where to be found.

Kevin once more glanced out the windows to assess the storm. From the south side, things seemed OK, but on the north side he could see the trees and debris falling and flying through the air, cars—even SUVs—were under water; rain was coming in the cracks of the windows and the walls even on the fourth floor, and Kevin knew in his heart, without even checking, that the first floor had to be flooded.

Without power there was no oxygen. Back-up batteries wouldn't last forever. They had to find some oxygen tanks. *But where?* If they didn't locate some soon, people would die. Every second counted. Without cell phones or walkie-talkies, there was no communication among the medical staff. Kevin would have to find some oxygen tanks himself. He raced to the temporary police department that had been set up on the other side of the building. The officers had walkie-talkies. He frantically screamed, "If you don't get some oxygen tanks up there, there's gonna be a whole lot of dead people!"

When he realized that he was being ignored because he was *just a family member* and had no authority, he ran to find the head nurse and led her to the police officials. They listened to her urgent appeal. That's when Kevin learned the oxygen tanks were downstairs—in the water. He started down and pleaded with the police who had flashlights, "Come with me!" Two officers started with him, but when one saw the depth of the water, he backed out, saying, "There's no way I'm going down there in all that water."

"Then give me your flashlight," Kevin demanded, and he and the other officer waded into the murky water and found five or six tanks.

Now Kevin really grew concerned. There was no way that many tanks were going to meet the overwhelming need, and there were far too few staff to even think of hand bagging the patients to keep them alive. They would have to evacuate or his mother would die. The enormity of the task was overwhelming. He realized he couldn't save them all, but he would do everything that was humanly possible to save his mother's life. They were on a countdown to death!

The officer with the walkie-talkie began making calls; he finally got through to the army. "We've got to get these patients out of here. There's no power. They're on ventilators and are going to die. We have no food for them. The downstairs is flooded. We've got to evacuate NOW!" The decision was made that it would take too long if they had to wait for helicopters. So amphibious army vehicles were sent.

Now began the nightmare of trying to get the patients out of the building. Each one had to be carried down four flights of stairs on a rescuer's shoulders. When they got to the first story, Kevin had to wade through water up to his chest to get out to the amphibious truck. He got his mother safely into the back of the vehicle and went back for another patient—and then another and another. When the truck was filled with five patients, they took off through the flooded streets to find a hospital that would accept them. Kevin and a New Orleans policeman stayed in the back with the patients, hand bagging them—pumping oxygen into their lungs to keep them alive.

When they arrived at the closest hospital, the staff had orders not to accept any more patients. They were at full capacity and under water. Kevin directed the truck to the Superdome—where they were refused entrance. They went to the VA hospital, which was operating, but the staff refused to open their doors. For two-and-a-half hours they drove around the flooded dark streets trying desperately to find someone to help them.

Finally, they went back to Charity Hospital, a part of the Louisiana State University health care system. Charity operated a Level 1 trauma center and served one of the nation's largest metropolitan concentrations of indigent residents and people without health insurance. The hospital was already responsible for caring for, feeding, and providing water and restroom facilities for hundreds of people—staff, patients and family—not to mention those from the community who had come for

Kevin Young and his baby daughter, Jade Myrietta Young, born November 15, 2005. Her middle name is the name chosen for her by her grandmother on her deathbed.

protection. When they said they had orders not to admit anymore patients, Kevin's heart dropped. When he saw the overwhelming needs the staff was already trying to deal with inside the hospital, their decision was understandable—but not when he was outside the hospital doors hand pumping oxygen for five people and one of them was his mother!

Through it all Kevin was trying to reassure his mom. She was calm and at peace. At one point she said, "I've seen the baby, and her name is Myrietta." At the time, Kevin's wife was about six-and-a-half months pregnant. It was as if his mom were preparing herself for death. She was a praying lady, loved the Lord, and was active in her church. She asked her son, "Are you all right?"

"Yes," Kevin replied, trying to mask the desperate feelings whirling around inside.

"I'm all right, too," she said with a smile.

This was the third time they had come to the doors of Charity Hospital. But Kevin wouldn't give up. He pleaded with the army officials to do something. A call was made to Mayor Ray Nagin, and orders were given, "Let the patients in."

The staff tried their best to follow patient registration protocol, but with no medical records, no social security numbers, and no knowledge of previous medications, it was a challenge to know just how to treat them. As Kevin watched the process, he had a whole new respect for the ER staff that was able to work so efficiently in such dire circumstances. He and his mom were frightened enough by the experience; how must all the other patients have felt who had no loved ones with them and no knowledge of whether or not their families had survived the storm? It must have been agony for them!

Once everyone was stabilized, the doctor came around and confided to Kevin, "We are doing the best we can, but we're probably going to have to evacuate this hospital. The main water line has burst, and by tomorrow we'll be out of water and food." In addition, the hospital had lost power, and water was rising. The doctor said he was going to meet with the staff to determine what was going to happen. As he left, the stark reality of their precarious situation began to sink in. The water was rising—and they were on the first floor. They were going to have to evacuate once more! Then Kevin noticed the medical staff around him was packing up.

Horrified, he asked, "Are you just going to leave the people down here to die?"

"Don't worry," he was told, "we're going to figure out something." But one by one the staff began to leave.

Kevin turned to his mother, "Mom, how long are you able to breathe without oxygen?"

She answered, "Maybe six to ten minutes."

At that point, with the staff leaving and the water rising, Kevin, realizing the gravity of their situation, broke down and cried. "Mom, we're going to have to move again. But don't worry, I'm not leaving you down here."

One of the staff came up to him. "If we help you move your mother upstairs, will you come back and help me move the others?"

"Oh, yes, yes," Kevin replied. "I'll definitely come back down and help you." The man left in a hurry to make the necessary arrangements. Kevin gently brushed a wisp of hair from his mother's face, tenderly kissed her cheek, and whispered, "I love you, Mom. It's going to be OK." Exhausted—not having slept more than a few minutes in the last thirty-six hours—he laid his head down beside her and dozed for a few minutes.

Still holding her hand, he woke with a start and realized his mother had stopped breathing. "Mom, Mom," he called as he began shaking her, hoping against hope for some kind of response. His heart was racing. He broke into a cold sweat. "Mom, Mom, talk to me." He felt for her pulse. There was nothing. She was gone.

Kevin's chest began to heave. He had tried so hard to save her and was making plans to evacuate her to a higher floor. She had heard the whole conversation. It was almost as if she realized the futility of it all. Not wanting to burden her son further, she closed her eyes and went to sleep.

He laid his head against her chest and sobbed. Her struggle was over. God had allowed him to be with her at the end. That had been his wish ever since his mother had become ill. It was as if God had it all arranged. Kevin knew he had done everything humanly possible to save her. He would never have forgiven himself had his mother died alone. He had no regrets. He breathed deeply, looked once again at the peaceful look on his mom's face, and in his heart said, "Thank You, Lord."

When Life Comes to an End

Life is precious. Sometimes it's a struggle to live. We go to amazing lengths to save others—as we should. Sometimes the thread of life takes hold, and it's as if the patient is resurrected from certain death—and we praise God for the miracle. But sometimes, the thread lets go.

How do we respond when so many are saved by medical miracles—and it is our loved one who dies? Can you say, as hymn writer Horatio Spafford did in 1876 when his daughters died at sea:

When peace, like a river, attendeth my way,
When sorrows like sea billows roll—
Whatever my lot, Thou has taught me to say,
It is well, it is well with my soul.

God has a plan for each of our lives, and it's not our place to second guess what that might be. Kevin's wish was to be with his mother when she passed. Yes, he prayed she would live, but it was as if God said, "Enough suffering! Myrtle is safe to save." As Kevin looked back, he was amazed how God had led him, instead of his sister, to be in New Orleans at the exact time when the hurricane hit. Of course, he wanted more than anything to be able to save his mother, but that was not to be.

God's plan is not that people should suffer and die. But until sin is eradicated from this old earth, we are reminded too often that one of the biggest consequences of sin is death. The good news is that with Christ, it's not the end!

God's Assurance Plan

"For the Lord Himself shall descend from heaven with a shout, with the voice of an archangel, and with the trumpet of God. And the dead in Christ will rise first" (1 Thessalonians 4:16, NKJV).

"For the hour is coming in which all who are in the graves will hear His voice and come forth—those who have done good, to the resurrection of life, and those who have done evil, to the resurrection of condemnation" (John 5:28, 29, NKJV).

"And God will wipe away every tear from their eyes; there shall be no more death, nor sorrow, nor crying; and there shall be no more pain, for the former things are passed away. . . . Behold, I make all things new" (Revelation 21:4, NKJV).

"For God so loved the world that He gave His only begotten Son, that whoever believes in Him should not perish but have everlasting life" (John 3:16, NKJV).

"Let not your heart be troubled; you believe in God, believe also in Me. In My Father's house are many mansions; if it were not so, I would have told you. I go to prepare a place for you, And if I go and prepare a place for you, I will come again and receive you to Myself, that where I am, there you may be also" (John 14:1-3, NKJV).

Kevin's mom went to sleep in Christ—accepting His gift of salvation for her—so she'll wake up on resurrection morning with no need of a ventilator! She'll be in the prime of her life. No aches and pains. For her, the time in the grave will be like a moment. That's how it is when you go to sleep; you're unconscious of anything going on around you. And with God's "assurance plan," Kevin and his family are looking forward to a wonderful reunion on resurrection morning.

Just as God planned Kevin's sojourn in New Orleans, God has a plan for your life. Here's God's promise to you: " 'For I know the plans I have for you,' says the LORD. 'They are plans for good and not for disaster, to give you a future and a hope' " (Jeremiah 29:11, NLT).

Chapter 10

THE LOST CITY

"The heavens declare the glory of God,
but the streets declare the sinfulness of man."
—Max Lucado

Human beings are both saints and sinners, people of dignity and depravity, filled with kindness and corruptness, laced with goodness and greed, with spiritual leanings and carnal lust—and looting. Crisis often causes people to respond in the extreme: It brings out either the best in human nature or the worst. And that's exactly what happened with Katrina—especially in New Orleans.

The good was not widely publicized—neighbors rescuing neighbors from their attics and rooftops, residents supplying boats to help with hospital evacuations, and the heroism of medical personnel trying so hard to save people who were utterly helpless. But much has been said about the bad! The world was shocked with the abhorrent evil that ran rampant through the streets of New Orleans in the first seven days after Katrina, before marshal law and an aggressive military presence was able to bring it under control.

How could such violence happen in America? Why was wickedness and crime so rampant at the Superdome and the convention center?

The story we're about to tell—the story of what happened in New Orleans immediately after the storm—is a sorry chapter that will be written into the history books of what many have considered to be a great and compassionate nation. Max Lucado put it this way, "Katrina blew more than roofs off buildings; it blew the mask off of the nature of humanity. The main problem in the world is not Mother Nature, but human nature. Strip away the police barricades, blow down the fences, and the real self is revealed. We are barbaric to the core."

Alice Jackson, writing from Ocean Springs, Mississippi, said it well when she exclaimed, "We may be in purgatory on the Gulf Coast, but those poor souls in New Orleans are in the inner ring of hell."

And that's exactly where Kevin Young was when his mother slipped away to her death in Charity Hospital right before she was to be evacuated for the third time in two days! But the agony of trying to keep his mother alive pales in light of the terror Kevin faced when he was forced to flee to the Superdome.

When Kevin realized that he had lost the battle for his mother's life, he broke down and sobbed over the futility of it all and over the cruelty of the storm that caused his mother's untimely demise. Then he took a deep breath and slowly exhaled. It was over! A physician had come to supervise the evacuation from the first floor. Kevin asked him, "What's next?"

"We'll send her down to the morgue."

Cold, icy words—THE MORGUE! Kevin knew that if it was "down," it was under water. He turned to say his last goodbyes, telling his mom how much he loved her. He then wrapped her body with blankets as tightly as he could. He wanted to make it easy for someone to identify her. After the physician once more reassured him that his mother's body would be taken care of, he directed Kevin to go upstairs to the seventh floor where there was some food. He knew it had been a long time since the man had eaten.

Despite the terrible situation at Charity Hospital, there was some food available for the attending staff. Kevin helped himself, then surveyed the surrounding rooms. Finding an empty one across the hall, he made a pallet on the floor and slept for two hours. By then it was Tuesday morning.

With the water continuing to rise, patients on the lower floors were now being moved upstairs.

Twice Kevin went back downstairs to find his mother's body; twice he failed. He searched unsuccessfully for the entrance to which the military truck had brought his mother and the four other life-support patients, thinking personnel might have moved her there. Water now covered the steps to where he had last seen her. He could do no more.

Having no place else to go, Kevin returned to the seventh floor, where he watched the behind-the-scenes drama of the medical staff coping with one of the worst disasters in United States history. He kept out of their way. When they left for their shifts, he used the hospital phone to check on his Dallas business and let his family know that he was alive. He decided to keep the news about his mother's death to himself until he could tell them in person. He ate when food was offered to him. One nurse, who must have thought he was a physician, kept him up-to-date with news from the outside.

Later that Tuesday morning, the hospital's power generator failed, plunging the massive hospital into darkness, except for those rooms lit during the day by sunlight. If people were terrified before, now their anxiety escalated. Evacuation began by boat and helicopter, moving patients to other locations and transporting family and community members to their fate at the Superdome. At that time, everyone thought the Superdome was a safe haven. They had no way of knowing what was really happening in their beloved city.

Who would have thought that the hospital's evacuation would become the target of senseless violence? A CNN News bulletin on Thursday, September 1, 2005, reported, "The evacuation of patients from Charity Hospital was halted Thursday after the facility came under sniper fire twice. The first incident happened around 11:30 A.M. (CT) as [Dr. Tyler] Curiel and his National Guard escorts headed back to the hospital after dropping off several patients at nearby Tulane Medical Center to be evacuated by helicopter. Charity shares a helipad with Tulane Medical Center, which is across the street. They were traveling in a convoy of amphibious vehicles, and Curiel said the vehicle behind him was targeted. About an hour later, another gunman opened fire at the back of Charity Hospital. . . . Evacuations by boat were halted after armed looters threatened medics and overturned one of their boats."

Four days later, on Saturday, September 3, it was reported that "Charity Hospital, where about 200 patients and doctors were trapped in deplorable conditions, was fully evacuated of all patients and personnel. . . . The hospital had no power, no water and no food. Some patients were on ventilators being worked by hand pumps; the bodies of those who died were stored in stairwells, as the hospital's morgue had flooded," (CNN.com).

Now, for a moment, we are going to leave the plight of Kevin Young, who was one of those trapped in Charity Hospital and about to be evacuated to the horror of the Superdome, and describe what was happening in "the lost city" during the first seven days after the storm. The deplorable conditions at the Superdome (see chapter 11) can best be understood as a microcosm of the greater tragedy that New Orleans and its surrounding parishes were experiencing.

The Nightmare of New Orleans

The once flashy city, famous for its nightlife—where people came to toss beads, drink booze, and listen to jazz—had overnight become a place of despair, violence, drugs, foul play, and random shootings. Groups of armed men roamed the streets looting and raping and terrorizing. Crazy or desperate people fired at medical-relief helicopters; pirates captured rescue boats. Carjackings were common. Unsuspecting drivers pulled over to help people they thought were in need, only to have their families forced out of the car at gunpoint. Police stood and watched looters—or joined them. Beautiful southern mansions in the Garden District went up in flames—destroyed by the evil hands of arsonists.

It soon became obvious that those who chose to stay behind in New Orleans included other individuals besides those who had no choice, no transportation, or no place to go. Two days *before* Katrina hit, radio announcements made it clear that transportation out of the city was available to *anyone* who requested it. The fact is, most people stayed behind for one of two reasons: Either to protect their property or to take advantage of the situation. The latter group armed themselves and waited for the wind to die down enough to begin looting the thousands of residences and businesses whose owners had evacuated. When the flooding began, a good number of this criminal population suddenly became refugees and were taken to the Superdome—along with the innocent, kind, considerate people of New Orleans. This evil element soon made conditions intolerable at the Superdome and the convention center as they continued to take advantage of others.

By Wednesday, three days after Katrina, the beautiful Riverwalk Mall next to the Superdome, which had almost no water damage, had been ravaged and emptied by looters. The Super Wal-Mart in the Lower Garden District wasn't flooded either but did a booming business—in freeloaders. Some people emerged with shopping carts full of food, bottled water, and medical supplies. Others appeared with TVs and DVDs, fishing poles, and chainsaws. "Is everything free?" asked one woman arriving at the door. When told yes, she began chanting. "TV! TV! TV!" One gang chased away the security guards and emptied Wal-Mart of guns and ammunition, enough to arm a company of soldiers.

By Wednesday night the violence was so out of hand that Ray Nagin, mayor of New Orleans, ordered fifteen hundred policemen—virtually the entire city force—to stop trying to rescue people from attics and rooftops and to focus instead on stopping the looting—as looters were now threatening the heavily populated areas where the hotels and the hospitals were.

By Thursday, New Orleans was on the verge of anarchy. Policemen, many of whom had lost their homes, were turning in their badges rather than face the looters. Mayor Nagin issued a "desperate SOS" to the federal government for assistance in handling the violence and the crimes of opportunity.

As the floodwaters continued to rise throughout Monday night, Tuesday, and Wednesday until most of the area around New Orleans was underwater, people were forced to their rooftops and attics. During these long, hot, terrifying days some lives came to an end. Some people miraculously survived. And for others, life began. Years from now stories will be told about being born in a New Orleans attic—delivered by family members who had picked up a few birthing tips by watching cable TV.

Following Katrina, much of New Orleans looked like a ghost town—with mud-covered streets and widespread devastation.

Newsweek, commenting on what it called *the lost city,* described the situation this way: "Day after day of images showed exhausted families and their crying children stepping around corpses while they begged: 'Where is the water? Where are the buses?' They seemed helpless, powerless, at the mercy of forces far beyond their control. The lack of rapid response left people in the United States, and all over the world, wondering how an American city could look like Mogadishu or Port-au-Prince. The refugee crisis—a million people without homes, jobs, schools—hardly fit George W. Bush's vision of the American Colossus" (msnbc.com).

The levees were breached in at least three places. Trying to plug one three-hundred-foot gap on the Seventeenth Street Canal, the Corps of Engineers dropped giant sandbags and concrete blocks from helicopters. But the choppers were called away on Tuesday to rescue people crying for help from rooftops, and the engineers were never able to get ahead of the flooding. As the water rose, New Orleans's Canal Street literally became a canal!

Stranded residents became resourceful. Because there was no electricity, people tore off chair legs and used them as torches after dark. Some brave souls, trying to wade through the garbage-strewn water to higher ground, screamed when they saw giant rats and poisonous snakes in the water. Others improvised, making boats out of empty refrigerators or Styrofoam.

More than eight thousand inmates from New Orleans-area parish jails had to be evacuated to thirty-four local jails around the state. But their criminal records were under water. Sorting out who had been charged—and with what crime—became a nightmare. Many were sent out with color-coded arm bands to designate the seriousness of the crimes they had committed, only to realize that the authorities at arrival destinations had no idea what the colors meant! It was likely that shoplifters were incarcerated with rapists. And some jails were likely compelled to let some suspects go free. Stories spread that rapists, murderers, and others with major offenses had escaped in the storm.

A month after Katrina, the headlines were screaming, "Where Have All the Prisoners Gone?" "More than 500 From New Orleans Jail Still Unaccounted For." Some did escape. We know that because two criminals on the "wanted list" were caught in Knoxville, Tennessee—one had already enrolled at the university! Louisiana lawyers stated that other prisoners were abandoned to die in the flooded Orleans Parish Prison. And that's just one of the many Gulf Coast prisons that weren't able to account for all their inmates!

Meanwhile, at Memorial Medical Center, food was running low; sanitation wasn't working; and temperatures inside were soaring. Flood-waters had isolated the hospital where about 312 patients—many of them critically ill—were being treated when Katrina hit. It was reported that conditions were so desperate that a few of the medical staff discussed euthanizing patients they thought might not survive the ordeal. The question remains, Why had forty-five of these patients suddenly died?

In nearby St. Bernard Parish a day before Katrina hit, a vehicle was sent to evacuate the patients at St. Rita's Nursing Home. Apparently, the owners of the facility turned it away stating that the residents had chosen to remain where they were. Thirty-five residents died when the facility flooded!

Many of those needing evacuation from New Orleans were taken to airports. The New Orleans Lakefront Airport was basically a desolate airstrip and not an official evacuation site. The problem was, no one communicated this to the rescue teams. Hundreds of refugees plucked from parking garages, apartment buildings, highway overpasses, and the roofs of their homes were shuttled to this dark runway, waiting for someone to take them somewhere—anywhere but where they were! Fights broke out among the refugees for seats on outbound helicopters. Jimmy Dennis, a Lakefront Airport firefighter who had been up two nights trying to care for the sick and keep order, shook his head, "People couldn't understand that we had to get the sick people out first!"

Col. Timothy Tarchick, commander of the Air Force Reserve 920th Rescue Wing, was reported as screaming into the phone to the New Orleans emergency operation center above the thump-thump of coast guard and military helicopters bringing more and more desperate souls into the airport, "It's absolute chaos. It's not safe here. I've got a thousand people who have been dropped here. We're out of food, and they're starting to get tense. I've got women separated from their children. We have no medicine. We need security. It's like Baghdad here. You have got to take control of this."

The New Orleans International Airport, an official evacuation site, had tents and medicine available; planes and buses were transporting people to shelters in Texas, northern Louisiana, and elsewhere. But that scene proved to be another nightmare. Refugees were forced to put their names on sign-up sheets, but no one knew where they were going until they were in the air or on the bus. Families became separated, with some going to one destination,

Notice the marks left by flood waters on these houses. At the height of the storm, little more than the roof would be visible above the water.

and the rest to another—sometimes thousands of miles apart.

When helicopters airlifted people from attics and rooftops, children were given first priority, and with limited space available, parents were often left behind. That's what happened to twenty-four-year-old Natrena Lewis, a home health aide who had stayed in New Orleans to help a patient get into a shelter before Katrina hit. Five days after the levees collapsed, she found herself with her two young boys, twenty-two-month-old Ty'iyr and five-year-old Telly, stranded on the roof of a motel. When little Ty'iyr had an asthma attack, he was airlifted to a hospital, but there was no room for his mother and brother. Natrena and Telly were eventually rescued and ended up in Houston, but no one had any idea where Ty'iyr was. Days later he was found at an Atlanta hospital. But can you imagine the utter terror Natrena experienced during the time her child was lost? Like Natrena, a week after Katrina many families were still desperately searching for their loved ones. At one time there were over two thousand names on the missing children list—and thousands more on the missing person list for other family members.

One woman in Waveland, Mississippi, told the story about how her aunt had narrowly escaped death in New Orleans: "My seventy-eight-year-old aunt Frieda was knocked unconscious in the storm and was so badly scratched and bruised that rescue workers thought she was dead. They took her to the morgue and placed her among the decaying corpses.

When she came to, she didn't realize where she was until she touched the cold hard body next to her. She screamed with terror, 'Somebody get me out of here. Please, get me out of here.' But her screams for help went unheard among the chaos. Finally when a paramedic came close enough, she grabbed him by the leg and pleaded with him to get her out of there. Not even looking down, he tried to shake his leg free. She refused to let go. Their eyes met, and as the tears spilled down her cheeks, she pleaded, 'If I were your mother, would you leave me here to die? I'm begging you. Please help me.' Compassion filled his heart. Quickly he scooped her up in his arms and carried her to the nearest medical facility. Other than her scrapes and bruises, her only injury was a broken ankle. Yet, had she not been rescued, she most certainly would have died."

Ozro Henderson described the condition of New Orleans well: "I do not have the words in my vocabulary to describe what is happening here—'castastrophe' and 'disaster' don't explain it."

What the World Needs to Survive Crisis

Max Lucado makes this thought provoking comment: "You don't have to go to New Orleans to see the chaos. . . . When you do what you want and I do what I want, humanity and civility implodes. And when the Katrinas of life blow in, our true nature is revealed and our deepest need is unveiled: a need deeper than food, more permanent than firm levees. We need, not a new system, but a new nature. We need to be changed from the inside out."

When Mark Umbehagen, whose parents had lived in St. Bernard Parish and lost everything, was asked, "What's the answer to the crime, looting, and violence that erupted in New Orleans after Katrina?" he simply said, "Jesus."

Perhaps this is the time to reevaluate your true nature. Would you have been tempted to take advantage of others in your struggle to better your own lot or save yourself? Or has Jesus changed you from the inside out, so even though you are hurting and empty, your first thought is: What would Jesus do? (WWJD?)

If you'd like Jesus to polish your values and motives so they reflect Him more clearly, He's knocking at your heart's door. Jesus is saying to you, "Behold, I stand at the door and knock. If anyone hears My voice and opens the door, I will come in to him and dine with him, and he with Me" (Revelation 3:20, NKJV). Jesus is a gentleman. He won't take advantage of you. He won't force Himself on you. He's willing to transform your life if you'll invite Him in, but it's your choice.

Although salvation is by grace, the test of whether you really love God has to do with obedience. Are you willing to do what He asks you to do? The more you love Him, the more you will desire to be like Him. That means you'll choose, through the power of His Holy Spirit, to change your thinking and your behavior to conform to His character, which is reflected in His moral law of Ten Commandments found in Exodus 20:2–17, and to follow His example of how to live here on this earth.

Only when you have Christ living in your heart will your first response in crisis be to do God's will, to be Christlike, to do what Jesus would do, regardless of personal pain or pleasure. Regardless of gain or loss.

Now it's time to return to the drama that was unfolding in the Superdome as thousands of refugees fled there thinking they would be safe, only to discover that they had jumped from the proverbial frying pan into the fire. Trapped! This was the plight of Kevin Young, who was forced to leave Charity Hospital. Read on.

-Chapter 11-
SUPERDOME—CRIME AND CHAOS

"The city's pain is a nation's shame."
—*Time* Magazine

The Louisiana Superdome is a large, multipurpose sports and exhibition facility located in the central business district of New Orleans. It opened in 1975 with a seating capacity of up to 75,000. The Superdome was home to the New Orleans Saints (NFL), the Sugar Bowl (NCAA), and Tulane Green Wave (NCAA) until it closed indefinitely on September 2, 2005, because of the structural damage inflicted by Katrina and the possibility that it could be a biohazard because of the human waste and trash from those who sought refuge there during and after the storm.

For seventeen years the Superdome was the largest domed structure in the world until it was overtaken by the Georgia Dome in Atlanta in 1992. More Super Bowls were played at the Superdome than at any other sports facility. It also hosted the New Orleans Bowl and Tulane University college football home games.

In 1998, the Superdome was used by 14,000 people as a temporary shelter from Hurricane Georges. The building survived the weather, but the human element resulted in looting and other damage—imagine people stealing the seats! Officials also had difficulty supplying the people with necessities—just as they did seven years later!

In 2005 when Katrina was blowing toward New Orleans, the Super-

The New Orleans Superdome stands like a ghostly mirage in the mist following Katrina. The protection and safety many hoped to find there also proved to be a mirage as the situation there quickly turned ugly.

dome was once more designated as an evacuation center. Authorities thought it would be safe if there were security checkpoints and officials confiscated alcohol, weapons, and illicit drugs. But no one counted on the numbers swelling to an uncontrollable 30,000 inside the dome, a number that swelled on Friday, September 2, to approximately 60,000 waiting at the dome for evacuation!

On August 28, the day before Katrina hit, the Louisiana National Guard delivered only three truckloads of water and seven truckloads of MREs (meals ready to eat)—enough to supply 15,000 people for three days. There was no water purification equipment on site, no chemical toilets, no antibiotics, and no anti-diarrheal medication stored for the crisis. There were no designated medical staff at work in the evacuation center, no sick bay, and very few cots. The mayor of New Orleans had announced that the Superdome was a "refuge of last resort" and that people should bring their own supplies. Obviously, officials were expecting that Katrina would be like past hurricanes. The people would come to the shelter for a day or two and then return to their homes when the storm blew past. No one expected the water. No one considered the worst case scenario: What if there were no homes to return to?

The night before Katrina hit, approximately 9,000 residents and 550 national guardsmen were in the Superdome in preparation for the storm. It was thought that the Superdome roof should withstand winds up to two hundred miles per hour. But it didn't! Once Katrina's fury was felt, the roof began peeling off, and the rain started pouring in through two huge holes fifteen to twenty feet across. When the levees broke and the city started flooding, search and rescue teams began bringing the people to the Superdome, New Orleans' only official evacuation center, and the number immediately swelled to 15,000. Then 20,000. Then over 30,000.

On Tuesday, August 30, the water started coming in the elevator shafts and eventually flooded the entire field area. Later that day, Governor Kathleen Blanco ordered the city of New Orleans to be completely evacuated. She also announced that since the Superdome had no power, no water, and no food, and the sanitary conditions were rapidly deteriorating, the refugees would be moved to the Reliant Astrodome in Houston, Texas. In spite of that order, refugees kept coming, and the Superdome quickly became what *Newsweek* called "the first circle of hell."

With 30,000 plus people packed in the building during the hottest days of the year, temperatures soared to 110 degrees or more in the stadium when the air conditioning failed. When the lights went out, a generator kicked in, but with only enough power to keep the huge arena dimly lit. It was the kind of darkness that breeds evil and despair, an environment where crime thrives. The Salvation Army doled out thousands of ready-made meals—but not nearly enough. Bottled water was scarce, and with no facilities, the stench of unwashed bodies ripened in the steamy heat.

On Wednesday, August 31, there was no more running water, and the reeking toilets had overflowed. The walls and floor were smeared with feces. People began putting plastic bags on their feet to walk through the pools of urine. In a dank bathroom someone attacked a national guardsman with a lead pipe and tried to steal his automatic weapon. In the scuffle, the guardsman was shot in the leg. A black market grew up. Hot sellers were cigarettes at ten dollars a pack, and antidiuretics to enable people to go longer without urinating. Going to the dark restrooms was unsanitary, unsafe, and, in the opinion of most, life threatening!

Random gunshots were heard from time to time. A man fell or jumped from the upper deck onto the concrete below and died. Crack vials were scattered around the floor. At least two rapes were reported, one of a child. Fear gripped parents. Can you imagine not being able to sleep in the Superdome for fear that someone might try to rape your children? And most horrific: dead people lying face down in the sewage or left sitting in wheelchairs where they had died.

When some five hundred national guardsmen showed up to keep order at the Superdome, their first objective was to get those who were at highest risk out of there because they couldn't guarantee their safety. Their next objective was to establish some kind of presence on the outside perimeter, while they waited for reinforcements to arrive. Meanwhile, the violence and illegal activity escalated inside.

As the Superdome became a clogged mass of desperate humanity—and the people kept coming—individuals were routed to the Ernest N. Morial Convention Center, where 10,000 people crowded into that facility. Later the number there rose to more than 20,000. Some say conditions at the convention center became even worse than at the Superdome—total chaos, no food, no water, no bathrooms, no structure, no organization, no command center, nothing! The reason for this deplorable state is that the convention center was never designated as a shelter. There was no security, food, water, or medical care until troops secured the building on Friday after the storm!

Finally, on Friday, September 1, five days after Katrina hit and five days late, national guard reinforcements, along with 475 buses and supply trucks, arrived at the Superdome. Thirteen thousand evacuees were taken to the Reliant Astrodome in Houston, until that facility could hold no more and buses were diverted to San Antonio, Dallas/Fort Worth, Arlington, and smaller shelters in communities across Texas. By September 5, when Katrina evacuees had reached an estimated 230,000, Texas Governor Rick Perry ordered that buses should be diverted to other shelters outside the state, resulting in 20,000 people being sent to Oklahoma and 30,000 to Arkansas.

By September 6, just a little over a week after Katrina hit, the last group of refugees at the Superdome had been evacuated. On this same day the number of evacuees reached an estimated 250,000, and Governor Perry was forced to declare a state of emergency in Texas and issue an impassioned plea to other states to begin taking the 40,000 to 50,000 evacuees that were still in need of shelter.

A Former NFL Player Survives the Superdome

With this background of the nightmare New Orleans residents experienced right after the storm and the sad scary saga of the Superdome, it's time to continue the story of Dallas resident and real estate executive Kevin Young, who, because of a twist of fate, found himself entangled in the chaos of post-Katrina New Orleans.

We'll pick up the story on Tuesday, the day after Katrina hit, as the power failed at Charity Hospital and there were no lights, no running water, and no restroom facilities. After Kevin's mother, who was on life-support, had died, Kevin stayed in the empty room on the seventh floor of Charity Hospital as long as possible. He slept and tried to make do with whatever he could.

When he had arrived at Charity Hospital in the wee morning hours of Tuesday, after evacuating his mother first from the Ferncrest Manor Nursing Home and then an abandoned hospital building, he didn't know the levees had broken. He presumed the rising water was due to the rain. But as the sun came out and the water kept rising, word spread that the levees had been breeched. By late that afternoon, he was told he that he had to leave the building and go to the Superdome.

Officials banded the hospital staff with one color and the visitors with another. About 7:00 P.M. Kevin's turn came to be transported by boat to the Superdome, about half a mile away. He had thought the Superdome meant safety. Imagine his shock when he arrived and saw the chaotic conditions there. He was horrified. The hospital accountant with whom Kevin had made friends at Charity took one look and refused to get out of the boat. Kevin pleaded for them to let him return to the hospital, too, but they flatly refused. They had strict orders about visitors, and no amount of begging was going to change their minds.

Slowly, Kevin began to walk around the mass of humanity outside the Superdome. Different subcultures had developed and were grouped together; fights were going on; drug deals were being made; gangs were forcing their will on the weak. Destructive, out-of-control kids were defacing the building. Foul language and cursing polluted the air, and feces, urine, and trash polluted the pavement. People were relieving themselves right out in the open. Trash was four or five feet high. People stepped over bodies, trying to find a place to lie down. Amid the noise of the crowd a few were trying to block out the chaotic mass and soothe their mounting fear by singing gospel songs. Everywhere Kevin looked, people were angry, threatening, crying, begging, and bitter!

This was the worst of the worst.

Kevin walked the perimeter of the Superdome twice, trying to assess the situation. At the entrance to the dome, the stench was so strong he gagged. There was no way he was going inside. He didn't belong here! He felt as if he were watching a horror movie being acted out in front of him. This couldn't be real! But it was! And his gut told him that when the darkness of night took over, all hell would break lose. For his own safety, he had to get out of there!

"God," he prayed, "what are You trying to tell me? I don't look like these people. I know I haven't shaved for a couple days. But these people are out of control. What have I done to deserve this?" He made his way back to the ramp, where boatloads of refugees were being dumped after being brought from rescue sites around the city. He found a fellow with a canoe, bought it for five dollars, and paddled his way back to Charity Hospital. When a doctor and a policeman at the hospital saw him try to return, they yelled, "What are you doing coming back here?"

"I would rather die here trying to help you guys evacuate others than stay at the Superdome. Please don't make me go back."

In no uncertain terms they told him, "You're not getting out of that boat. And you're not coming back here! We have instructions to evacuate—and that's what we're going to do!" He had no option but to turn around. Now where?

He considered trying to get to the west bank across the river. He had heard it was dry over there. He had credit cards and plenty of cash.

If he could just get there, he'd be gone in a second. He paddled around for two hours, trying desperately to get to dry land. But downed power lines, fallen trees, and other debris made it impossible.

Kevin's only option now was to go back to the dreaded Superdome—the place where he had once played defensive end. The place where the crowds roared with enthusiasm over completed passes and touchdowns. The place where people enjoyed themselves, ate hotdogs and popcorn, and slurped icy slushies. A place that held some of the best memories of his life. Where people cheered instead of cursed. Where people respected others, instead of taking advantage of them.

What a contrast! He would have feared for his life had he been forced to actually go inside the Superdome itself. At any moment he could have been attacked or could have been the victim of a stray bullet. Not even armed military personnel were willing to risk entering the Superdome alone. Those who did entered en masse for the purpose of getting those who were in the greatest danger out of there—since they knew they could offer them little or no protection within the dome.

As Kevin paddled toward that fateful place, a survival plan began to form in his mind. The military had taken posts around the outside perimeter of the dome. If he could just stay close enough to them, perhaps he would be safe. After leaving his canoe, he walked up to one of the national guardsmen and asked, "How long are you planning to be here?" When he learned they were there for the duration, he began talking and making friends with some of the military personnel.

As the night hours ticked away, he looked for someplace safe where he could sleep. At the end of the Superdome, he noticed a parked bus. He went to investigate and found five or six people inside with children. No one said anything as he entered. "What's going on?" he asked.

"The driver left a while ago and hasn't been back," they answered.

Kevin surveyed the situation as he made his way to the back of the bus. No one was messing with this bus. The military were positioned behind it, and an ambulance was parked by the side. "If you all will be quiet and don't hang out the windows or do anything to attract attention, and keep the doors closed, we might be able to keep people from discovering this bus and coming in here and crowding us out." The others didn't question his authority and did what he said.

During the long hours of the night, the people on the bus began to tell stories of the terrorizing things they had witnessed. One told of a police officer who got shot in the head. Others talked about the terrible conditions inside the Superdome the night before—of the fights in which people were critically hurt or left for dead; of the girls that got raped; of the sick, the dying, the heat, the stench! And then there were the stories about the shootings.

Kevin asked, "As I came to the Superdome, there were military helicopters flying in. What were they here for?"

The people had heard different rumors, but most said, "There are some white kids from Tulane University in there that they're getting out."

"Yeah, that's why people are shooting at the helicopters. It doesn't seem fair that they're getting out, and we're left here to die."

"What about the buses lined up on the bridge?"

"They're shooting at those too."

"Do you think they're evacuating anybody?"

No one seemed to know.

By Thursday, Kevin was beginning to get paranoid. *Could the buses be a trap? Could they be taking people out and drowning them? Why are they telling us they're going to get us out of here, but nothing is happening?* He didn't know what to think.

That night he was on "his" bus trying to get some sleep. It was getting later and later, but sleep eluded him. He decided to get up and investigate. He took the flashlight he had been given at the hospital and made his way to the line of people waiting to get on one of the evacuation buses. "Is the line moving?" he asked them.

No one seemed to know, and he didn't see buses leaving. It seemed like a lot of promises—and no action. Confused, he got back on "his" bus, laid down as best he could, and began figuring out a plan of escape. Suddenly, he woke up out of a deep sleep with an urgent need to call his sister who worked with him in the business. There were bills that needed to be paid. He had to tell her. By now it was one A.M. He found his cell phone, but it was dead. He had accidentally left his charger by his mother when she died. As long as he was in the hospital, he hadn't needed his phone. Now he felt a desperate need to make this call.

He went down to the generator light where everyone was charging up their phones. But without a charger, it seemed his luck had run out. Then amazingly, a woman came up to him and mentioned that a young lady had just dropped off a Nextel cell phone charger. She was using it to charge her phone. "Do you need a charger?" she asked him. "Maybe this one will work." Kevin tried it—and it worked! *Incredible,* he thought. *Just incredible that at the very moment I want to make a call, God provided a charger.* He plugged into the generator power and called his wife, Olga, and his sister, Roxanne, to let them know where he was. He avoided telling them just how bad the situation was at the Superdome. No need to worry anyone!

While he was waiting for his phone to be charged, a guy came by with whom Kevin had gone to high school. They exchanged small talk, and the man lamented, "I lost my mother yesterday." Kevin sympathized but didn't burden him by telling him that he, too, had lost his mom the day before. "I'm just trying to use the phone, but I don't have any money."

"You can use mine," Kevin offered. Then he asked the man, "You don't know me, do you? But I know you. You're Jonathon Green."

"How do you know me?" the man asked.

"We went to the same high school. You were a couple years ahead of me, but I remember you played basketball." There was not even a glimmer of recognition on Jonathon's face. Kevin thought, *This guy was on top of the world in high school. Now look at him in those baggy clothes—and the people he's with.* Kevin had heard that Jonathon had made some bad decisions and had gotten hooked on drugs after being a star athlete. Kevin could now see that this was probably true. How sad to live such a wasted life! Once again Kevin realized how out of place he was at the Superdome and resolved to get out of there as soon as possible—somehow.

As he reflected on his situation he thought, *How ironic that I once played in the Superdome and now I'm sleeping like a tramp on a Superdome ramp!* "God," he prayed, "What is it You're wanting to tell me? Why am I still here?"

Later, as Kevin recalled his ordeal, he commented, "In spite of all the things I was going through, it was clear to me that God's hand was with me, ordering my steps. I should have been scared, but I wasn't. It would have been a wonderful miracle if my mom had survived. That was not to be, but the Lord was with me through it all, even giving me power for my cell phone. There was never a doubt that God wasn't going to deliver me. This was just something I had to go through."

All day Thursday and Friday Kevin watched the helicopters come in. They were bringing in troops by the droves. When were they going to start the massive helicopter evacuation that was so desperately needed? But instead of leaving, the choppers just sat there lined up in the parking lot. There went the idea that he could escape this hell hole by air.[1] During the worst part of the Superdome ordeal, Kevin was conscious, but really "unconscious." The agony of it all was too much to bear. It was surreal. It was as if he were walking around in a fog. He mentally zoned out! All he could think about was helping himself. He kept as far removed from the deplorable Superdome environment as he possibly could. It was survival of the fittest. It wasn't safe to be noticed. If someone died, you left them. He felt he couldn't take time to help anyone or he might look weak and be taken advantage of. *Whom could he trust?* So, for his own safety, he continued to stay removed from the crowd, talking mainly to military personnel.

On Friday, he decided to walk around the dome to the place where people were lining up to be evacuated. He wanted to see if the guy he had met earlier in the line had moved closer to the end of the procession. The guy wasn't there. *Had he gotten out of line? Or maybe this line was moving! Something may be happening.* For the first time during that reign of terror, Kevin felt a glimmer of hope. He made a decision. *At eight o'clock tommorrow morning, I'm going to get in that line. I've got to get out of here!*

That's just what he did. Hours went by. As he was standing in line, all of a sudden he saw a man jump from the ramp of the Superdome. The man fell two stories and landed on his head. The military rushed down and got him. Kevin watched the whole episode from a distance. Later, he heard that the man had been playing cards and just got up and jumped off the ramp. Was this really happening? People were getting desperate. Many had given up all hope. By eleven o'clock that morning many exhausted, hot, thirsty people started leaving the line. As the day grew hotter, some collapsed. Kevin himself felt dizzy. He needed water. He needed to go to the restroom. But he couldn't risk losing his place in line. It stretched for half a mile, block after block.

As Kevin was standing in line, he began to hear people talking about FEMA. "FEMA's going to take care of us." *What is FEMA?* he wondered. "FEMA's going to cut me a check for all this?" *Who is FEMA?* Kevin had never before been in a situation where he needed aid. *Who is this powerful FEMA that is going to do all these wonderful things?*

At last Kevin began to see the end of the line. Relief flooded his soul. Maybe this nightmare would end after all! Finally, he got to the security checkpoint—similar to airport security. At the end of the line people were told that they would be given "real" food in preparation for boarding buses, which were to take them away from the misery and deprivation of New Orleans. But that turned out to be a lie, too. He had to walk in two feet of water to board the bus.

Kevin was the first one on his evacuation bus. He put his bag in a place where he could easily grab it and took the front seat. He immediately struck up a conversation with the driver. "Where are we going?" he asked.

"Man, I still haven't gotten word," the bus driver replied.

"Think it will be Dallas or San Antonio?"

"Don't know."

The bus finished loading and fell in line behind the other buses. Their route took them past the dry west bank of the Mississippi River; wind damage here had been severe, but the area hadn't flooded. Then

Kevin Young stands with his mother, Myrtle Jackson, and his best friend, Walter Mitchell. Through his friend Walter, Kevin was finally able to leave the hell that New Orleans had become.

they moved out onto Highway 190 and came back the long way to get onto I-10 heading to Baton Rouge. Occasionally the driver used his walkie-talkie to communicate with the other drivers.

"Any word?" Kevin kept asking. "If I can get to Baton Rouge, I'm out of here!"

As the bus got closer to Baton Rouge, Kevin was on the phone with his friend Walter Mitchell, trying to coordinate where they could meet. Without warning, Walter asked where Kevin's mama was. Caught by surprise, Kevin broke down and told him he would call him back. Walter called Kevin back a minute later, and Kevin told him what had happened. They stayed in contact as the bus got closer to Baton Rouge.

"Where are you now?" Walter asked.

"Just passing Blue Bonnet exit."

Walter ordered him, "Get off the bus at the next exit. I'm just a few minutes behind you."

When Kevin told the bus driver he wanted off, the driver thought he was crazy.

"I can't drop you off like that," the driver argued. "Everyone's got to have a place to stay."

"I have a place to stay! My friend's picking me up, and I'm staying with him," Kevin announced with jubilation in his voice.

Reluctantly, the bus driver pulled over. Kevin quickly grabbed his bag and jumped from the bus before the driver could change his mind. He took a deep breath. The fresh air of freedom was wonderful.

The bus pulled back on I-10, and a minute later his friend Walter picked him up. Their first stop was at Wal-Mart to buy Kevin some clothes. His had become contaminated when his bag fell into the polluted floodwaters.

When Kevin finally arrived at his friend's home, he sighed. *What comfort!* He took a long, hot shower—his first in over a week—and ate a delicious meal. At last he was able to let down his guard and fully relax. He was so exhausted he fell asleep on the floor while everyone around him was talking. The next morn-ing, he woke refreshed and had a big country breakfast, and then he and his friend headed toward Dallas! Home sweet home!

But that's not quite the end of Kevin's New Orleans saga. Finding his mother's body after the water receded turned out to be a challenge. The

The Young residence in New Orleans after Katrina.

hospital was now closed. No one had a clue where she might be. That's when Kevin learned what FEMA was! After a month of searching, it was FEMA who finally located her body in a city outside of New Orleans where bodies had been transported!

After Hurricane Rita, when New Orleans was pumped dry for the second time, Kevin went back to meet with the insurance agent concerning the condition of his mother's flooded home. Entering New Orleans was like entering a ghost town. Volunteers from a church in Georgia had begun clearing his mother's house, removing the water-damaged furniture and debris. Mold was growing everywhere. The place that he had diligently worked on over the years was gone. Sadly, he and his friend Keith sorted through the belongings that remained and loaded up a rental car with what they had retrieved—a few pictures and keepsakes. It was emotionally draining to close the New Orleans chapter of his life. Never again would it be home to him. The neighborhood was a disaster—and was deserted. Conditions were so toxic that they had to drive forty-five minutes across the river to safely wash their hands or grab a bite of food. And even then, they couldn't order what they wanted, since very little was available on the menu.

Adding insult to injury, as Kevin was driving back home to Dallas with his friend Keith Morgan in the passenger seat and his nephew, Duce, in the back, they were involved in a four-car collision. Kevin saw a car jump the median and head straight toward his car. There was a terrible impact when it ran into a car ahead of Kevin, spinning it out of control, and then flipped another car as if it were a toy. Kevin slammed on his brakes and swerved just as the car smashed into the side of his fender and broke his mirror. Panic swept over him. *Was this the end?*

Somehow he was able to bring the car under control. He slowly edged into the right lane and pulled over. The other cars involved were totaled, and their passengers were airlifted or driven to Baton Rouge. He, Keith, and Duce had to go to the police station to be drug tested. Kevin thanked the Lord for His protection. They could have so easily been killed. For the second time, God had delivered him from disaster in New Orleans. *What was God trying to tell him?* He shook his head and sighed, "I'll never go back. Never!"

On November 15, 2005, Kevin's wife, Olga, gave birth to a beautiful healthy baby girl. They named her Jade Myrietta Young—using the middle name his mother had chosen on her deathbed. A new chapter—and hopefully a much happier one—had begun.

What Is God Trying to Tell Us When Everything Goes Wrong?

Kevin questioned God's purpose for him in having to go through his New Orleans ordeal. That is something people have been asking since sin entered the world. Job and his friends questioned God. And what was the answer?

First of all, it's clear *God* didn't design Job's troubles to test him.

That was Satan's idea. God already knew Job's heart was true to Him. Their relationship was secure. Job loved God in spite of what life dealt him. Job was a righteous man because of that love relationship—not because he wanted to see how many blessings he could get from God.

It was Satan who came to God with the accusation that Job served God only because God rewarded him. Satan was sure if Job's blessings were taken away, he would curse God. God's character was being questioned! Since Satan made this accusation publicly in some heavenly counsel room before the "sons of God," God trusted Job with whatever troubles Satan would bring to him so the universe could see more clearly the contrast between God's character and Satan's. The question is, Can God trust you to be an example to the universe, as He trusted Job?

When bad things happen to us—such as being trapped in a terrifying situation like the Superdome—God can use it for good. For it's in the peaks *and valleys* of life that a relationship with Him is strengthened most.

God calls His children to the peaks. He wants us to stand on the quiet mountaintops away from the hustle and bustle of the crowds, feel His presence, commune with Him, and shout, "O Lord, You are my God. I will exalt You, I will praise Your name, For You have done wonderful things" (Isaiah 25:1, NKJV).

Remember Moses? It was on a mountaintop—Mount Sinai—that he and God really got close—so close that after forty days Moses' face shone with God's presence! (See Exodus 34:29–35.)

The problem is that, although we want a deeper relationship with God, we're often too busy to listen to His invitation to come away to the mountaintop. We don't take the time and effort to climb to the peaks, away from our daily activities to where we can really spend the necessary time to be so filled with His presence that our countenances glow.

Instead, our wake-up call comes when Satan does a number on us and plunges us to the depths of the "valley of the shadow of death" (Psalm 23:4). At the place of our greatest difficulties, struggles, troubles, and trials, God meets us! The truth is, that for far too many of us, our relationship with God is deepened most in times of deepest tragedy.

What is God trying to tell us when everything goes wrong? Maybe it's simply this:

My child, you may not know Me, but I know everything about you (Psalm 139:1). I know when you sit down and when you rise up (Psalm 139:2). I am familiar with all your ways (Psalm 139:3). Even the very hairs on your head are numbered (Matthew 10:29–31), for you were made in My image (Genesis 1:27). In Me you live and move and have your being, for you are My offspring (Acts 17:28). I knew you even before you were conceived (Jeremiah 1:4, 5). I chose you when I planned creation (Ephesians 1:11, 12). I determined the exact time of your birth and where you would live (Acts 17:26). You are fearfully and wonderfully made (Psalm 139:14). I knit you together in your mother's womb (Psalm 139:13). I brought you forth on the day you were born (Psalm 71:6). I have been misrepresented by those who don't know Me (John 8:41-44). I am not distant and angry; I am the complete expression of love (1 John 4:16), and it is My desire to lavish My love on you (1 John 3:1) simply because you are My child and I am your Father (1 John 3:1). I offer you more than your earthly father ever could (Matthew 7:11), for I am the perfect Father (Matthew 5:48). Every good gift that you receive comes from My hand (James 1:17), for I am your provider and I meet all your needs (Matthew 6:31-33). My plan for your future has always been filled with hope (Jeremiah 29:11) because I love you with an everlasting love (Jeremiah 31:3). My thoughts toward you are countless as the sand on the seashore (Psalm 139:17, 18), and I rejoice over you with singing (Zephaniah 3:17). I will never stop doing good to you (Jeremiah 32:40), for you are my treasured possession (Exodus 19:5). I desire to establish you with all My heart and all My soul (Jeremiah 32:41), and I want to show you great and marvelous things (Jeremiah 33:3). If you seek Me with all your heart, you will find Me (Deuteronomy 4:29). Delight in Me, and I will give you the desires of your heart (Psalm 37:4), for it is I who gave you those desires (Philippians 2:13). I am able to do more for you than you could possibly imagine (Ephesians 3:20), for I am your greatest encourager (2 Thessalonians 2:16, 17).

I am also the Father who comforts you in all your troubles (2 Corinthians 1:3, 4). When you are brokenhearted, I am close to you (Psalm 34:18). As a shepherd carries a lamb, I have carried you close to my heart (Isaiah 40:11). One day I will wipe away every tear from your eyes, and I'll take away all the pain you have suffered on this earth (Revelation 21:3, 4). I am your Father, and I love you even as I love My Son, Jesus (John 17:23), for in Jesus My love for you is revealed (John 17:26). He is the exact representation of My being (Hebrews 1:3). He came to demonstrate that I am for you, not against you (Romans 8:31), and to tell you that I am not counting your sins (2 Corinthians 5:18, 19). Jesus died so that you and I could be reconciled (2 Corinthians 5:18, 19). His death was the ultimate expression of My love for you (1 John 4:10). I gave up everything I loved that I might gain your love (Romans 8:31, 32). If you receive the gift of My Son Jesus, you receive Me (1 John 2:23), and nothing will ever separate you from My love again (Romans 8:38, 39). Come home, and I'll throw the biggest party heaven has ever seen (Luke 15:7). I have always been Father and will always be Father (Ephesians 3:14, 15). My question is, Will you be My child? (John 1:12, 13). I am waiting for you (Luke 15:11–32).

Love, your heavenly Father.[2]

---

1. Shortly after Katrina, Ivan Wolfe was in Washington State, using a helicopter service to fly him into remote areas where he worked. The pilot told him that when all the people were trapped in the Superdome, his company received a call from a desperate person who begged the company to send a helicopter to get him out of New Orleans. When they told him how far away from Louisiana they were and that there was no way they could help him, the caller insisted he would make it worth their while if they would just come and rescue him. Apparently, Kevin was not the only one hoping for rescue by helicopter!

2. Author unknown.

Chapter 12
THE BIG EMPTY

"They knew New Orleans was a fish bowl. Now it's a toilet bowl."
—Vickie Johnston

Watching Katrina's Fury

Not all Katrina survivor stories were from those who stayed behind and somehow made it through the storm. There were those who packed up their most precious possessions and essential legal papers and left—even though they doubted this was the *big* one. What they returned to, however, was a shock! Their whole world had turned upside down. Such is the story of Monique and Jamall Dayries.

Monique and Jamall Dayries (right), their children Dominique, Danielle and Devin, along with her brother Reggie Dupard and his son Jonathan and friends celebrating Devin's birthday at the Seventh-day Adventist Southwest Region campgrounds in Athens, Texas, where many of the evacuees were temporarily housed after Katrina.

When Monique and Jamall first heard that Katrina was heading toward New Orleans, Jamall suggested they leave. Monique didn't want to. She was complacent about the whole thing. "It will turn," she said of Katrina. "They always do." But he was persistent. She was certain they'd be safe if they stayed, but the words, "What if . . ." kept nagging at her. Finally, because of their three children, Devin, eight; Danielle, eleven; and Dominique, thirteen; she relented. "OK, we'll go up to Uncle Reggie's in Dallas for a couple days. Kids, pack your bathing suits and a couple changes of clothing."

They ended up taking their two cars so they could take Jamall's mother and his younger brother. And just in case she was wrong about Katrina, Monique decided she'd take all their important papers, their family pictures—both the albums and those hanging on the wall—and the video of their house and its contents that they made every year for hurricane season.

Friday, August 27, Monique went to work as usual as a supervisor at Whitney Bank in New Orleans. Even though some of the employees mentioned the coming storm, no one seemed particularly concerned. Saturday night, about seven o'clock, she and Jamall started boarding up their home in Marrero in Jefferson Parish—not so much because they were worried about the hurricane, but to keep it safe from looters since so many of their neighbors had left town.

By four o'clock Sunday morning the roads were already clogged! They crawled out of the city via I-10 over the causeway to I-20 and headed toward Shreveport, stopping only once for gas before continuing on to Dallas. The usual nine-hour trip took fifteen hours!

Not once during the drive did Monique ever seriously consider that Katrina was a threat to New Orleans. It was such a great city in which to live. She loved the spirit of the people in the Big Easy, and she loved the culture, the museums, the zoo, and the parks. After all, she was born in Jefferson Parish's Third Ward and grew up in Kenner, a suburb of New Orleans.

When she was a kid, most of her extended family lived in New Orleans's Lower Ninth Ward that was tucked into a deep depression between two canals, railroad tracks, and the Mississippi River. In fact, her aunt Lynn and uncle Rolland Clemens still lived there when Katrina hit. And her aunt Brenda and uncle James Chapman lived nearby in the Upper Ninth Ward.[1] When she and Jamall got married, there was no question that New Orleans would be their home.

As they drove toward Dallas, little did Monique realize the force of the winds that were being driven toward her beloved hometown. Nor could she have imagined that in less than twenty-four hours the places she knew as a child—the corner grocery where they stopped for goodies after school and the playground where they played sports—would all be destroyed. Entire houses would be knocked off their foundations, cars tossed inside living rooms, roofs blown away, and shortly after, everything—even her childhood home—would be under polluted mucky water, a mixture of canal water, sewage, human and animal rot, toxic chemicals, oil, and dirt. Deadly black mold would begin rapidly devouring the interiors of those few structures that managed to stand.

That night when the family finally reached their motel in Dallas and flipped on the TV, Monique stared at the screen—stunned! This

This is the home where Monique grew up. It was destroyed under seven feet of water. All that she has left are memories!

storm was huge. "My goodness," she gasped, "I think it's going to hit New Orleans. It's not turning. It always turns. This can't be happening!" Their whole family was spellbound by the reports coming out of New Orleans as Katrina's fury was beginning to be felt. Exhausted, they fell asleep with the TV still on.

The cell phone awakened them at seven o'clock in the morning. The alarm company was reporting a disturbance at their home. The wind was so strong it had set off their security system! Monique froze with fright. The unthinkable was happening. Katrina was hitting New Orleans. Anxiety gripped her heart. This was going to be bad—very, very bad! For two days the family stayed glued to their TV. Even Dominque, who is not a TV person, was mesmerized by the storm coverage.

Back in New Orleans, thousands of residents who stayed behind were experiencing 145 miles per hour winds that were literally tearing their lives apart. Then, just when they thought the worst was over—that Katrina had merely given New Orleans a glancing blow as the eye of the storm shifted east toward Mississippi—the levees broke, and the water from Lake Pontchartrain began pouring in, flooding everything below sea level. Not only was most of New Orleans under water, but so were surrounding parishes, such as St. Bernard Parish and Plaquemines Parish. Some places had as much as twenty to twenty-six feet of water! Even Kenner in Jefferson Parish was under seven feet of water. And then, three weeks later, just when the Army Corps of Engineers thought the pumping task was almost complete, Hurricane Rita hit, and once again everything was under water!

New Orleans: Six Weeks Later

Six weeks after Katrina hit, the Big Easy was now the Big Empty! Even those who had stayed during the storm had now evacuated to other places as New Orleans was drying out. For some areas, such as St. Bernard and Plaquemines parishes and the Lower Ninth Ward of Orleans Parish, it could be months—or even years—before power, water, and sewage facilities would be ready to support residents. People were being told, "Don't come back for a year!" But realistically, where the flooding was the worst, it could be five, ten, or even twenty years!

Will They Return?

Nearly half of the one million people who evacuated from the areas that Katrina decimated have indicated an unwillingness to return. A full 40 percent of those surveyed among the 250,000 evacuees in Texas indicated that they intended to remain in Texas permanently. Another 15 percent indicated that they would probably relocate to other areas of the country instead of returning to Louisiana. Even New Orleans Mayor Ray Nagin admitted that he expected New Orleans would likely be only about half its pre-Katrina population of 560,000—even after several years of rebuilding. This is a very disturbing reality for politicians to accept, because it will likely mean their jobs! Louisiana could stand to lose half of its congressional seats!

Returning "Home" to a Whole New World

As September turned into October, Monique and Jamall decided it was time to go home. Their house hadn't flooded, and their employers needed them. But the city they returned to was very different from the one they had left!

The once bright and beautiful city was now drab. Instead of brilliantly colored blossoms and giant, vibrant green, live oaks with their grand canopies and graceful lines delicately draped with graying Spanish moss, the grass and leaves, which had marinated for weeks in saltwater, were a dreary gray-brown. And many of the giant century-old oaks that gave New Orleans such character were gone—toppled over, exposing huge root balls ten feet or more in diameter.

Parking lots looked like drought-starved lake beds, with cracks in the mud. Within a few hours, anyone working outside was covered in a fine layer of grit.

Just driving through the decimated neighborhoods was depressing. One could not help noticing the giant red Xs that had been sprayed on the houses accompanied by numbers indicating the toxicity level and how many corpses had been found inside. It was a grim reminder of the real tragedy of the storm.

As various regions dried out sufficiently, residents were allowed to survey their damaged homes, determine with insurance adjusters what they might expect to recoup, and then shut the door once more until electricity, water, and sewage facilities could be reestablished.

Many people who came back to survey the damage in their houses couldn't unlock their doors because the locks were jammed with dirt and sand. One of Monique's bank customers said that when she and her husband tried to open the door, it was warped shut. When her husband finally shoved hard enough, it opened, and at that same moment the whole ceiling collapsed. They stood there, horrified. What if the door had opened easily and the kids had run in like they normally did? They would have been killed! The family took one look and walked away from everything they had known.

Six weeks after Katrina, because of the strict curfews, identification checks, and patrolling national guard, the threat of looters was lessened. Now the biggest threat to the residents whose houses weren't water damaged were the alligators that were trapped in backyard swimming pools and the poisonous snakes who inhabited the piles of rotting debris and the packs of wild dogs that roamed through the neighborhoods. Wild dogs? Yes, beautiful dogs—the terriers, the retrievers, the Dalmatians, the German shepherds, the Rottweilers, and the Dobermans—still with collars and tags. But now, instead of being people's pets who walked the neighborhoods on leashes or barked behind secure backyard fences, they had, in just a matter of weeks, gone wild, surviving in packs and attacking whatever threatened them. Gone were the fences; gone was their link to caring humanity; gone was their easy source of food supplied to them each day by people who loved and petted them. Gone was civilization as they knew it—instead, pack instinct had taken over.

And gone were the stores and shopping malls. Monique said there used to be seven Super Wal-Marts in New Orleans; now there was only one, and it closed by 5:00 P.M. because of the lack of employees. The best time to shop was in the morning because shelves tended to empty by 7:30 or 8:00. The check-out lines sometimes stretched to the middle of the store, and it could take up to two hours to get to the register!

Most stores closed at 4:00 or 5:00 in the afternoon. Pharmacies closed at 6:00 P.M. and gas stations at 8:00 P.M., when the curfews went into effect. Monique said her whole lifestyle changed. Before Katrina, if the kids got hungry, they went to a restaurant. Now she said, "If I have food with me, I swallow my pride and go into a gas station and ask if I can use their microwave to warm it up for my family. Or we go without! One time we missed the 8 P.M. curfew to get back into our neighborhood and had to spend the night in our car! Public restrooms are a thing of the past. Now, I just tell my kids, 'You've got to hold it!' Or we might put toothpaste on a finger when we can't find water to brush our teeth! There's no place to get your hair done—mine looks horrible! Some days I don't even bother with make-up!"

The Dayries may be experiencing some major inconveniences, but they are young, have a home, cars, legal papers, pictures, keepsakes, family, and friends. They're going to make it. It may take years, but for them life will eventually fall back into a comfortable routine. They were the lucky ones. Seventy-four-year-old Elmer Umbehagen and his wife, Rose, were not!

I'll Never Go Back

Thirty-three years ago Elmer and Rose Umbehagen had built a beautiful brick home in Chalmette, a middle- to upper-class neighborhood in St. Bernard Parish. Elmer had lived in the area all his life and remembered when everyone knew each other.

His daddy grew okra and a little corn, while their Italian neighbors grew tomatoes and parsley. The Domino Sugar refinery was about the only industry in the area when he was a boy. Then in 1953 Kaiser

Aluminum moved in, and the farming community gave way to housing developments. After forty years as a salesman in the area, Elmer knew many of the business people of the community. Life for the Umbehagens was filled with loving family and friends, and comfortable surroundings—until Katrina washed it all away!

Elmer Umbehagen sits with Kay Kuzma in the ICU waiting room. As he tells of his experience with Katrina, Kay enters the story on her computer.

We found Elmer sitting alone in the ICU waiting room at the Methodist Medical Center in Oakridge, Tennessee. We were there because Kay's husband, Jan, had taken a terrible fall. Between visiting times, we settled into a corner in the waiting room and continued working on our Katrina project. After a few hours, we noticed Elmer was intently listening. We introduced ourselves and told him about *Between Hell and High Water*. He mentioned that he and his wife had lost everything in St. Bernard Parish. We asked for his opinion about conditions in the New Orleans area. This is what he said:

> The beginning of the end of this beautiful farming area started in 1921 when the Industrial Canal was built to connect the Mississippi River with Lake Pontchartrain. Before long the Industrial Canal lock had became a bottleneck for shipping, as it sometimes took ten hours for ships to get through, and it wasn't deep enough for the larger ships. To remedy the situation, the Mississippi River Gulf Outlet (MRGO) was built in 1965. This seventy-six-mile-long man-made navigation channel connected the Gulf of Mexico to the Port of New Orleans's

Inner Harbor Navigation Canal in eastern New Orleans. Now ships didn't have to go through the Industrial Canal lock. But this shortcut to the city destroyed the marshlands and barrier outlets. Because of erosion, the mouth of the outlet has widened to over two thousand feet now, and it constantly needs dredging. The result is that MRGO is continuing to destroy wetlands and is bringing the Gulf waters closer to the city, making it easier for a major hurricane surge, like Katrina's, to breech our levees. As long as MRGO is there, St. Bernard Parish will never be safe! And even though the levees are holding for now, their strength has been compromised, and they are still oozing water. Who knows what the next hurricane will do?

It was the break in the Industrial Canal levee, caused by Katrina's gigantic surge, that destroyed not only Elmer and Rose's house but a whole way of life.

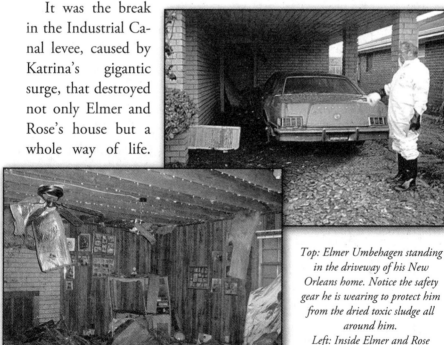

Top: Elmer Umbehagen standing in the driveway of his New Orleans home. Notice the safety gear he is wearing to protect him from the dried toxic sludge all around him.
Left: Inside Elmer and Rose Umbehagen's home that was totally destroyed by Katrina's fury.

The current was so strong that across the street, a concrete slab foundation for a house was raised up far enough that the front end of a car was wedged beneath it! Just a few blocks away, a van sat on top of their son Jonathan's house!

As soon as the water was pumped out of the neighborhood, Elmer and his two sons went to investigate. They wore boots, gloves, and masks to protect them from the toxic mud. The door had already been kicked in by officials looking for bodies, and a large red X was spray painted on it. Elmer took one look inside. When he saw everything covered with oily polluted muck, he turned around and walked out. It was too much. He began to cry. Everything dear to him was gone.

It's too late to start over at my age. We can't go back. Our past has been washed away. Who knows how many years it will take before it's safe for people to live there. So we went ahead and bought a little house next to my son Mark here in Tennessee. We've met a couple friends, but it was common for us to have 150 to 200 family members over for Thanksgiving or Christmas Eve since we all lived within about twenty minutes from each other. Now they're scattered across the continent! And here I sit alone in the ICU waiting room. My wife's had a stroke, and there's no family here—except Mark.

To me it all feels like a bad dream. I'm going through the motions of living, but it doesn't seem real. Waiting for the water to recede was like being on death row waiting to be electrocuted and wondering just how bad it was going to be! When I finally went back and realized it was worse than I had imagined, something in me died. A way of life was gone.

I'm one of the lucky ones; I have flood insurance. It took me and my sons four weeks to complete sixty pages of inventory items that we lost. But that doesn't replace our family and friends that Katrina scattered across the nation. Life for us will never again be the same.

One of the biggest concerns that Elmer voiced was the long-term health risk of untreated sewage and decomposing bodies and livestock, as well as a complicated mixture of toxic chemicals and oils originating from domestic, agricultural, and industrial sources that mixed with the floodwaters contaminating the groundwater, soil, and everything it came in contact with. He told about the crude oil container from the Murphy Oil refinery that broke during the storm and left as much as three inches of crude oil on top of the toxic mud in about eighteen hundred homes in Chalmette. There was a reason the EPA wouldn't let anyone go into the area without wearing masks, boots, and gloves to protect them from these hazards.

How to Thrive and Not Just Survive!

Every survivor has a story. Some, like the Dayries, lost a way of life for a while, but they didn't lose their possessions and the people who make their lives meaningful. They've come back to their beloved New Orleans, and in time, by working together, they will make a new, safer, and healthier New Orleans for their families.

Some, like Elmer and Rose, are too old, have lost too much, and face too many unhealthy environmental conditions to ever go back. They are forging a new life for themselves. It will never be the same, but if they don't dwell in the past, they will survive.

Others say they'll never leave. For example, eighty-two-year-old Marguerite Simon. She worked hard all her life cleaning other people's homes. Finally, she earned just enough to buy a house in the Ninth Ward, one of New Orleans poorest neighborhoods—and one that was hit hardest with the flooding. Three months after Katrina, Marguerite was staying with her daughter in nearby Algiers at night, but she hated the loss of her independence. "I miss having things my way," she lamented. During the day she came back to her cherished home in New Orleans, wearing rubber gloves, rubber boots, and a paper face mask. She was determined to clean off all the black amoebic splotches of mold from her precious family treasures. "Inside her small house, her well-made furniture, with its carved arms and curved legs, lay scattered as if some giant mixer had been whirling away. Sitting on her tiny porch, she managed a laugh. "You have to laugh," she said, "but it doesn't come from the heart."[2]

There are many, like Marguerite, who are coping with post-Katrina's tragedy by working hard and laughing—even if it doesn't come from the heart! If they took time to think of what they lost, depression could easily drag them down. If they worried about the future—about whether there would be jobs to support them or whether the levees would hold—they could easily develop post-traumatic stress disorder.

Then there are those who are having a very difficult time dealing with the tragedy of Katrina. Some of these merely shrug their shoulders and say, "Here today, gone tomorrow." But adopting a martyr syndrome doesn't promote healing.

Some look as if the light has gone out of their lives. They're numb. Hopeless. Withdrawn. However, retreat is seldom a successful strategy for winning, unless it's to take a short break before coming back with renewed energy and a determination to overcome.

Others try to pretend it didn't happen. They refuse to talk about it and refuse to make responsible decisions for their future. They are living in limbo and will likely find their shadowbox existence collapsing on them sometime in the future.

If you were caught in Katrina's wake, How would you cope? Although no one knows for sure how he or she might react in a massive disaster such as Katrina, one thing is certain: the only way to make it through the storm and remain emotionally healthy is *to dwell on that which you still have and not on that which you have lost.*

In lean times, praise the Lord for the little things that you might take for granted in prosperous times.

Choose to sing rather than sigh. Laugh rather than cry.

Be thankful for what's in your cup, rather than complaining over that which isn't.

Count your blessings, not your burdens.

Sing His praises, not the blues.

Share your joys, not your sorrows.

Focus on your friends, not your foes.

Give of yourself to those in need, rather than getting for yourself that which you want.

Pray for wisdom, rather than for wealth.

Hold on to God, because with Him "all things are possible," rather than holding on to things that give temporary pleasure and blow away in adversity.

Max Lucado puts it this way, "Raging hurricanes and broken levees have a way of prying our fingers off the stuff we love. What was once most precious now means little; what we once ignored is now of eternal significance."

King David put it this way, "I would have lost heart, unless I had believed that I would see the goodness of the LORD in the land of the living" (Psalm 27:13, NKJV).

Peter put it this way, "Now we live with a wonderful expectation because Jesus Christ rose again from the dead. For God has reserved a priceless inheritance for his children. . . . So be truly glad! There is wonderful joy ahead, even though it is necessary for you to endure many trials for a while" (1 Peter 1:3, 4, 6, NLT).

James put it this way, "Dear brothers and sisters, whenever trouble comes your way, let it be an opportunity for joy. For when your faith is tested, your endurance has a chance to grow. So let it grow, for when your endurance is fully developed, you will be strong in character and ready for anything" (James 1:2–5, NLT).

Paul put it this way, "Fix your thoughts on what is true and honorable and right. Think about things that are pure and lovely and admirable. Think about things that are excellent and worthy of praise" (Philippians 4:8, 9, NLT).

And one old-timer from southern Louisiana put it this way, "You gotta thank God for whatcha got, not for whatcha ain't got!"

Seven-year-old Owen Betz from Pass Christian, Mississippi, asked his mom the question so many survivors have asked: Will anything ever be the same?

The answer is simple. No, it will never be the same. But it will be OK. In fact, it can be even better, if that's what you believe, hope for, and work toward. New Orleans may be the Big Empty for a while, but just because *it's* empty doesn't mean *you* have to be empty. Regardless of circumstances, with Jesus in your life, you can be filled to overflowing with His joy!

---

1. James and Brenda Chapman's home in the Upper Ninth Ward had four feet of water throughout, and almost everything was lost. Rolland and Lynn Clemens's house in the Lower Ninth Ward was completely submerged and knocked off its foundation.

2. Cathy Booth Thomas, "Hurricane Katrina: The Cleanup," *Time* Magazine, November 28, 2005.

-Chapter 13-
ACTS OF COURAGE AND COMPASSION

"Inasmuch as you have done it unto the least of these,
My brethren, you have done it unto Me."
—Matthew 10:40

Truckers to the Rescue

Rhonda West's oceanfront house in Long Beach, Mississippi, disappeared in Katrina's wake. Knowing her house was at risk, Rhonda survived the storm by going to her sister's house, where thirteen people huddled

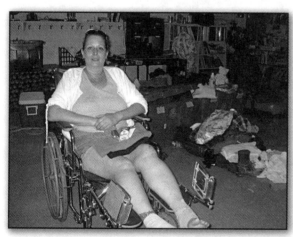

together in one room for more than twelve tension-filled hours, praying for their lives. Almost all the members of her family, eleven generations, had lived along the Gulf Coast. Two weeks after Katrina, Rhonda had located twenty-six of them who were alive. Her blond-headed cousin, Denise Carver, who was a nurse, had to be air-lifted out of the Superdome by the military to ensure her

Rhonda West helped to turn the Quarles Elementary School into an emergency rescue station and called her trucker friends to bring in lifesaving supplies.

174

safety. Her cousin, Herbie Carver, in New Orleans survived in his attic for six days, eating raw eggs and bacon he salvaged by swimming below to his refrigerator and forcing open the door. Five had drowned in their living room in New Orleans. And eleven were still missing.

Rhonda had been through hurricanes before, and she knew what they could do to large tractor-trailer trucks, so she had parked her eighteen-wheeler in a sheltered place more than a mile away from her sister's. Getting back to it after the storm was something else! The piles of debris were so high and so treacherous it was like walking through a landmine—splintered wood, shards of broken glass, mangled metal, stinking sewage, and always, the threat of snakes.

Other than her truck and the clothes on her back, Rhonda had nothing. That's when she discovered that the Quarles Elementary School on Commission Road in Long Beach hadn't flooded. Maybe she and the other homeless individuals who were wandering the streets could stay there. Without any governmental authority, she and her friend, Jake, and others from the fire department set up an emergency rescue shelter. They also broke into the school cafeteria to find whatever supplies they could in order to feed the people. Finally, they set up a little first-aid clinic to provide care to those in desperate need.

Rhonda administered CPR to a forty-seven-year-old man who had a heart attack. Thankfully, he survived. She helped a twenty-two-year-old girl who had a miscarriage. Then she cared for Trina, a lady with a severely abscessed tooth. Trina was burning up with fever caused by the infection and was in so much pain that she was almost out of her mind. Her jaw was so swollen it looked like she had a golf ball in her mouth. Professional help was needed—and needed now. But in the first week or so after the hurricane, there was none. Yet, the homeless people—rich and poor—started coming.

One was Elizabeth Stone, a well-to-do eighty-one-year-old woman whose antebellum mansion on the beach had been destroyed. She would have fled before the storm, but she had no one to help her transport her handicapped, wheelchair-bound adult son, Jason, who was suffering from multiple sclerosis—so she stayed. Rhonda watched as this mother tried to care for her son. For three days he sat helplessly in his wheelchair. And although his whole body was wracked with pain, he never once complained! He, along with the other evacuees, had no food, no water, and no place to sleep. Surely, any minute now, someone would come to help. After all, this was America! Where was FEMA? Where was the Red Cross?

Finally, Rhonda could stand it no longer. It dawned on her that no help was coming. She grabbed her cell phone and started pushing the buttons down the preprogrammed numbers of her trucker friends. She told it like it was. "This is hell here. I'm talkin' *hell!* And there ain't nobody comin' to help us!"

They asked only one question, "Tell us, what do you need?"

She mentioned the basic necessities and one thing specifically for Jason—a bed.

What Rhonda had no way of knowing was that seconds after she made her first few calls, the truckers' CB radios were ablaze. From coast to coast, in every direction, Rhonda's plight was being passed on. "I've got a load of blankets, do you think they could use some cots, too?" "Hey, I have a truck full of water. What's that address again?" "Someone just donated ten thousand dollars. I'm stoppin' by Wal-Mart and loadin' up!" And the semis started rolling in.

When the first one backed up and opened its doors, and the people could see all the cases of food, water, blankets, personal items, and clothing, Rhonda exclaimed, "It's like God Himself just opened the windows of heaven." You can't imagine the celebration. The whooping and the hollering! But the best part of all was when the truckers carried in the bed for Jason. Gently they lifted him out of his wheelchair, and for the first time in ten days, he was able to stretch his legs. Tears of relief rolled out of his eyes. His face shone with unspeakable joy.

It was too much. Everyone cried. As Helen Keller once said, "As long as you can sweeten another's pain, life is not in vain."

But the most touching experience of all was when three young children (two girls, sixteen and eight, and a small boy, seven) were brought to the Quarles Elementary School shelter. As a nurse was helping them, Rhonda overheard this conversation with the little boy.

"Where were you during the storm?"

"We was swimmin'."

"But the storm lasted many hours ma'am; were you swimming the whole time?"

"Yes, Ma'am, we was."

"Didn't you get tired?"

"Yes, Ma'am, I did, but my sister kept screaming at me to keep swimmin'. But my mama, daddy, and mam-ma, they got tired and quit swimmin'. But my sister wouldn't let me quit. She just kept yellin' at me."

"You are my hero, Sweetie," the nurse commented. "How did you learn to swim like that?"

"Miss Peggy Lassabe taught me, Ma'am."

At that point, Rhonda stopped what she was doing and asked the boy, "What did you say?"

"I says, Miss Peggy Lassabe. She taught me to swim."

That was too much. Rhonda got weak in her knees when she heard the name Peggy Lassabe. She knew her. She was a Red Cross swimming instructor. And Peggy Lassabe was her sister!

Rhonda immediately called her sister. "Peggy, do you know what you have done? You have just saved three little kids' lives!"

"What?" Peggy asked. And Rhonda related the entire story. By then both Peggy and Rhonda were sobbing. Isn't it amazing how something you may have done years before, without realizing the significance, could mean the difference between life and death to three precious children?

Rhonda and her friends, manning that "unofficial shelter" in Quarles Elementary School, made a significant difference to hundreds of Katrina survivors because they cared enough to be used by God to bring comfort, shelter, food, and care to those who could not help themselves.

The Ice Man

John Gooding survived Katrina with three other families in a twelve-by-fourteen-foot underground bunker he had dug and equipped with its own ventilation system. It was so quiet down there, they couldn't hear the ear-piercing shriek of the hurricane, nor did they have any idea that their world above was being flooded and swept away. Coming out after the storm was like seeing Hiroshima after the atom bomb.

Immediately John began searching for his missing friends. Other people were doing the same. On the roof of one house was a spray-painted sign. "Symore is alive. Call . . ." A cell phone number followed.

John found Charles in a daze sitting on a pile of debris on what used to be the beach. He'd ridden out the storm in his neighbor's boat. His own home was crushed. His hands and arms were covered by chemical burns from the spring on Nicholson Street in which he'd tried to wash.

John Gooding, "The Ice Man," loaded his truck with water and ice and started making deliveries. He kept up his rounds of mercy for several weeks.

On the second day, still looking for their friend Chris, John and Charles filled containers with well water, loaded them in John's truck, and started delivering them to the people who were literally dying of thirst in the hundred-plus degree weather. When the truck tires blew out because of the sharp debris, they took two tires from Charles's van, siphoned his gas, and refilled John's tank so they could keep helping people. Gas stations were out of service, like all the other businesses!

Later in the day, John was helping someone repair his roof, when an old man came up and asked for a ride to a shelter. "I'll be glad to help you," John said. "Just let me finish here." Twenty minutes later, John looked around and couldn't see the man. He entered what was left of the old man's house and found him in his bathtub, delirious, beating his head against the faucets. Not able to lift him out by himself, John cushioned his head with pillows and ran for help. He found the sheriff and a FEMA agent, and the three of them pulled the man out of the tub and got him into John's truck. John drove around for two hours trying to find someone to help the old man. At last he found a make-shift clinic that was willing to take him. A few days later John heard that the old man was safe at a senior citizens' center. If it hadn't been for John, he would have surely died of a heat stroke.

On the third day, John found Chris in an abandoned K-Mart parking lot and was able to reunite him with his family. Now, with John's personal mission accomplished and no place to call home, he focused entirely on helping others.

At first he signed up with the city's volunteer agencies to deliver water and food, but he soon became discouraged because it was so poorly organized. One day it took more than four hours just to get a load! That's when he hooked up with Lt. Randy Brooks of the U.S. Army Reserves and the Florida Forestry Brothers. In five minutes they loaded his truck with ice, and he was on his way. Ice to the Gulf Coast survivors was more precious than gold! John had heard stories that desperate people had even held volunteers at gunpoint to get more ice than they were allotted. So John didn't mess around. He gave it away as fast as he could, rushing back for more. In one hour he delivered three loads!

Three weeks later, John was still delivering ice, not only to the homeless existing under makeshift tarps next to their abandoned homes but to other helping agencies, such as the army, air force, the U.S.

Coast Guard, FEMA, the Red Cross, emergency medical clinics and hospitals, and dozens of church groups and volunteer organizations that were feeding people and handing out supplies. By now people had dubbed him The Ice Man!

When asked why he was working so hard, John smiled and exclaimed. "Well, it's certainly not for riches, fame, and glory!" He hesitated then and simply said, "These are my neighbors."

Acts of Compassion

Others came to help who didn't live in the Gulf Coast "neighborhood." They came from every state of the union and from many foreign countries—Canada, Mexico, Russia, Sweden, France, and others. The rich and the poor; the professional and the laborer; the young and the old. From different churches, social clubs, schools, and racial and ethnic backgrounds—they came.

Why did they come? Because their hearts were filled with compassion as they heard about the plight of so many people who had lost everything. They could not live with themselves enjoying the comforts of life when fellow human beings were suffering. When they heard that Katrina had left people helpless, hurting, and slowly dying from exposure, lack of food and pure water, and unsanitary conditions, they felt *compelled* to come. They had to do what they could to ease another's pain. In some small way, they wanted their lives to make a difference to somebody.

And for most, they came because the Lord of their lives said, "Go, take My gospel of love to the world. Be My hands and My feet. Let them know through your care that I still care."

By Helping Others, He Helped Himself

When James Wicker—better known as Red—moved out of his home in Myrtle Beach, South Carolina, and sold all his possessions, it wasn't with the intention of helping others nor did it have anything to do with wanting to be a good Samaritan. It was because his own life was falling apart. It had no meaning. He had thrown away the God of his childhood and was into drugs, drinking, smoking, partying, and living irresponsibly and was just plain hard to get along with. He would promise to shape up—at least for his child's sake—but the devil always got the best of him, taking him further and further down the path to failure and rejection. Finally, his wife had enough and divorced him. But instead of shaping up, Red sank lower into his addictions and depression. Angry at God, he had nothing to live for. All he wanted to do was end his misery. Suicide seemed like the only way out.

Before Katrina hit, Red Wicker was thinking about taking his own life. He was angry with God and felt he had nothing to live for. But after pitching in to help others, he found a reason for living. Red says, "God brought meaning back into my life."

Then Katrina hit.

As Red heard about the plight of the Gulf Coast people, he thought that maybe he could help someone before killing himself. So he packed up his few remaining things of value, got into his car, and headed south. When he reached the wasteland of Waveland, he had no contacts, no organizational support, and no place to stay—so he slept in his car. Each morning he'd wake up with only one agenda item: to find people in need and help them. One day you would find him on a roof helping an elderly gentleman with repairs or cleaning out a mud- and mold-infested house for a single mom. The next day he might be taking someone to see the doctor or getting needed food or supplies for a family. If someone was scared to stay alone at night in the shell of their home or their tent that offered no security, he'd sleep nearby on the floor or in his car. He had nothing to lose since he was planning to kill himself, anyway.

If someone needed the shirt off his back, he'd give it away. The needs of the survivors were so great that what little money he had was soon gone. Then just as he'd think he had no more to give, someone would hand him a few dollars, and he'd find someone else in worse shape and be compelled to help them out. When he ran out of personal resources, he went looking until he found what was needed.

When someone needed something, the word was, "Go, find Red!" They knew he would help—or die trying! People talked, and his reputation spread. "Hey, man, that Red is an awesome guy. He'll help anyone!" It didn't take long for the government officials and charitable organizations to notice what Red was doing. They gave him a gas card and arranged for him to stay at the Stennis Space Center.

Over the weeks, something awesome began happening in Red's life. He began to realize that God was alive and that He cared about people! The God that he had rejected had never rejected Him. The more he did for others, the more Red began to sense that God was using him. Helping others is a God thing. He began to feel God's Spirit inside as he ministered to the hurting and the lost. God was working through him. What an incredible thought that such a messed up and miserable man like himself was actually being used by the God of the universe! Instead of depression, he began to feel a vital force within. His energy was renewed. The more he worked for others, the better he felt.

At last, he couldn't deny the power that was working within him, and he rededicated himself to God. "Lord, You died for me on the cross. If I'm that important to You, why should I kill myself? Instead, I want to live for You and do what You want me to do!"

Now he shares Jesus with everyone he meets. He prays with them and gives them something to read about Jesus. And when he runs into someone who feels like giving up, he tells them his story: "Several times I was ready to kill myself, but God saved my life. Look what He's done for me. He's given me an important work to do. He's given me self-respect. He's given me a purpose for living. He's brought meaning back into my life. I may not have a home or money, but inside I'm excited about living. God has given me everything I need. I used to dread the long lonely night hours. Now, I can't wait until tomorrow to see what new experiences God has in store for me. If He can bring hope and love and dreams back into my life—He can do it for you, regardless of what Katrina took from you."

There are many ways to find Jesus. Most of us try to do it ourselves. We pray. We try to be good. We try to please God. But the good news is that it doesn't matter where we begin our journey. In fact, we might be running in the opposite direction, like Red was. But if we stop to help those in need, which is the work Jesus gave us to do, *God will be in us.*

How many worldly possessions did Jesus have when He walked the dusty roads of the Middle East two thousand years ago? None! When He needed a donkey or a boat, He had to borrow one. When He needed food, He ate with friends. Instead of thinking of His own needs, He spent His time meeting the needs of others. And when He asks us to follow His example—He doesn't just mean to dress up and worship Him in a large cathedral!

Jesus said that He came to help others—to add quality to their lives. (See John 10:10.) If we just do what Jesus did, meeting other people's needs and adding a little quality to their lives, God has an exciting journey that He's going to take us on—with an awesome ending! If we just do what He asks—feed the hungry, give pure water to the thirsty, find the homeless a place to stay, give clothing to those who need it, minister to the sick, and visit those who can't visit us—we're going to get God's blessing splashed back on us! And there is no doubt but that we'll enjoy the journey. (See Matthew 25:34–40.)

The more we do for others, the closer we'll feel to Jesus who is working through us! And someday soon, Jesus will say to those who do what He asks, "Come, you blessed of My Father, inherit the kingdom prepared for you from the foundation of the world" (Matthew 25:34, NKJV).

John 17:3 sums it up in the words that Jesus prayed for us so long ago: "And this is eternal life, that they may know You, the only true God, and Jesus Christ whom You have sent." What is eternal life? A growing relationship with Jesus—and it happens naturally when we have a heart to help others. Just ask Red!

Today, Jesus is pleading with us, "Don't let the enemy steal your health and kill your relationships by enticing you into addictions, partying, and living for your own self-pleasure. Don't let him destroy you with envy, anger, and bitterness! Instead, give Me a chance, and I'll take you on the most incredible journey you can imagine. Cast your bread upon the waters by helping others, and blessings will be returned to you more numerous than you can count. With Me, today is the start of eternal life for you!"

ACTS: The Hurricane Trackers

Dale and Dianna Bass have been on an incredible journey since the summer of 2004. For seventeen years they had been in the Florida fruit-packing business. As founders of the Golden Harvest Food Company, their main mission was to provide wholesale citrus to over 850

Dale and Dianna Bass found God was pushing them into disaster relief efforts even before Katrina struck.

Christian schools throughout the nation for fund raisers. Without the money they made by selling their product, many of these schools would not be able to survive.

Harvesting season, from November until May, was their busiest time, but the months just prior were filled with mountains of paperwork that were necessary to coordinate the ordering and delivery of the fruit! Theirs was not a small operation. Over the years it had grown into a thriving business with annual sales of over fifteen million dollars—with 120 employees in the packing house and another 60 in the field. But for Dale and

Dianna, it was more than just work—it was their mission—until a hurricane changed everything.

Hurricane Charlie came ashore in August 2004 while Dale and Dianna were attending a large meeting in Oshkosh, Wisconsin. Charlie hit Florida's west coast, so didn't affect their citrus crop. However, as they watched the news about the devastation in the Fort Charlotte area and later saw some of the damage as they drove south on I-95, they commented, "I hope God sends someone to help those people." But they never once considered it to be their responsibility. After all, their fruit season was just getting organized.

Then on September 4, Hurricane Francis swept into Central Florida's citrus country—St. Luci County, Indian River County, and St. Martin County. Dale and Dianna prayed for protection and weathered the storm in their brick and concrete home with friends. They survived, but the damage around them was severe, and their citrus crop was destroyed! That changed the whole course of their lives—and their ministry!

Suddenly, they found themselves in the middle of a major disaster relief program in their own backyard! As soon as the winds died down, they

Diane Epperson and David Canther serve hot meals to hungry volunteers with Adventist Community Team Services (ACTS)—an organization that quickly arrived on the scene to provide emergency services to Katrina victims.

were out in their truck checking on their neighbors' safety, chain-sawing their way through hundreds of fallen trees and clearing downed power lines. Never before had they realized how important it was for volunteers to come into a devastated area and help the survivors. The overwhelming appreciation they received from those they helped softened the terrible realization that their thriving business was gone. In its place, God put upon their hearts a burden to help those who were worse off than they were.

A couple years before, when Hurricane Andrew hit Florida, few were prepared for a massive hurricane disaster relief program. Right after that, God impressed David Canther, a pastor in Florida, to begin working with people of different faiths to establish a Christian disaster relief organization that would be ready to meet any emergency. The result was ACTS (Adventist Community Team Services), a lay-driven/lay-funded group of volunteers trained to go into disaster areas with food, water, supplies, and other essential services.

Dianna Bass moves supplies that will help meet the emergency needs of the victims of Katrina.

In 2004 David became director of another organization, Adventist Community Services (ACTS), for the Florida Conference of Seventh-day Adventists. At that time the leadership of ACTS fell on the capable shoulders of Dale Bass and his wife, Dianna.

The timing was perfect—but isn't that the way it is with God? Just as Dale and Dianna's business was blown away by Hurricane Francis, God gave them a new and more exciting mission—and prepared them as well. Having survived a number of hurricanes, they knew what the survivors needed, and they immediately began shaping ACTS to be even more effective. That's why, when Katrina hit a few months later, they were ready with a massive force of volunteers—including hundreds of students from Christian schools around the country.

Knowing Katrina was a big one, they began tracking her course as she came ashore, hitting Miami, the Keys, and Ft. Lauderdale. One day later ACTS was there. When Katrina blew out to sea, ACTS regrouped at Camp Kulaqua in Central Florida, and the ACTS trucks and volunteers left for the Mississippi Gulf Coast early Monday morning,

ACTS volunteers from Mount Pisgah Academy in North Carolina unload supplies.

the day Katrina hit. Tuesday they found themselves chain-sawing their way into the Gulf Coast counties—supporting the rescue teams that were searching for bodies. With eleven emergency supply–filled vehicles, including two mobile kitchens, they immediately began feeding the rescue workers. They also had heavy equipment to help clear Highway 11 so they could get down to Bass Memorial Academy in Lumberton, Mississippi. It was there that the volunteers set up their base camp and during the first week served over 70,000 hot meals to the residents of Lamar County.

Almost immediately, ACTS moved some of its equipment down to the hard-hit coastal towns of Waveland and Purvis, where they set up other distribution centers, feeding stations, and emergency medical clinics. All this happened within the second day after the hurricane. In fact, ACTS moved into operation so quickly that it was feeding people and handing out water and ice before the Red Cross, FEMA, or any of the other disaster relief organizations got there.

Volunteers came from Seventh-day Adventist high schools and colleges across the nation. Semi-trailers from Florida, loaded with donated food and relief items, were taken to Mississippi by commercial trucking companies free of charge.

By September 23, more than 235,000 hot meals had been served at the three mobile kitchen sites. And during this time 182 semi-truck loads of supplies had been received and unloaded, organized and distributed by students from dozens of schools nationwide.

God was there working through the volunteers of ACTS, just as He was at the hundreds of other Christian relief sites established in the first few weeks throughout the Gulf Coast region. People were prayed for, hugged, encouraged, and ministered to. Many survivors voiced the same observation, "It was the churches and Christian people who were there first and helped us the most." And the miracles happened! Here are just a few examples:

One Saturday night at the ACTS food service station in Purvis, the cook surveyed his supplies and figured he had enough food to serve twelve hundred meals the next day. The volunteer staff decided to just keep serving the food until it ran out. The team prayed and kept returning to the supply room for more. At the end of the day, they were shocked when they realized they had prepared fifty-five hundred meals! When the cook asked how many meals he could prepare the next day, he checked his inventory, and he still had enough to feed twelve hundred!

Another miracle: A few days after Katrina, the ACTS distribution center on the Bass Memorial Academy campus in Lumberton was running out of bottled water. The volunteers began praying, but continued handing out water as the people requested. The next afternoon students from Andrews University and Southern Adventist University were getting ready to go through neighborhoods to help people who couldn't get to the distribution center. David Canther challenged them to go get the bottles of water that they had brought for themselves but hadn't yet opened and, in faith, give them out to the people. He told them, "The principle of the kingdom is, you need to give first in order to receive." The thermometer registered over a hundred degrees as the students gave their water away. When they returned, two semi-trucks of water had miraculously arrived. The truck drivers said they had no idea where to go and were directed by the police to take the water to Bass Memorial Academy.

And one more miracle: There were no showers for workers or community members for two weeks. Everyone was hot and sticky. Some residents still had mud on them from the tidal surge wave that had flooded their homes. ACTS immediately began building showers. The very day the showers were completed, a prayer team

Volunteers load food, water, and clothing into people's cars as they drive through the ACTS distribution center.

asked God for an unusual request—a gas-powered pump for the showers. That day, Tom Hayes, chaplain and Bible teacher at Walker Memorial Academy in Avon Park, Florida, arrived at the Bass Memorial Academy distribution center with an enthusiastic group of student volunteers. As they were unloading, Tom casually mentioned to Dale

Bass, "Can you use a gas-powered-pump?"

"A what?" Dale exclaimed.

"A gas-powered pump!"

"Look over there," Dale said, pointing to a group of praying people. "That's exactly what those people are praying for right now!"

Tom said that about a week before, God impressed someone to donate

There are always lots of pots and pans to wash after serving hundreds of hot meals.

the pump for the Katrina effort, even though they had no idea whether or not it would be needed! And he just happened to have room on the truck, so he had brought it along. And there it was on the very day it was needed!

But the miracles didn't happen just for the sake of the survivors. Volunteers who unselfishly gave of their time and energy in the sticky hot, bug-infested, smelly Gulf Coast walked away with a blessing. Here's just one example:

Two weeks after Katrina hit, Joshua Haley, boys' dean from Heritage Academy near Monterey, Tennessee, had a van load of students who were handing out water, food, and other essential supplies to the survivors who couldn't get to one of the ACTS distribution centers.

At one location, when Joshua got out of the van, vicious dogs began barking and nipping at his feet even though the owners of the dogs were right there. The students hesitated to get out of the van, even though it was obvious the people needed the supplies they had come to give them.

"Come on, gang," Joshua urged, "let's do the work God brought us here to do." Without hesitation, the students jumped out of the car and began passing out supplies with the dogs barking ferociously at their heels. They acted confident and made sure everyone got what was needed.

Later, they talked about how God must have given them courage because they would have never faced those dogs in any other situation. Over and over again they saw God working in their lives as they met people's needs.

There was no doubt that God was there in the midst of chaos and disaster, showing His care and concern for those whose lives had been torn apart. Almost every volunteer went back home with a testimony. They experienced the truth of the often-quoted proverb, "It's more blessed to give than to receive" (see Acts 20:35).

-Chapter 14-
BRENDA'S SURVIVAL STORY

*"Everyone's life story is out on the curb, soaked and stinky—
furniture and clothing, dishes, and rotting drywall,
even formerly fabulous antiques."*
—Cathy Booth Thomas

It wasn't until I stepped from the air-conditioned truck onto the crusty, parched mud-covered pavement of a parking lot in Waveland, Mississippi, that it hit me. The smell! Putrid, foul, hot, humid air blasted me with nauseating sensations. It was a briny fishy odor—a mix of oil, gas, raw sewage, feces, and decaying flesh. The smell of death.

It reminded me of the time I worked with a pathologist when a body was found after two weeks decaying in the hot July sun. The stench was so overwhelming we had to wear gas masks. But now I had no gas mask. Instead, I had a tape recorder and microphone. And this wasn't the morgue. It was the Gulf Coast eighteen days after Katrina wreaked havoc on one of the most beautiful coastlines in the world. And I was there to interview the survivors and to weep with those who had lost everything—including loved ones.

I had known in my heart that this was not going to be an easy task, but now more than ever I sensed the magnitude of what I was facing. This was surreal. *Could this be the United States?* Everywhere I looked was total devastation. I'd seen pictures of war ravaged lands and television footage of cities destroyed by bombs, yet somehow this seemed even worse. This was not just a city that was decimated—but miles and miles and miles of utter destruction in every direction. Waveland was gone, Pass Christian was no more, and on and on—everything destroyed all the way east to Biloxi. Then to the west—New Orleans and surrounding parishes were still under water! It was incomprehensible!

But more heartbreaking than all of the physical devastation around me was the knowledge of what this hurricane had done to destroy the lives of thousands and thousands of precious people. People who loved this land. Who for generations had built homes and businesses and raised their families here. People who knew no other way of life. Their past was literally washed away. Everything familiar, destroyed. Not just material things, but their hopes and dreams—vanished. Life as they knew it was gone forever.

I wept as I thought of the thousands of my fellow Americans whose lives had been needlessly snuffed out. And among those who survived, many had lost everything but the clothes on their backs, and these were now ragged, torn, and smelly. Mothers and fathers were grieving the loss of their children. Children, the loss of their grandparents. Friends were missing. Neighbors, gone. No wonder the spirits of so many were crushed. No wonder so many thought that life for them was over; they had no reason to live.

What difference could I possibly make in their lives?

The futility of it all started to sink in. This disaster was too awful, too massive. And the hurt, too deep. I might be able to put on a bandage, give a vaccination, or hug a sweaty body. But only God could heal their wounded hearts.

Why was I really down here?

The bug-infested smelly world that I stepped into that blistering hot September day was obviously far from what I considered my comfort zone. You've got to know me to understand the reality of this statement. I hate bugs—and any other creepy, crawly thing! And talk about being infested—I thought I had stepped into one of the seven last plagues! Personally, I don't think locusts or frogs could possibly be any worse than those Gulf Coast love bugs during mating season. I never did get their scientific name. But I sure found out why they called them love bugs. They were lusting all over the place—and then dying! I couldn't even talk without waving my hand wildly in front of my face, hoping to deter the little critters from getting inside my mouth!

Love bugs made life miserable for Brenda—and others. Here, hundreds of these insects "decorate" a bus from Southern Adventist University.

In addition to putting up with the miserable environment, I had other challenges. I'm what you might call a "high-maintenance" woman. Don't ask me to go anyplace without at least a two-hour notice. It takes me that long to put on my face and fix my hair! I don't even go out to my mailbox without blow-drying, curling, combing every hair into place, and spraying to make sure it stays that way! And we haven't even talked about the decision-making process of what to wear. This is more challenging than you might think. The color of your top determines the color of your shoes. And the choice of shoes will determine the necessity of a purse change!

By now you have probably analyzed me as having a slight hint of compulsiveness. Yes, I'm well aware I need therapy! But that's me! Can you can imagine how mortified I was that first morning? My mission was to collect stories from Katrina survivors, but how was I ever going to survive? Little did I know the lessons that God had in store for me.

My Rude Awakening

It all started at five o'clock Thursday morning, September 15, when my bare feet touched the floor of the dorm room where I was staying. Crunch! Crunch! Crunch! **YUCK!** I couldn't believe it. *I swept up a* *bucket full of those dead love bugs last night. How could there be so many covering the floor this morning?*

With no broom in sight, I finally found a piece of paper and swept a path through the bugs so I could get to the shower. Two hours later, with every hair in place, and my shoes and purse coordinated with my blue silk blouse and black designer pants, I stopped for one quick look in the mirror. After all, I was representing 3ABN. Of course, had my mission been to muck out houses, I most certainly would have opted for something more comfortable! Satisfied that I indeed looked like a "professional," I made my way down to the makeshift food tent that the ACTS relief organization had set up on the campus of Bass Memorial Academy in Lumberton, Mississippi.

I was ravenously hungry, having missed supper the night before. But my appetite disappeared completely when the volunteer server put the first spoonful of applesauce on my plate—sprinkled with love bugs! The volunteer, surmising that this was a problem for me based on the green color of my face, quickly reached over and scooped off the unwanted guests!

That did it. That was my first and last trip to the food tent during my entire stay! I survived on Tennessee-purchased pretzels, wheat crackers, and the few apples I had in my car. It's not a diet I'd recommend! And it may not have been fat-free, but it *was* love-bug free!

With two cameras, two tape recorders, and a video recorder, high heels, and a very heavy color-coordinated purse, I marched forth and thought I was prepared for anything. But I couldn't have been more wrong!

The two-hour drive to Waveland had been an eye-opening experience. The closer we got to the coast, the more severe the conditions. Demolished forty-thousand-dollar cars stuck out of the debris. A semi-truck trailer was wedged in the tops of trees; another one was plopped in the middle of a house. Big heavy expressway signs were bent in half. I saw cars on top of houses and hundreds of them upside-down in ditches. Huge business signs—Taco Bell, Burger King, K-Mart and many more— were mangled so badly you could hardly identify them.

Trees had all kinds of debris hanging from the few remaining limbs. Even a refrigerator had been washed up and imprisoned among the branches. And can you believe there were boats four and five miles inland, in the most unusual places, like sticking halfway out of a living room window or on top of what used to be someone's garage? An entire riverboat casino had been washed in three blocks and was sitting on top of a house. And dark grey smelly sludge was everywhere! I was reminded of Jesus' question in the Bible: What good will it do you to gain the whole world, yet lose your own soul? (See Matthew 16:26.)

Left Behind

So there I was, standing on the crusty, parched, mud-covered pavement of the Waveland parking lot that had been converted by ACTS into a massive disaster relief center. There was such a whirl of activity my mind couldn't comprehend it all. Energetic students bounded out of the school buses, eager to contribute in whatever way they could. No job was too lowly. In minutes they were washing dishes, pots, and pans; taking out the trash; sweeping the pavement; unloading semis in the hot sun. Never once complaining. There must have been at least two hundred volunteers, each with their own task to accomplish.

The FEMA trucks were delivering fuel for generators and volunteer transport vehicles. Semis were being unloaded. Big fork lift operators were moving pallets of bottled water, food, personal items, diapers, and other supplies. People were unpacking boxes and taking the items to

Each of the nearly two hundred ACTS volunteers had his or her task to do in making sure that emergency services and supplies were delivered efficiently and promptly.

Supplies were organized on parking lots so that people could drive through and receive items without ever having to leave their cars.

where they were needed. There was a semi-trailer that had been converted into a mobile kitchen where volunteers prepared thousands of meals a day. To shade the people from the blazing hot sun, a huge tent had been erected to serve as a dining area, where long lines of grateful Gulf Coast residents and volunteer workers were fed daily.

But the heart of the operation was the distribution line. It stretched across the parking lot as far as the eye could see. Supplies were organized in stations and positioned so that drivers would never have to leave their cars. As they passed, three or four volunteers would quickly load what was needed and move them along to the next station. Another three to

ACTS volunteers unload ice—more precious than gold in the Gulf Coast heat.

four volunteers were needed for restocking. Police were posted at each entrance and exit to maintain a steady flow, enabling thousands of vehicles to pass through each day. It worked like a well-oiled machine. David Canther, as part of his responsibilities as Director of Florida's Adventist Community Services, had designed this ACTS distribution center. Government officials were so impressed with its efficiency that they asked him to consult with other disaster relief centers.

In one corner of the parking lot was a semi-trailer that had been converted into a medical clinic—once again staffed by volunteers. These doctors and nurses came from all over the world to use their skills to relieve the suffering of others.

In addition to this beehive of activity that surrounded me, ACTS had organized a home delivery program bringing much needed supplies to those who had no transportation. Only the lucky ones had cars that still worked. Since it was unsafe to send volunteers out alone, teams were organized, each stocked with its own set of supplies: tents, food, water, ice, toilet paper, bug spray—and more.

And there I was in the middle of all this, shaking my head in amazement. Each volunteer was moving with purpose, dedication, and urgency to help someone. It was as if this terrible crisis had somehow united strangers in a bond that made them family.

But this was not the

ACTS volunteers clean the mobile kitchen where they prepared thousands of meals daily in this small space.

time to wonder at the magnitude of this operation. I had work to do. People with amazing stories were out there in the surrounding wasteland communities—and my mission was to find them, record their stories, and in some small way let them know that Jesus loves them.

Just when I was beginning to wonder, *Where do I begin?* David Canther approached me. "How would you like to team up with Andrea Matthews, another nurse, and the two of you can give medical care and get your interviews at the same time?" It sounded good to me. I had already asked

Sonya Reaves, a photography student from Southern Adventist University, to help me. So David introduced the three of us to a school principal and his wife and a group of students. Their van was already loaded with supplies. Before taking off, David emphasized the importance of staying together for security reasons. "We have been told there are prisoners who escaped during the storm. We have no idea who's out there." He also reminded us to wear our paper masks if entering any homes due to the toxicity levels from mold and decay. "Be careful what you touch."

Sonya Reaves surveys the damage inside a destroyed home, now covered with mold and toxic waste.

"Where do we start? Is there any certain area you want us to go to first?" I asked.

"No, just go anywhere God impresses you to go." And with that, Andrea grabbed two medical kits, and we were off.

Even though we began the day with prayer, I prayed silently asking God to lead us to just the right homes that He wanted us to go to. I pleaded with God to send His Holy Spirit to guide us each step of the way. Little did I know how important this prayer was and how God was going to work that day in mysterious ways."

"Where should we go?" Andrea, who had already been there for a week, told us about a hard-hit neighborhood. She had been there the previous day but hadn't had time to visit every house. It sounded like a good place to start.

This particular neighborhood was near the ocean. The closer we got, the worse the devastation. I could not believe my eyes! Nothing I had seen on television was as bad as this! Why wasn't this being reported on the news? Dried mud and sludge covered the ground. Houses were so broken that you could look at the front and see all the way to the back. Most had no windows, doors, or roofs. Trees were broken and bare; debris was strewn everywhere. I gasped as I saw a couch high up in the branches of a tree that was still standing! People were out on their property digging through their destroyed homes, like archeologists searching for scraps and pieces of their past. Mold-infested furniture and once treasured possessions now lay in piles in front of every house waiting for FEMA or someone to carry it away.

There was something missing from this scene. But I couldn't figure out what it was. Then it struck me: The absence of color. Not a green leaf or blade of grass anywhere! This was a war zone! How could anyone survive this? I was about to find out!

The driver pulled up to the first street and parked the van on the side of the road. I use the word *road* loosely because the paved roads were not visible due to the heavy mud and sludge. Large equipment had gone through the streets removing just enough debris to make a path for cars to drive on. The stu-

As the volunteers went through neighborhoods looking for individuals to help, this is what they saw—destroyed houses and ruin everywhere.

dents divided up in twos to approach the houses, and Sonya, Andrea, and I went to the first house on the street.

Standing outside near a makeshift tent, which consisted of a blanket tied to the house and a standing tree, was a blonde, middle-aged lady who was fanning herself vigorously with a paper plate. She was wearing shorts and a sleeveless top that was drenched with sweat. As beads of

In many blocks not a single house was left standing; nothing but rubble remained.

perspiration rolled down her face, she would use the back of her hand to wipe it away. Looking into her eyes, I sensed a mix of hopelessness, anger, and despair.

For sixteen days Frieda Feigle hadn't changed her clothes, bathed, or washed her hair, except when she used one bottle of water to rinse off the toxic chemicals from her inflamed and irritated skin.

Nor had she left her property. What little she had salvaged could easily be carried away by looters. In addition, home owners had been notified that they must be present when FEMA came by or they wouldn't get their assessment to determine if they were eligible for a FEMA trailer. And no one knew when FEMA was coming. She said, "I feel like a prisoner on my own property."

I explained that I was interviewing those who had survived the hurricane in their homes, and she was eager to tell me her story. As Frieda shared her terrifying ordeal, tears ran down her cheeks as well as mine. My heart went out to her as she told how the water kept getting higher and

People wrote their names and dates on their houses to let others know they were still alive—and they added poignant messages such as this one.

higher until it forced her sister, son-in-law, and her to flee to the attic. Her son-in-law was able to kick out the attic window, and they crawled onto some floating debris and clung to the side of the house. As the water rose, so did the debris, until it finally was high enough that they could climb onto the roof. They held on for dear life!

She described their terror as they fought against the strong winds and prayed that the flying debris wouldn't kill them. When the storm subsided, they crawled down from the roof, only to discover they had lost everything!

Frieda invited us into what was left of her house to look for ourselves. You could see the water marks on the walls. Caked mud was everywhere. The smell almost made me pass out! Mold was growing so thick that it was hard to breathe. I had left my paper mask in the van, so she quickly handed me a washcloth to put over my face. Furniture, clothes, pictures, appliances, lamps—everything was strewn around. It looked as if someone had filled the house with water, shaken it up, then set it back down with a thud, leaving its contents to fall where they might. I

Furniture and other items from houses ruined by floodwaters line the streets.

walked around a refrigerator that was now in a back bedroom, and I stepped over filthy clothes, drapes, and pieces of broken dishes.

I had to leave the house quickly because the smells were overtaking me. Once outside I noticed an outdoor thermometer lying by the side of a lawn chair under the tarp. "It's 104 degrees!" I was thinking it felt more like 204 degrees! It was HOT!

I asked the lady if I could pray with her. "Please do," she said. We

Andrea Matthews with Frieda Feigel, the lady whose home was the first she and Brenda visited after leaving the van and the other volunteer workers.

formed a circle with our arms around each other. I prayed that God would give her strength, protection, and courage to face whatever lay ahead. When I finished, I gave her a hug. She began to sob. "It feels so good to be hugged. No one wants to touch us or be near us because we are so filthy and stinky."

She was right about the smell, but I had felt impressed that this lady needed more than my prayers and words of encouragement. She needed to feel loved!

I had heard the engine of the van start up during our prayer but thought nothing of it. I figured it was just moving down the street to keep up with the students. When we finished and said our goodbyes, we looked for the van. *Where was it?* The street was empty. I didn't panic. There must be some good explanation why they moved the van without telling us. *Maybe they went to the next street.* But when we got to the next street, the van wasn't there either!

What about the street in the other direction? We quickly turned around and walked toward that street. But again, no van!

For hours we walked up first one street and then down another, but the van was nowhere to be found! *Where were they?*

"You don't think they would leave us do you?" Andrea asked.

"Oh no," I assured her, although I wasn't feeling so certain anymore.

The heat and humidity were unbearable. I could hardly breathe. My head ached from my sunburned scalp. I rarely sweat. But let me tell you, the sweat was running down me in rivers. My clothes were sticking to me like glue. That's how hot and humid it was.

I thought about how silly I was to have awakened two hours early just to fix my hair! Now wet with perspiration, the sticky hair spray plastered it to my face! The love bugs must have been enjoying it. My hand was getting tired swatting them away! I was miserable and getting more than a little annoyed that we were even placed in this predicament. I was desperately thirsty, but our water bottles were in the van—and my stomach was beginning to growl. How much longer could we take this? I looked at Sonya and Andrea and could see that they were not faring any better. I prayed, Lord, please help us find a ride out of here!

As we were passing what was left of a house, a man came out and called to us. "Hey what are you gals doing out here? Don't you know it's not safe for you to be walking alone?" We stopped to talk to him and ask him if he had seen our van. He hadn't, but he told us we needed to get out of there quickly because there were pit bull dogs loose in the area that had mauled several people. Some of the men in the neighborhood had tried to shoot them but so far had been unsuccessful. "They were psycho dogs before the storm," he said, "but now they've gone plumb crazy. I'm telling you that it just isn't safe. And there are prisoners out here, too, raping women. I'm serious, you gals need to *git outa here!*"

We could hear the dogs barking in the distance, and we had every reason to believe that he was telling the truth. We thanked him, prayed with him, and then quickly headed in the direction where we were first dropped off. By now we had been wandering the streets for several hours, and our feet ached. *Oh, why had I worn high heels!* If that weren't enough, we had to go to the bathroom, and there was no place to go! The sound of barking dogs grew closer. Fear gripped our hearts. We picked up our speed considerably!

When we finally reached the street where we had started that morning, we saw that there was now a truck parked on the corner with a volunteer giving out sandwiches to the neighborhood residents. We introduced ourselves, and the volunteer told us he was with the Baptist church. He offered us egg salad sandwiches—which I quickly declined after a vision of food poisoning from hot mayo flashed through my mind! He,

Brenda gives a woman a tetanus shot. Disease was a real problem following Katrina.

too, told us it wasn't safe for three women to be walking alone in this neighborhood and that we should hitch a ride back to the disaster relief center. We assured him that we were certain our ride would come for us, and we waited another long hour! Finally, seeing men coming by and staring at us, the volunteer took matters into his own hands. Without us realizing what he was doing, he flagged down the next car that came by and asked if they would give three ladies a ride. I bent down to look in the car and breathed a sigh of relief to see it was a woman driver! She graciously offered us the seven-mile ride back to the Waveland distribution center. I never appreciated air conditioning and soft seats so much in my life.

When we told her that we were interviewing survivors of Hurricane Katrina, she was quick to tell us her story and was just finishing when we pulled into the parking lot. She, too, had narrowly escaped with her life! We helped her find items that she needed and prayed with her. After thanking her profusely for her kindness, we headed to the main office to find out what had happened to our van.

Imagine my surprise when I turned the corner and passed the pallets piled high with supplies. There was the van we had spent all morning looking for! I couldn't believe my eyes. "Well," I thought, "they must have been so scared they lost us that they came back here to get help and start a search party!"

I asked one of the volunteers walking by if he had seen the principal and his wife that we were looking for. "Oh, yes," he said. "I just saw them in the main dining tent over there."

What? How could that be? How could they be calmly eating their lunch under a nice cool tent after having abandoned us—leaving us in the sweltering heat, in a dangerous area with no water, food, or means of communication? They know there is no cell phone coverage down here. What were they thinking?

Later that day when I saw David Canther, all my frustrations spilled out as I relayed each detail of the morning's horrific ordeal we had endured. He listened very intently to every word. When I finished my story, I looked up into his kind eyes for what I was sure would be sympathetic assurance. Nothing could have shocked me more than the three words that came out of his mouth. He simply said, "Isn't God good!"

What? Wasn't David listening to me? My mind was reeling. *Did he not hear one word I said?*

Seeing the look of confusion on my face, he quickly continued. "Brenda, God must really have His hand on the book you're preparing. Isn't it amazing that before you can even write your first story, God placed you in a position to really *'feel'* what these survivors are feeling? You didn't have any water; neither do they. You had no place to go to the bathroom; neither do they. You were hot and sweaty, with no place to get out of the heat; so are they. You had no security; neither do they. They don't even have walls to surround them for protection. They have to sleep out in the open where any criminal, wild animal, or dog could attack them! You felt abandoned; so do they! Everything you described is exactly what these people are living with on a daily basis! Isn't God good!" he said again.

This time I felt all my righteous indignation melt away, and with tears in my eyes, I nodded and said, "Yes, God is so good!"

Wow! That put everything in a whole different perspective. The morning hours that I thought were wasted were not wasted at all. God allowed this to happen so I would have the compassion and empathy I would need to listen to each one of these hurting people. My interaction with them would not have been the same. I was not the same either.

The next morning, and every morning after that, started differently. I still cleared a path through the love bugs but sliced an hour off my get-ready-for-the-world routine by throwing my hair back in a pony tail and applying minimal make-up. Gone were the designer pants, silk blouse, and high heels—replaced with blue jeans, cotton top, and sensible shoes.

An Answered Prayer for a Man

My sister Linda called me the next morning, and after I relayed my previous day's ordeal, she pleaded with me to ask a man to go with us for

security. She was terrified, knowing the potential danger I had faced. I told Linda, "There is no way I'm going to ask for a man to be our security guard when every able-bodied man is desperately needed for all the lifting that's required here."

Again, my sister pleaded with me. "It's just not safe for three girls to be going around those neighborhoods by themselves." She had heard on the news about women being raped and robbed. "Please, just ask! You won't know if you don't ask."

Katrina survivor Dennis Strong (second from left) stands with ACTS volunteer workers (left to right), Andrea Matthews, Thea Stoia, and Kevin Komarniski.

I flatly refused. "Just pray for us. God is the only protection we need."

She knows me well enough to know that trying to talk me into it would be useless. We prayed together on the phone. As Linda finished her prayer, she added, "Please Lord, send a man to go with Brenda and her friends today as they go about Your work, and I thank You in advance for what I know You are about to do. In Jesus' name, Amen."

We said our goodbyes, but not before Linda added, "Remember Sis, God answers prayer!"

I grabbed my purse and headed out the door to meet Andrea and Sonya. They laughed when I told them I was no longer going to depend on anyone else for transportation! I wanted my own wheels! I was almost to my car when a red-headed man approached me and said, "Excuse me, would you mind if I tagged along with you today? I missed my ride to Waveland, and besides I've been volunteering here for ten days now and could use a change of scenery!"

What? Had I heard right? You could have knocked me over with a feather! God had answered my sister's prayer! Kevin Komarniski stayed with us the entire time I was there, never letting us out of his sight. When I told him that he was an answer to prayer, he choked up a little and said, "You know what? That feels pretty good!"

The challenges I faced were many. I cried more in the next seven days than I had in years. I heard so many heart-wrenching stories that my emotions were raw. Never had I prayed so intensely. Every morning I pleaded with the Lord. "Where do You want me to go today? Help me be a blessing to everyone I meet. Let them see Jesus in me." I never went to a town or turned down a street without silently praying for God's direction. I knew God had a mission for me. My time here was so short. I didn't want to waste a minute.

And I prayed for safety. Driving was a major hazard. Only the main roads were completely cleared. The back roads were barely passable, increasing the possibility of a flat tire. Gas stations were few and far between, and those that were open were rationing fuel. I was constantly watching my gas gage. But fuel wasn't the only thing that was scarce— so were restrooms.

Because there was no electricity or water, no one in any of the Gulf Coast towns had bathroom facilities! Instead, each town had a line of port-a-potties placed in deserted parking lots. But there was never enough to meet the demand.

Believe me when I say that the mere mention of the word *port-a-*

potty, makes me nauseous. Trust me, I'm not exaggerating. My first experience was a nightmare. Let me paint the picture! I opened first one door and then the next trying to find one that didn't have a pile above the seat or smeared feces on the toilet paper. Not able to find one "potty" that was better than another, I was forced to enter the hottest, smelliest, filthiest place I had ever been. With outdoor temperatures around 104 degrees, inside was like a sauna. Steam was literally rising from the decaying feces and urine. Flies were everywhere! The stench was overwhelming. I started to gag! I could see I wasn't the only one. Vomit was all over the floor. This sick sour smell combined with the odor of "cooking" human waste was too much. I thought I would pass out.

But when you gotta go, ya gotta go! *Oh, Lord, please help me!* I held my breath as long as I possibly could and completed this mission in record time. But then the worst possible thing happened. By now I was sweating profusely, and my jeans were sticking to my legs. I pulled and I pulled, but I couldn't get them up. I was starting to panic. I knew I wasn't going to last much longer. Every cell in my body was screaming for fresh air. I pulled and tugged—and started to cry. *Lord, please help get these jeans up before I throw up all over myself! I can't take it in here another minute!* With that I made one more try, and my jeans easily slipped up into place! *Oh thank You, Jesus! Thank You for caring for something as trivial as pulling up my jeans!* With that I almost broke down the door to get out and gulp some fresh air.

From then on, I considerably limited my water intake and prayed for strength before ever approaching those dreaded "blue sweat boxes!"

Looking at Life Through Holy-Spirit Glasses

In spite of it all, I wouldn't trade that week spent on the Gulf Coast for anything in the world. Every day God showed me in some new way that He was with me. He led me to so many people who needed to know that Jesus loves them. That He was with them, before, during, and after the storm! I watched hearts soften that were once bitter toward God, and I prayed with everyone I met. There was so much suffering that it was hard to comprehend.

In a way, I felt guilty. I knew I was going home with all the comforts it entailed, but these people were home! They had no options! I felt powerless to help them, but I could show them Someone who would. People who didn't believe in God never refused my offer of prayer! I wanted so much to be a blessing to others, but truly—I received the greater blessing!

God has a way of taking the most terrible conditions you can imagine and turning them into something you can look back on and say, "Isn't God good." I still don't like bugs and port-a-potties, mold and sweat, but I made it—and my trip to the Gulf Coast has become one of my best memories. In a way, "all things work together for good" (Romans 8:28) if you choose to look at your troubles through Holy-Spirit glasses: What can I learn from what I'm going through? How can I be a better person? How can this help me have a closer relationship with Jesus? With my family? With my friends?

God has put within each one of us a tremendous power to cope. Like the inflated toy clown with a heavy rounded bottom that always bounces back when hit, *so can you*. Who knows what you might be asked to go through in the future—or what God is asking you to go through right now? You might not think you have the discipline or courage to make it. Well, you're probably right. But with God, you can do anything. (See Mark 10:27.) Once you factor God into the equation of your troubled life, even the most heart-wrenching experiences can become the most meaningful. As tough as it is today, if you're growing closer to Jesus because of your circumstances, tomorrow you will be able to say, "It was worth it all."

Those who sow in tears
Shall reap in joy.
He who continually goes forth weeping . . .
Shall doubtless come again with rejoicing . . .
(Psalm 126:5, 7, NKJV).

Chapter 15

BURIED
TREASURE

"For where your treasure is, there will your heart be also."
—Luke 12:34, NKJV

Sherry and Harold Helveston's house in Biloxi, Mississippi, was completely destroyed. The night before Katrina hit, they thought it would be safe to ride out the hurricane in their home, but once the wind and the rain started, they quickly changed their minds and raced to the nearby Wal-Mart and spent the night there. It was a good thing they did, because when they got back to where their house was supposed to be, it had been picked up by the wind, whipped around, and thrust back to earth in their neighbor's yard. Totally demolished!

As they surveyed the mess, Sherry shook her head in disbelief and sighed. "Thank goodness, I grabbed a few of the grandchildren's pictures—it's the only thing I've got left! These photos mean the world to me. I just wish I had grabbed my Bible too. But thank God—and I give Him all the praise and glory—we still have our lives. We can replace all this, but we can't replace our lives." Taking a deep breath, she straightened her shoulders and stated, "As bad as it looks, we're coming back here. God's going to help us."

At that moment, Sherry had no idea how God was going to bring them back. And the end of the story may still be years away. But just a few days later, God gave Sherry a sign that He was with her and her family and that all would be well again. Here's how it happened.

Since the storm had destroyed not just their home but all their clothing, Sherry and Harold decided to go over to one of the relief centers to see if they could find something that would fit them. Sherry looked at the piles of boxes and had no idea where to begin. Where would she find her size?

Brenda Walsh (left) stands with Harold and Sherry Helveston. On the right are volunteer workers Andrea Matthews and Thea Stoia. Sherry is holding her "miracle" Bible.

Just then she noticed a pair of cowboy boots along with some clothing, so she went over to investigate. She took the boots out of the box and began to rummage through the contents. As she got close to the bottom, she felt something. Pulling the clothes out of the box, she couldn't believe her eyes. There was a Bible! She opened it and found, to her utter amazement, that it was a large-print edition. "Look, Harold!" she exclaimed. "Look what I found! It's exactly what I've been wanting to get—a large-print Bible."

Sherry carefully opened the Bible and was surprised when a piece of paper fell out. She picked it up and read the first line: "A Note from Sherri."

A note from Sherri? she thought. *That's my name. Strange isn't it, that a "Sherri" wrote the note—and another Sherry found it! This is not a coincidence. This Bible is meant for me!* Then she read the message:

"To whomever finds this Bible: I feel so helpless to help you. You are so very far away. Please accept our meager offerings and please accept this Bible. It was my grandmother's. She is 101, suffering from Alzheimer's and probably would have been one of the first to die if East Tennesseeans

211

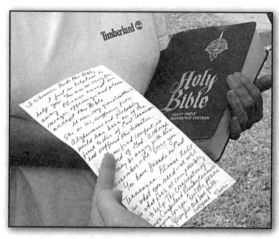

Sherry felt that the letter she found inside the Bible was a special message to her directly from God.

had suffered this disaster. Please find comfort in the Word of God. Although you may be angry with Him, remember He loves you. You have friends in East Tennessee. Please tell us what you need. We will do whatever we can possibly do to help. The congregation of Union Cumberland Presbyterians are praying for you. Feel the power of our prayers and have faith. Godspeed, Sherri."

Tears came to her eyes. What an inspiration that message was. It was as if God had reached down and said, "I am with you, Sherry. I know how hard it is for you to have lost everything. I just want you to know that I will see you through."

"Wow!" she exclaimed. "God put this Bible in that box just for me!"

Two weeks later when Brenda interviewed her, Sherry was still

Brenda Walsh surveys storm damage inside the home of Harold and Sherry Helveston.

beaming from the treasure she had discovered buried in the welfare box. "Isn't it just amazing," Sherry commented, "how God can take all the broken pieces of our lives and turn them into good? He has blessed us with wonderful volunteers who have come to help. I know God has sent them to encourage us. I just can't tell you what this has meant. And then on top of everything, God gave me His Word—in giant print so I can read the good news of His love and claim His promises—without my glasses!" Then she added, "One day I hope to meet Sherri from Tennessee. Maybe we'll be neighbors in heaven. Each day, through her note and my precious Bible, God is giving me strength to go on."

The Rest of the Story—in Brenda's Own Words

There's an amazing story behind the miracle of Sherry finding the Bible in the box. When I first came to Mississippi to collect stories for this book, I met Andrea Matthews, a volunteer nurse from Florida who, for the last week, had been helping people throughout the Gulf Coast. When I shared my mission with her, she immediately told me about this woman who had found a Bible in a box of clothing.

When I heard her story, I knew that God wanted it in the book. I can't really explain it, I just knew! So I asked Andrea, "Where does this lady live?"

She looked at me and said, "I'm sorry, Brenda. We'll never find her again. I don't even know what town she was in, much less what street. I've been working all over the Gulf Coast area. It would be like finding a needle in a haystack."

I said, "You know what, Andrea? My God has counted every hair on my head, so if that story's supposed to be in the book, God can find that needle in a haystack."

So as Andrea and I started out that next morning to continue our interviews, we had a special prayer. "Lord, if you want us to meet 'the Bible lady,' would You please allow our paths to cross today."

As the day wore on, I kept praying, "Lord, if it's Your will, please show me where to go." In each town there were curfews that were strictly enforced by the military. To prevent looting, absolutely no one was allowed on the streets after dark. I could see that the sun would be setting soon, and I had only a short amount of time left. "Lord, what street should I go down?"

At the next corner, piles of water-logged furniture and debris in front of each of the houses caught my attention. I turned and slowly drove past first one house and then another, praying, "Lord, is this were you want me to go?" I almost drove by a camper parked on an empty lot because it didn't look like anyone was home. Then out of the corner of my eye, I noticed a man walking toward the camper. I quickly pulled over, threw the car into park, and with my tape recorder in hand went to approach him. Like I had done with others hundreds of times before, I started interviewing him and his wife. It was so hot outside that Andrea had stayed in the air-conditioned car, thinking this would be a quick stop.

The man's wife was in the middle of telling me how they survived the storm, when all of a sudden, Andrea jumped out of the car and ran toward me, yelling excitedly, "Brenda, this is the Bible lady. It's the Bible lady!" The two of them started hugging each other and jumping up and down. "I can't believe it; I can't believe it! God brought us here," Andrea exclaimed. Then turning to me, she said, "I didn't recognize this place because when I was here before, they didn't have a camper. They only had a small, makeshift tent."

At that point, Sherry said, "I've got to show you my Bible." She quickly disappeared into the camper and came back proudly holding the Bible against her chest. Her face was beaming. "You have no idea how precious this book is to me. I will always treasure it. Let me tell you how God gave me this Bible. It's an absolute miracle." And with that, the story just spilled out—this time with even more details than I had heard from Andrea. When she was finished, Sherry held the Bible close to her heart. "I may have lost everything," she said with tears streaming down her face, "but then again, I haven't really lost everything. I haven't lost my connection with God."

Have You Found God's Treasure for You?

Just how precious is God's Word to you? When the storms of life hit, do you have that connection with God that Sherry was talking about? The kind of relationship that's so close that you never feel alone? The kind of friendship that can pick you up when you're discouraged or calm the storm in your heart when the wind is blowing and a flood of problems is threatening to drown you?

How long do you think a couple would stay happily married if they spoke only once or twice a year or whenever there was a crisis in their lives? The answer is obvious. In any relationship, communication is key. If you really want to grow closer, you have to spend time together. So it is with a relationship with Jesus. The more time you spend with Him—the more you talk together—the closer you'll get.

Perhaps you're thinking, *I wish I had that kind of relationship with Jesus, but I find reading the Bible is sometimes boring. How do I get started?* The best way to jump-start your friendship with Jesus is *not* to just read the Bible. It's best to follow a daily three-step approach: (1) Read His Word, (2) think about what He's saying to you, and (3) share with Him how you're feeling about what you've read.

Regardless of what's happening in your life right now, God has something He wants to tell you. He's got something in His Word that will add meaning to your life. He has a message for you. A promise you're going to want to claim for yourself. Or maybe just something interesting that you're going to want to think about and share. Unless you open His Book and dig for buried treasure, you'll never know what you're missing. So here goes. . . .

When troubles hit, God wants to give you these messages. Read each one. Think about what God is saying to you and write it down. Then tell the Lord how you're feeling. (All texts are from the New King James Version.)

Nahum 1:7. "The LORD is good, a stronghold in the day of trouble; and He knows those who trust in Him."_____

_____.

2 Corinthians 4:8, 9. "We are hard pressed on every side, yet not crushed; we are perplexed, but not in despair, persecuted, but not for-

saken; struck down, but not destroyed." _____

_____ .

Psalm 138:7. "Though I walk in the midst of trouble, You will revive me; You will stretch out Your hand against the wrath of my enemies, and Your right hand will save me." _____

_____ .

John 14:1–3. "Let not your heart be troubled; you believe in God, believe also in Me. In My Father's house are many mansions; if it were not so, I would have told you. I go to prepare a place for you. And if I go and prepare a place for you, I will come again and receive you to Myself; that where I am, there you may be also." _____

_____

_____ .

Isaiah 43:2. "When you pass through the waters, I will be with you; and through the rivers, they shall not overflow you. When you walk through the fire, you will not be burned, nor shall the flame scorch you."

_____

_____ .

Romans 8:28. "And we know that all things work together for good to those who love God, to those who are the called according to His purpose." _____

_____ .

Psalm 31:7. "I will be glad and rejoice in Your mercy, for You have considered my trouble; you have known my soul in adversities."

_____

_____

_____.

Hebrews 4:15, 16. "For we do not have a High Priest who cannot sympathize with our weaknesses, but was in all points tempted as we are, yet without sin. Let us therefore, come boldly to the throne of grace, that we may obtain mercy and find grace to help in time of need."

_____

_____.

1 Peter 5:6, 7. "Therefore humble yourselves under the mighty hand of God, that He may exalt you in due time, casting all your care upon Him, for He cares for you."_____

_____

_____.

Matthew 6:34. "Therefore do not worry about tomorrow, for to-morrow will worry about its own things. Sufficient for the day is its own trouble."_____

_____

_____.

2 Corinthians 1:3, 4. "Blessed be the God and Father of our Lord Jesus Christ, the Father of mercies and God of all comfort, who com-forts us in all our tribulation, that we may be able to comfort those who are in any trouble, with the comfort with which we ourselves are com-forted by God."_____

_____

_____.

Philippians 4:6, 7. "Be anxious for nothing, but in everything by prayer and supplication, with thanksgiving, let your requests be known to God; and the peace of God, which surpasses all understanding, will guard your hearts and minds through Christ Jesus."

_____

_____.

Isaiah 51:11. "So the ransomed of the Lord shall return, and come to Zion with singing, with everlasting joy on their heads; they shall obtain joy and gladness, and sorrow and sighing shall flee away."

_____

_____.

Lamentations 3:21–24. "Therefore I have hope. Through the Lord's mercies we are not consumed, Because His compassions fail not. They are new every morning; Great is Your faithfulness. 'The Lord is my portion,' says my soul, 'Therefore I hope in Him!' "

_____

_____.

Jeremiah 29:11–13. "For I know the thoughts that I think toward you, says the Lord, thoughts of peace and not of evil, to give you a future and a hope. Then you will call upon Me and go and pray to Me, and I will listen to you. And you will seek Me and find Me, when you search for Me with all your heart."_____

_____

_____.

-Chapter 16-
HOPE FOR THE HOPELESS

"Do not gloat over me, my enemies! For though I fall, I will rise again. Though I sit in darkness, the Lord himself will be my light."
—Micah 7:8, NLT

As you read the next few stories, put yourself in the "shoes" of the survivors. They had lost everything—family members, friends, homes, jobs, keepsakes! And realistically, for most there was no hope of recovery. Their lives were forever changed. How do you instill hope in the hopeless? What could you say that would make a difference? What could you do?

Surviving After Katrina

Frieda Feigel survived Katrina from her home in Bay St. Louis, Mississippi. Here's what she says about living through it—and the frustration of trying to survive afterward:

> Thank goodness Katrina hit when it was daylight, because if that tidal surge had hit at night, the people would have been swept from their beds and would not have been able to make it through. The water came up so fast we didn't have time to grab anything—no medications, no tools to break a hole in the attic, no clothing, no nothing. And neither me nor my sister can swim a lick.

This house, like so many others, is covered with mold and toxic bacteria. People were warned not to enter their houses without protective clothing and face masks.

For three days all vehicles were under water. We didn't know if any of our neighbors were alive. When we came out of that attic, it was like the end of the world.

FEMA tells us to stay here and wait. For what? For some idiot to come out and tell us our house is destroyed! Every one of these houses will have to be condemned because of the mold spores. We're sleeping in a tent. A shower would be wonderful. Just to get out in the rain with shampoo and soap would be heavenly.

It Happened on Racetrack Road

Right after the storm, with the wind blowing thirty or forty miles per hour, Terry found herself in shock walking down Racetrack Road in D'Iberville, cradling her little wiener dog in her hands. She came upon Dennis Strong, whom she had worked for at one time in the casino, and told him this story, "When the water came up so fast, I grabbed my dog and climbed up into the attic. When the water started coming into the attic, I knocked a hole in the roof. That's when I noticed that my neighbor had a little skiff, so I swam to it with my dog. I got a stick and paddled down Racetrack Road and found me a pine tree. I stayed in the boat and held on to that pine tree through the entire storm—holding on to my little dog the whole time. I was terrified. Just terrified. I thought I was gonna die."

Two weeks after the storm, Dennis Strong made this comment from outside his house in D'Iberville. "Do you see what's going on over there? They're moving debris a little at a time, looking for bodies. They've got to go slow to see if they can find any people. Just three days ago, about one block over, they found a little boy's body under the debris, and I watched them as they searched for his mother and two sisters. The next day an ambulance came again. I suppose they found them."

They Thought He Was the Wind

In the South Beach, Mississippi, area, a man was in his attic, forced there by the rising water, when the wind ripped away the roof and his house began to crumble. He was swept away with his dog in his arms and was pushed inland by the wind and waves. Somehow, he was able to keep his head above water. Finally, he felt himself bumping against something. He had been pushed against the balcony railing of the second story of a house. He grabbed hold and was able to get onto the balcony with his dog.

Hearing voices inside, he began banging on the door. The frightened family, confused by the banging of debris against their house and the incessant whine of the wind, thought the noise was from the wind and water, so they got mattresses and started cramming them in front of the door. The desperate man began screaming. Still holding on to his dog, he began pounding more frantically. It was not until the storm died down a bit that they were able to hear the screams, remove the mattresses, and drag the half-drowned man and his dog into the safety of their attic.

This family, too, lost everything. Their possessions were washed away; the home was knocked off its foundation, and within days black mold was growing in the walls, forcing authorities to condemn their house. Two weeks later, like thousands of others, they sat hopelessly under a makeshift tarp beside their mold-infested home that held so many memories—waiting for the bulldozers!

Sixty-two Years in a Green Box

Boyd Cook and his family lost everything except the camper in which they drove to Montgomery, Alabama, the day before Katrina hit. Their idea was to go about eighty miles north, just far enough to miss the fury of the storm, and then immediately return to their home in D'Iberville, Mississippi, before anyone had a chance to loot it.

His stepdaughter Karen Burgess said, "When we started coming back, we had to pull off under overpasses because the wind was so strong. We were at Moss Point on Pascalusa Bridge on I-10 when a gust hit us and almost knocked us over. We went swerving on the road, and I was crying and praying in the back seat. I didn't think we were going to make it."

Brenda Walsh interviews Boyd Cook whose life possessions were reduced to little more than a single green box.

When the family drove into their old neighborhood, they could hardly recognize that it was the same place they had left just a few hours earlier. They asked the people across the street, "How bad was it?"

"It was bad," came the reply. "We just got down out of our attic about an hour and a half ago. Your house was completely under water." At that Karen's heart sank. She tried to hold herself together but lost it when her dad broke down the front door. "Furniture was everywhere," she said. "It looked like the house had just been picked up, flooded with water, shook

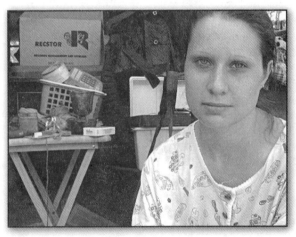

Boyd's stepdaughter, Karen Burgess.

up, and sat back down. It was like our stuff had been through the spin cycle in the washer. The refrigerator even jammed a huge hole in the ceiling." She broke then, put her head in her hands, and wept. After gaining her composure, she went on with her story, saying that for the next three days they mourned their loss—and bitterly accepted the reality that no one was coming to help them. They had no home, no food, no water—and no hope!

Boyd Cook's home following Katrina.

Two weeks after Katrina, Boyd described the condition of his house: "It's so filled with mold that it looks like a smelly old piece of cheese that's been lyin' out in the yard too long. See that green metal box over there?" he said, pointing to a box about eighteen by twenty-four by twenty inches. "That green box is worth sixty-two years of my life. That's all I've got left."

This was what was left of the kitchen in Boyd Cook's home when he returned following the storm. Notice the marks on the ceiling left by floating appliances.

Karen explained, "My dad suffers from asthma. Just twenty minutes inside, and he can't breathe! How is he going to clear this place, as FEMA requires? I'm glad to be alive, and I know there are people who are worse off then we are, but I wish they would send us help. We hear about all these people raising money, like the Red Cross and FEMA. But where is the Red Cross when you need them? And FEMA, FEMA, FEMA! Where is FEMA? The national agencies have been absolutely no help at all. It's the church people who are feeding us and keeping us alive with food, ice, and water."

"And what really hurts," Boyd interrupted, "is all these businesses who are gouging prices on things we really need. Trying to make a buck off our bad luck. Last week, I had to stand in line forever to try to buy a five-hundred-dollar generator, only to find out that now they are charging almost a thousand dollars more! Can you imagine? Can you imagine that? Talk about kicking a dog when it's down. How do they sleep at night? Go talk to all my neighbors, they'll tell you the same thing. It's happened all over. Except the neighbors over there," he said, pointing across the street. "They all died in their attic!"

It's Really Tough When You've Lost Twice

It was sad losing everything that Katrina washed away, but the greater tragedy was having that which you were able to salvage stolen from you. That happened to so many of the Gulf Coast residents. It happened to Dennis and Betty Strong from D'Iberville. Although they lost their home, they searched through the rubble during the days after the storm and found a few pieces of furniture and some dishes that could be salvaged. Then there were some wrought iron pieces that they thought they could use when they rebuilt. So they borrowed a trailer from a friend, backed it into their yard, loaded it, and covered it with a tarp. Then they had to go to work. When they returned, the trailer was stolen. They reported it, and even though Dennis's sister gave police a description of the vehicle that hauled it away, the officers were far too busy dealing with life and death matters to look for a missing trailer.

Now I've Lost Everything

Lee Garvey, an emergency physician from Charlotte, North Carolina, told the story of a sixty-seven-year-old man who stumbled

224

into a mobile hospital in Bay St. Louis after spending the first five days following Katrina sleeping in his truck, which didn't even have a working battery. He was dehydrated and disoriented. After receiving IV fluids, a snack, and then a meal, he seemed to come back to life.

Then he asked about his bike that he had ridden five miles to the hospital and left parked outside with a blue-and white beach towel draped over it. After searching, all that could be found was the towel, neatly folded on the ground. No bike.

Dr. Garvey thought the old man might go berserk when he heard about the loss of his last significant possession. To his surprise, the man simply said, "That's it. Now I've lost everything."

Many of the survivors found that the only way to cope with their devastating losses was to adopt an attitude of "whatever will be, will be." Lorraine Landry, a seventy-year-old retired nurse, expressed her resignation to fate with the phrase "Here today; gone tomorrow!"

Once people accept this defeatist attitude, depression often lurks around the corner. What might it take for the old man who lost his last worldly possessions to once again find life worth living? To experience joy? To find the contentment that comes when you hold in your heart the hope that tomorrow will be better?

You Loot, I Shoot!

Fifty-two years old, with two master's degrees, Sam Brothers had a well-established photography business which he ran from his home in Waveland. He loved living on the Gulf Coast—the smell of the ocean, the gentle sea breezes, and the beautiful white sandy beaches. Sam had it made—you might say.

Hurricanes seemed his only threat. He weathered Katrina from Picayune, Louisiana. A few days later he returned home . . . to nothing! Waveland had been hit by the eye of the hurricane. His $175,000 home, which was almost debt free, was destroyed. The only thing he had was $800 in his pocket.

Looting was such a problem that signs like this one could be found throughout the area devastated by Katrina.

Feeling life had dealt him a bitter blow, he was looking through the moldy rubble of his possessions, hoping to find some keepsake to remind him of the life he had once enjoyed, when two guys came up to him and tried to make conversation. They told Sam a hard-luck story, saying that they were from New Orleans and had lost everything. "We haven't eaten in days; do you have anything you can give us to eat?"

"I've got some rations from the government," he said. As he turned to share with them the little he had, they hit him in the head with a hard object and beat him so severely he passed out. They grabbed his wallet and the $800, leaving him for dead.

Sam has no idea how long he was unconscious, but when he came to, his assailants were gone. He somehow managed to stumble over to his friend's house. Shocked at Sam's condition, his friend called an ambulance. He was taken to a temporary treatment center. His head wounds were so severe that the physicians feared brain damage. Just a few weeks after Katrina, none of the Gulf Coast hospitals were equipped to provide treatment for head trauma, so the physicians ordered that Sam be flown by medevac to a hospital in Mobile, Alabama. As he was being carried out to the helicopter, Sam protested, "I don't have any money to pay for this."

"Don't worry," he was told. "FEMA—or someone—will pay!"

Sam arrived at the trauma center in Mobile, Alabama, with no identification, no money, no medical records—nothing! When his condition was stable and plans were being made for his release from the hospital, the hospital administration bought him a bus ticket and sent him home to . . . nothing! He didn't even have flood insurance, which would have made it possible for him to rebuild someday!

Sam was trying to put his life back together and clear his house of the mold and mud, but he lacked the physical energy and psychological spirit to bounce back. And it

Sam Brothers stands beside the only photo he has left of his son. Sam's troubles didn't end after the storm passed. Life had more disappointments for him—but God had a blessing in store for him as well.

didn't help when he received a bill for $11,500 for the medevac!

By November the weather had turned cold. Someone had given him a cot and a couple of blankets so he wouldn't have to sleep on the floor. And he had taken in a stray cat for companionship.

That's the condition Sam was in when Pastor Ken Micheff and his dedicated group of Michigan volunteers went to his house, ignoring the big sign he had posted out front—"YOU LOOT, I SHOOT!" They were looking for those with the greatest need, to help them strip the moldy siding and flooring from their homes, pull all the old nails, and get the homes cleaned up and ready for rebuilding.

Sam was skeptical at first. The last time someone stepped on his property, it almost cost him his life. He hesitated, stepped back, and looked them over carefully. But at this point, what more could he lose? Besides, he had no other options. Grudgingly, he accepted their offer.

At the time Sam had some major questions about why God hadn't come through for him. After his house was cleared and cleaned, the trashed furniture and rubble hauled away, the nails removed from the existing studs, the ten fallen trees cut up, the branches and stumps removed, and his yard cleaned, Sam shook his head. "I cannot believe that a group of people all the way from Michigan would volunteer to help me." He was visibly moved. He then said, "And you've done all this, without any charge! You know," he hesitated, "those scalpers were gonna charge me a thousand dollars a tree—and they weren't even gonna remove the stumps! You did it all for nothing!"

"We did it," Pastor Ken explained, "because Jesus wanted us to let you know that He still cares for you and loves you supremely."

"I'm beginning to get that feeling!" Sam mused. "How can I thank you enough for what you've done?" And then the unbelievable happened: Sam asked for prayer. The group gathered around, linked arms, and asked that God put his protective arms around Sam and continue to let him know just how much he was loved.

How can you splash a little hope into the lives of people like Sam who have lost everything?

Pastor Ken later commented, "It's being there. It's not saying the right words. It's just being there and letting these people know that you care. Our presence for Sam was like a jump-start to a spiritually dead battery. So many people are angry at God. They need to communicate their feelings. And they need to know that the Lord sent us to them because He loves them. That's the real reason we came.

"We live in a sinful world. Bad stuff happens to good people. Bad things happened to God's Son when He came to earth. No one is immune—because the devil is trying to assassinate God's character. He wants people to think God brought these natural disasters and that God kills people. But Jesus made it clear that it's the enemy who has come to steal, kill, and destroy. (See John 10:10.)

"God sent His Son so, someday, earth would be free from sin and the effects of sin—disease, disaster, and death. In Romans 5:8 it says, 'But God demonstrates His own love toward us, in that while we were still sinners, Christ died for us.' Satan is behind all the bad stuff that happens. Not God!

"We're caught in the middle of a terrible war. And every time there is a war, there are casualties. The beautiful thing about the spiritual warfare that we're experiencing is that even though we have lost loved ones, we can have hope. We've read the back of the book. Christ won the war at Calvary. Now we just have to wait until sin has run its course, until every one knows just how evil it is. We're close—very close—to the end. One day very soon, God is going to stand up and say, 'Enough!' and evil will be done away with forever. All the mess that Katrina dumped into the lives of the Gulf Coast residents is just temporary. We came to shovel as much away as possible—and give the people hope that things will be better. But what's really important is leaving them with eternal hope!

"One man I talked to said, 'This has made me refocus my life. I wasn't a church-going man, but I am now. I was crying out to God during that storm—I was! And I'm not ashamed to say it. I'm thinking about life in a whole new way. I screamed out to God, and I'm here. I better go do what I know I should, don't you think?'

"I try to let people know that the most important thing is not 'being good.' Sure that's important, but what's really essential for salvation is that they feel God loves them so much that He sent His Son to save them, and all they have to do is be willing to put self aside and humbly accept that sacrifice of love. When they do that, they will experience eternal hope—which is the best hope of all!"

"Yet I still dare to hope when I remember this: The unfailing love of the LORD never ends! By his mercies we have been kept from complete destruction" (Lamentations 3:21, 22, NLT).

-Chapter 17-
DO YOU KNOW WHO HOLDS YOUR HAND?

"You have also given me the shield of Your salvation;
Your right hand has held me up."
—Psalm 18:35, NKJV

Not since the end of the Civil War in the 1860s and the Dust Bowl of the 1930s have so many Americans been on the move from a single event. Similar to the way God disbursed the builders at the tower of Babel by confusing their language, Katrina disbursed people in the twenty-first century by destroying their homes!

Two weeks after Katrina, over half the states were involved in providing shelter for evacuees. And by four weeks after the storm, evacuees had been registered in all fifty states—as well as in many foreign countries. It's interesting that three-fourths of the evacuees stayed within two hundred and fifty miles of the Gulf Coast, but tens of thousands had located—or were in the process of relocating—more than a thousand miles away.

Roughly 150,000 people were not able to evacuate from New Orleans, partially because the four hundred school buses that were supposed to be used for evacuating the city if a disaster struck were stranded and useless in a flooded parking lot in the middle of the city.

Although we might tend to criticize the residents of the Gulf Coast who appeared to ignore the mandatory evacuation orders, we seldom realize that for many it was impossible to leave. They had no transportation and no place to go. Then, think of the thousands of tourists who were stranded there because fuel and rental cars were in short supply and the services of the Greyhound bus and Amtrak train system were halted well before the hurricane made landfall. Even the airports closed early!

Most of those who evacuated before the storm found themselves in turmoil and with few options for the future. They had thought they'd get far enough away to escape the brunt of the storm and then immediately turn around, head home, and pick up their lives where they had left off. They hadn't expected that the officials would be warning, "Stay away at least a week." Ivor van Heerden, director of the Center for the Study of Public Health Impacts of Hurricanes in Baton Rouge, Louisiana, said the flood zone was like a wilderness. "There are no utilities, and it's infested with poisonous snakes and fire ants. If your house is gone, it's gone. If you come back in a day or a week, it's not going to make any difference."

Those who tried to make it home often found re-entry routes blocked by military personnel who were allowing entrance only to emergency workers or those who could prove without a doubt that they were residents. And even then, there were strict curfews. Many returned for a few hours—or a day or two—to sift through the rubbish of their homes hoping for some little treasure from their past, and to grieve for what was lost. Most had to face the fact that the lifestyle they had previously enjoyed was gone forever!

You may not always be able to get out of disaster's path. Sometimes people don't get adequate warning to evacuate before they're hit by impending doom. You may get caught in the wind and water with no way of escape. Or by planning ahead, you might be able to escape a direct hit, thinking you'll immediately return to life as you've always known it, only to find that your return is blocked by circumstances beyond your control. Regardless, you can hold on to the promise found in Isaiah 59:1: "Behold, the Lord's hand is not shortened, that it cannot save."

On a highway in Tennessee, trucker Mike Dowdy shared sandwiches with a couple displaced by Katrina—and learned a valuable lesson.

The Survivor's Song

A week or so after Katrina, Mike Dowdy, a trucker from Hartselle, Alabama, found himself with a load to be delivered in New Jersey. He headed through Knoxville and then, approximately forty minutes later, picked up Interstate 81. Around Bristol, Tennessee, just below the Virginia state line, he found himself halted by a fatal traffic accident involving a tanker truck hauling hazardous material that had developed a leak. He learned from the Tennessee State Police that traffic would be stopped until the clean-up was completed. Obviously, they weren't expecting to go anywhere for hours.

He set his brakes and got out to stretch his legs. Other truckers were doing the same. At one point, five truckers were chatting beside his truck. Sitting beside them, in a Silverado pickup, were two elderly people. The man, Joe, lowered his window and asked what was going on regarding the traffic situation. Soon the truckers were including this couple in their conversation.

At one point, Mike made the comment that if he had known this was going to happen, he'd have made sure he had some water with him because he was really getting thirsty. Joe's wife, Anna, immediately said, "We've got plenty of water and sodas in the cooler in the bed of our truck. Would you all like something?" She immediately hopped out of the truck and started rummaging around in the cooler. "And by the way, I have plenty of tuna salad, how about a sandwich?" After some urging from Joe, the truckers agreed to accept their offer.

While Anna was making the sandwiches on the tailgate of their truck, she was singing like a songbird. She had a remarkable voice. After they finished the sandwiches and Joe raised the tailgate of their truck, Mike noticed the Mississippi license plate.

Curious, he inquired, "So, what part of Mississippi are you from?"

"Biloxi," Joe said.

Knowing that Biloxi had been ravaged by Hurricane Katrina, Mike asked, "Was your place damaged at all?"

Joe replied, "We lost everything except this truck and what's in it—some clothes, a few family pictures, some of Anna's china and silverware, and this antique grandfather clock, which is a family heirloom. We were lucky!"

As soon as the truckers heard their story, they immediately offered to pay the couple for the lunch they had provided for them. Joe and Anna flatly refused!

"Tell me, how did you make it through the storm?" Mike asked as they stood there munching their sandwiches.

Joe then told about seeking refuge behind a block wall that he had built years ago. From there, he and Anna watched their belongings and their home disappear in the winds of Katrina. Then Joe added, "During all this, I had one hand holding on to Anna and the other holding on to God."

"Where are you going?" Mike asked.

"Our son has a real estate business near Harrisonburg, Virginia, and we can live in his home. We're heading up there to start over."

Mike shook his head as he began to comprehend their plight. At forty-eight years of age, he couldn't fathom how he would cope if forced to start over again. How much more difficult it must be for those who have nothing but a retirement check! And yet, these people wouldn't accept any money for their food and drinks! What an incredible couple! How selfless to be thinking of others when they, themselves, had nothing. Mike later reflected, "I have never eaten a tuna salad sandwich with side orders of such reality and humility. And I probably never will again."

Mike would never forget the lesson he learned that day—it is better to give than to receive! And Joe and Anna will probably never know how far-reaching their kindness stretched.

Today, as Mike thinks back to that experience on Interstate 81 and how these two dear elderly people blessed his life with a cool drink and a tuna sandwich, he can still hear Anna's sweet voice singing *I Don't Know About Tomorrow*—the old familiar gospel lyrics and music by Ira Stanphill.

"Many things about tomorrow, I don't seem to understand:
But I know Who holds the future, and I know Who holds my hand."

When troubled times come to you, it is our prayer that your heart will be so filled with the joy and peace of Jesus that you, too, can sing with assurance, "I know Who holds my hand."

EPILOGUE

"I believe there's a lesson and a blessing in everything.
We just haven't found it yet."
—Sharon Welch

Katrina will forever by synonymous with sorrow, destruction, heartache, loss, looting, and pain. For those who lived through its fury, "between hell and high water" will never be just a cliché. It was reality! The terror and agony of Katrina was so intense that words are powerless to express just how awful it really was. It will not be forgotten. Terror has a way of haunting memories and becoming the subject matter for nightmares. Weeks after the storm, Alice Jackson commented, "I still get a little edgy when I hear water running in the bathtub!"

But as horrendous as Katrina was, through it all, *God was there*. Not in the storm, but beside those who were storm-beaten, broken, and bruised. If you question that, read what God says in Isaiah 57:15: "I dwell in the high and holy place, with him who has a contrite and humble spirit." Do you know what "contrite" means? It means to be broken; to be ground into powder; to be crushed. God Himself says that He dwells with brokenhearted people. Those who are suffering, discouraged, angry, or rejected, or who have lost everything. Whatever the cause of your brokenness, *God is there*.

In other words, when you're at your lowest—when you think you can't go on—that's when God is closest to you. And that's why God was there when Katrina struck—because thousands of people were being pulverized by the power of the storm.

God goes on to say that He is there "to revive the heart of the contrite ones." In other words, to lift the spirits of those who have been broken and crushed! So, if, for any reason, you feel you're being battered by a storm, God wants to comfort and encourage you and mend your brokenness.

Two weeks after Katrina hit, Danny Shelton, president of Three Angels Broadcasting Network (3ABN), visited the disaster zone to record the testimonies of Katrina survivors for 3ABN's worldwide television audience. As he began to hear the heartbreaking stories, his own heart broke. "Mending Broken People" has been the motto and theme song of 3ABN since it began in 1984. The more Danny heard, the more convinced he became that the messages of these people, the faith and courage they displayed, and the lessons they learned were a story that had to be told. That's when the phone call came. "You have to write a book about Katrina survivors. There's a story here that we all need to read!" And so this book was conceived to spread the word that whatever the circumstance of your life, no matter what storm you're going through, *God is there!*

God promises, if you will just seek Him, you'll find Him. (See Lamentations 3:25.) That's what Elijah did. But he looked in all the wrong places. He looked in the big noisy catastrophic places—the hurricane-force wind, the earthquake, and the fire. But God wasn't in the elements that destroy. Instead, God was found in a still small voice. First Kings 19:11–13 tells the story: "Then He [God] said [to Elijah], 'Go out and stand on the mountain before the LORD.' And behold, the LORD passed by, and a great and strong wind tore into the mountains and broke the rocks in pieces before the LORD, but the LORD was not in the wind; and after the wind an earthquake, but the LORD was not in the earthquake; and after the earthquake a fire, but the LORD was not in the fire; and after the fire a still small voice" (NKJV).

When Katrina hit, many called the storm an act of God. But it wasn't God's act. Killer storms are acts of nature—an earthly atmospheric event that occurs in a world that has been compromised by sin. It's much more accurate to call killer storms acts of Satan. God was *not* in the storm. God wasn't in the hurricane-force wind, the earthquake, or the fire. Instead, God was there, whispering encouragement to the hurting; He was mending broken people!

The Escalation of Crisis

You may be thinking, *I don't live in hurricane country. I don't have anything to worry about. Disasters happen to others—not me.*

Unfortunately, you're wrong. As long as you live in this world, you are a target of Satan's increasing fury, for he knows Christ is coming and his reign of terror is about to end. He's bent on bringing as many people down with him as he can. His strategy for winning your soul is the same as was his strategy regarding Job so many years ago: He wants to hurt you enough—take away your loved ones, your money, your home, your job, and your health—until you will end up becoming discouraged, cursing God, and dying.

But just as Job overcame the tough times and was able to say, "Though He slay me, yet will I trust Him," *so can you.* (See Job 13:15, NKJV.)

It's going to get worse. From highway accidents to lightning strikes to the threat of terrorism, we've been told what's ahead. "For when they say, 'Peace and safety!' then sudden destruction comes upon them. . . . And they shall not escape" (1 Thessalonians 5:3). Until Jesus returns and does an extreme makeover on planet Earth, catastrophic events can—and will—happen to all of us!

Jesus predicted that there would be wars, famines, pestilences, earthquakes, and lawlessness just before His coming. These things have been common ever since sin entered the world. But you can't argue with the fact that it's getting worse! Just consider the rate and intensity of the disasters that have hit the world in the last decade!

Hurricanes. In 1995 Opal hit. Then the next year, Fran. Floyd came in 1999; Allison in 2001; and Andrew in 2002. But the string of deadly billion-dollar storms blowing in from the Atlantic was far from over. In 2004, the furious four—Charley, Frances, Ivan, and Jeanne—ravaged Florida in rapid succession and set records for damage. Then Katrina hit! Quickly on its heels came Rita and Wilma—both more intense but, thankfully, less destructive. There were so many hurricanes in 2005 that meteorologists ran out of alphabetical names and had to begin using the Greek alphabet—Alpha, Beta, Gamma, etc. And did you know that 2005 racked up more storm deaths and destruction than the previous ten years combined? Did you know that hurricane power has roughly doubled in power over the past thirty years? And did you know that, worldwide, the number of Category Four and Category Five hurricanes, the strongest categories, has nearly doubled over the past thirty-five years?

Tsunamis. On December 26, 2004, a roaring monster wave washed hundreds of thousands in southern Asia to their death and affected over five million people in eleven countries. The most experienced soldiers in the modern wars against catastrophe call this the greatest challenge of their lifetimes. The U.N. warned that disease could kill as many as the tsunami did, a number now reaching upwards of 150,000.

Earthquakes. More than 73,000 people were killed, 69,000 injured, and as many as 2.5 million people left homeless by the 7.6 magnitude earthquake that struck in Pakistan on October 8, 2005.

Violence and Wars. With the current climate of terrorism around the world, human beings have come to exist in what is essentially a permanent state of war. The following are just some of the most recent and violent incidents.

On April 19, 1995, at 9:03 A.M., just after parents had dropped off their children at day care in the Murrah Federal Building in downtown Oklahoma City, the unthinkable happened. A massive bomb inside a rental truck exploded, blowing half of the nine-story building into oblivion. A stunned nation watched as the bodies of men, women, and children were pulled from the rubble for nearly two weeks. When the smoke cleared and the exhausted rescue workers packed up and left,

168 people were dead in the worst terrorist attack on U.S. soil until September 11, 2001!

On September 11, 2001, terrorists highjacked four commercial jets filled with unsuspecting passengers. The first two planes were flown into the World Trade Center towers in New York City, causing them to collapse. The third hit the Pentagon. The fourth crashed in Pennsylvania farmland instead of the White House or Capitol, because passengers attempted to take back control of the plane rather than let terrorists kill more innocent people. By the end of that fateful day, 2,986 people were dead!

Since the September 11, 2001, attack on the World Trade Center and Pentagon, terrorism has become a part of our world to an unprecedented extent. The United States has gone to war in Afghanistan and Iraq. As this book goes to press, dozens—if not hundreds—are dying every day in the fighting that has developed in these countries.

It's hard to imagine that all this—and much more—happened in just a ten-year span. Think of the hundreds of thousands of people—the hurting, the homeless, and the dead—that are the casualties of these events! Yet we know from reading Bible prophecy that the world situation will not get better; it will only get worse. Our only safety and salvation is in Jesus Christ.

What Can We Learn From Katrina?

Before closing the book on Katrina, perhaps we should search through the rubble for lessons God would have us learn so that we can become better—not bitter—when faced with crises in the future. Here are our picks for the top ten lessons all of us should learn from Katrina:

1. We don't need all our stuff.
2. Lost possessions can be replaced; people can't.
3. Relationships are more important than things.
4. You can survive more than you think.

5. Worry doesn't mop up the muck; work does.
6. Clean water is more precious than gold.
7. Comfort is having a clean bathroom.
8. Be thankful for the little things.
9. Immediate disaster relief cushions the terror and the pain.
10. What the world needs is Jesus.

For those caught between hell and high water, life will never again be the same. But with Jesus, life can be filled with blessings. Our prayer is that God will continue to bless His Gulf Coast children through their sojourn in the wilderness and bring them home—to the mansions that He's preparing for them in heaven.

THE REST OF THE STORY—
ONE INCREDIBLE WEEK

Sometimes it's interesting to learn the story behind the story. This book has an incredible one. That's why we decided to take you behind the scenes. The publisher loved the manuscript for *Between Hell and High Water*. Everyone who read it couldn't put it down until the last page. We were expecting the book to be printed and in our hands in one month to coincide with a scheduled "live" television program on 3ABN when we would be announcing the book and talking about the Katrina stories.

And then, on Tuesday, February 28, we received an unexpected email from our publisher, saying, we definitely should NOT publish any story or picture of anyone without a specific written release that covers both the story and the picture."

"What?" Kay exclaimed. "This can't be. I've never had to get permission to use someone's story. A picture, perhaps, but not a story! The book is finished. We've prayed through every story. Each one is vital. Somehow we'll find a way to get it published," she told Brenda. "God will open a door. I wish I could help, but I'm here in Mexico until the end of March. Every phone call from here costs a fortune. I can't do much else, but I can pray!"

On Wednesday morning our publisher called Brenda, confirming the decision that each story and picture had to have a signed release form. Brenda pointed out, "We explained to each person that their story and picture would be in a book called *Between Hell and High Water*. Everyone willingly told their story knowing it was being recorded for publication. They even held up their printed names when we took their picture. Wouldn't all this be evidence that they wanted their story in the book?" But no amount of pleading on Brenda's part made a difference. The decision was firm.

"I'm so sorry," the editor said. "Without signed release forms, we can't publish the book. And the bad news is that you only have one week to get the signatures. Our deadline for releasing marketing information on all our new products is in just one week. I realize that this makes it impossible for you. I feel sick about it, but there's nothing we can do."

Hanging up the phone, the finality of the situation began to blanket Brenda like a dark, heavy cloud. All she could think of was the months and months that she and Kay had been spent working on this project—the hot sweltering days down at the Gulf collecting the stories, the hours transcribing the tapes, putting all the stories together, doing the research, checking out details, cataloging the pictures. There was no doubt in Brenda's mind that God had led to every one of these stories. She shook her head. "Surely God wouldn't have had us go through all this, and then not let it get published so people could read it!"

Brenda's first reaction was to lie down and cry. *There's no way we can find everyone! Homes are gone; phones changed; people have moved. Not to mention that we have no addresses, phone numbers, or contact information on any of these people. And in some cases, we only know first names.* Then the thought came to her, *I can either lie here and cry or get down on my knees!* So she got down on her knees and prayed and prayed.

That's when God brought to her mind an incident that had happened just a few days before. Brenda was in Texas for a speaking appointment when she got a call from Emily Schulz (see chapter 3). Emily said she was impressed to get back in touch with Brenda because she remembered Brenda's beautiful prayer for her when they talked together right after the hurricane. Now the authorities had contacted Emily because they thought they had located her mother and they needed Emily to identify the body. This had happened once before and had left Emily so emotionally drained that she feared she wouldn't be able to go through the process again. She desperately needed God's strength. She told Brenda that she was so shaken that she had been clutching her rosary in one hand and Brenda's business card in the other. "I know how busy you are, and I don't want to bother you, but I keep thinking about that prayer you prayed for me before, and I need it desperately again. I just can't get over how a stranger could come into my life and pray for me like that. That meant so much to me and gave me so much strength. That's why I finally made the call."

The story of the Schulz family was a vital chapter of the book, and God had brought Emily to Brenda with a current contact number just at the time it was needed! It was as if this was a sign to Brenda that if God could do that with one person, He could do it with the others.

Here's where the story really gets interesting as God began, through a series of divinely ordained circumstances, to prove that when Jesus said that all things are possible with God, He really meant it!

As Brenda was praying, the problem that was weighing on her mind was, *How can we get signed release forms when we have no idea where the people are?* Then it dawned on her, *But if I went back there myself, I might recognize some of the streets where I talked to people, and maybe I could get some signatures.* Just the memories of her first trip (see chapter 14) made her stomach queasy. The Gulf Coast was the last place in the world she wanted to return to. *But if I don't go,* she reasoned, *the project dies, and both Kay and I feel that God brought us the stories in such unusual ways, that His hand is on this book.*

Then resolve came. "Lord, make me willing. I believe Matthew 7:7. I believe if we ask, You will give us the signatures we need. Make me willing, obedient, and joyful, knowing that You will guide my every step."

She got up off her knees feeling that God must have some reason for her to go to the Gulf Coast. Maybe He had a divine appointment for her there. Maybe there was someone else that she was supposed to witness to. She consulted her calendar and started canceling appointments. She couldn't leave until Sunday, March 5. Then she had to be back for a speaking appointment on Friday, March 10. That would give her only four days. Could she find sixty signatures in only four days? It seemed impossible! She made some exploratory calls: ACTS (Adventist Community Team Services—see chapter 13) was still working in the area and would provide whatever assistance she needed. And the Morrell Foundation offered her a place to stay. Danny Shelton said 3ABN would pay expenses. It seemed as if God were opening doors for Brenda to go.

But those were just little doors, making Brenda's trip possible. What Brenda didn't know was that God sometimes opens the biggest door only after we prove we're willing to be willing. Here's how it came about.

On February 28, the same day the publisher's email came, Brenda received a call from Denise Wolfe in Idaho. "Please pray!" Little nine-year-old Sarah had suffered a seizure; her arm was numb, and her speech was affected. She had been rushed to the hospital. (Sarah Wolfe was battling a brain tumor and had recently met Miss Brenda when her wish to be on the *Kids Time* television program was granted by the Idaho Make a Wish Foundation.)

The next day, as Brenda was making her Gulf Coast plans, Denise called to thank Brenda for her prayers. Sarah was doing great and was back home. That's when Brenda asked, "Denise, will you return the favor? Now I need you to pray for me. I need a miracle." Then she explained about the impossible task of obtaining the release forms in one week. Denise said, "Of course I'll pray for you. God just gave us a miracle. We can do this! Let's pray right now." And they did.

When Denise hung up, she turned to her friend, Brenda Marie Abbott, and said, "We really need to pray for Brenda because she has to go to the Gulf Coast to find all the people whose stories are in the

Denise Wolfe and Brenda Marie Abbott, who made hundreds of phone calls tracking down individuals mentioned in this book

book before it can go to press." Her friend replied, "Quick! Call her back. Tell her, we will help her find them!" Little did they know how this generous offer would forever affect their lives—as well as that of others!

That was Wednesday morning, March 1, at 11:30 A.M. Tennessee time! At first Brenda gave her Idaho "detectives" only a few names. She didn't want to overwhelm them. All three prayed together on the phone that God would guide. Then Denise and Brenda Marie immediately hit the Internet search engines.

In less than an hour, they were emailing Brenda possible contact numbers to call. Again and again, she tried. "No. Wrong number." "Wrong number." "Sorry, we don't know the person you're looking for." There were far more wrong numbers than right numbers. Then after many failed attempts, all of a sudden Brenda asked, "Is this Sherry Helveston?"

"No this isn't Sherry, but this is her daughter."

"Really?" Brenda almost screamed with excitement. "Do you happen to know if this is the same Sherry Helveston who found a Bible?"

"Yes, that was my mom."

Brenda could not contain her joy and started screaming. "Praise the Lord! Praise the Lord! I'm sorry to be so excited, but I just can't help myself. I have been looking and looking for a phone number so I could get back in contact with your folks. Is there any way you could give me their number so I can call them?"

"Well, they are just next door in a FEMA trailer. I'll go get them right now."

You can't imagine the exhilaration in Brenda's voice when she realized she was actually speaking to Sherry Helveston. When Brenda explained the reason for the call, Sherry exclaimed, "The Bible story has got to be in the book. Email that release form to my daughter, and I'll get it signed and faxed back to you right away." Within thirty minutes, Brenda had the first signature. Only fifty-nine more to go!

The next phone call was to Denise and Brenda Marie. "We found the Bible lady! We found the Bible lady! I just talked to her. She's faxing in the release form right now." By this time Brenda was crying tears of joy. "If God gave us one signature, He's going to give us the rest of them. I just know it. Let's pray right now and thank Him." And that's exactly what they did!

By this time Denise and Brenda Marie were crying too. Brenda's husband, Tim, heard the commotion and came bounding down the stairs, bursting into Brenda's office wondering what was wrong. Seeing tears rolling down Brenda's cheeks, he anxiously asked, "What happened? What's the matter?" After she explained everything to him, Tim got caught up in the excitement, too. And that's basically the joyful process that was followed with every single person that was found.

Then, once a name was found, the group prayed over the next name that they needed. And the process started all over again. Brenda would then fax or email the release form to the person while Denise and Brenda Marie began searching for the next name; then the next and the next. All day the emails and the phone calls buzzed back and forth. "Try this number!" If it didn't work, they prayed again, came up with some new ideas of how to continue searching, and Denise and Brenda Marie went back to the search engines for sites that might provide the information needed. When all else failed, they paid for time on the most high-powered Internet search sites available.

By the end of Wednesday, everyone was feeling a spiritual high even though they were physically exhausted. One by one, the Katrina survivors were being found—and in a way that Brenda and Kay never thought possible. Everyone Brenda talked to was thrilled she had called and was more than willing to sign the form. Getting the form to them was not always easy, because computers and fax machines had to be found in a region that was still crippled by Katrina's fury. But volunteers offered to take forms to people; the Morrell Foundation donated the use of its fax machine; businesses cooperated; and within a day, the release forms began to pile up on Brenda's fax machine! Each one was greeted with screams of delight—and immediately Brenda would email Kay with the corrections in the spelling of names, locations of where the stories happened, and the addition of any new information—all of which Kay entered into the manuscript from Mexico.

Once Brenda realized that Denise and Brenda Marie were passionately willing to go the extra mile to obtain *all* the names within the time limit of one week, she decided to email them the manuscript as well as the entire list of all sixty names!

By eight o'clock the next morning Denise and Brenda Marie had the list and the manuscript so they could read the stories themselves and look for clues. Now they needed to print off a hard copy. Two weeks earlier, Denise's printer had broken. They had both tried to fix it, but failed. It still wasn't fixed. Now they desperately needed it for this project. What were they going to do? How could they get the job done with a broken printer? Brenda Marie brought her laptop over to Denise's house, where Brenda Marie homeschools their combined six children. She set it up on her desk next to the printer. They prayed earnestly, plugged it into the computer, and hit the print button—it worked perfectly!

Each morning, as soon as Brenda Marie got the kids started on their class work, she went online and started searching. When information was found, Denise would run upstairs, where she made the exploratory phone calls to see if she had located the right person. If so, she emailed Brenda to make the contact. Denise also was the person who kept the hundreds and hundreds of bits of information organized—wrong numbers, right numbers, possible addresses, who to find, who had been found, fax numbers of where to send release forms, neighbors or friends of certain people, and what Web search sites had been used for what people. The women used over twenty-five Web search sites to find the survivors! Then, while Denise was calling, Brenda Marie went back to teaching, answering the kid's questions, giving spelling tests, and grading papers.

Throughout that week, the children were very patient. They knew that their moms were doing this work for God. When it seemed like the team of detectives, Brenda, Denise, and Brenda Marie, had reached a dead end on one of the names, the kids went into a prayer huddle, and there was always a breakthrough—a neighbor that knew the person and was willing to run over to where they lived, or an address was found in a neighboring town that matched the name, or a name was found under a different spelling. When a person was found and new information became available, Brenda called or sent the corrections via email to Mexico to be entered into the manuscript by Kay. It was a team effort all the way.

On Thursday, the team put in more than twelve hours in their "search and find" operation. On Friday, ten hours! As the sun set, there was major rejoicing. God had helped them find all but eight people! Then everyone stopped to rest for the Sabbath.

Early Sunday morning Brenda was getting ready to pack her suitcase and start the long drive from Knoxville to the Mississippi Gulf

Coast, when she hesitated. "Lord, do You really want me down there?" She called Denise. "What do you think, Denise? Should I go?"

Denise was firm in her conviction. "Brenda, I don't think God wants you down there. I think He wants to show us that He can do this without you trying to retrace your steps. Let's step out in faith and work hard today and see how many names God will give us. Then you make your decision." Brenda called ACTS and the Morrell Foundation and explained that she would wait one more day before making the decision about whether or not to come.

Sunday, while Brenda was making phone calls as fast as she could from her home in Knoxville, Denise and Brenda Marie were in Idaho sitting in front of their computers for more than twelve hours straight. Denise would run upstairs and fix some food and bring it back to Brenda Marie to eat while she continued searching. By the end of the day, they had only four names to go. And Brenda exclaimed with joy and amazement, "I guess God doesn't need me down there, after all!"

On Monday and Tuesday, Denise and Brenda Marie continued searching, with Brenda Marie stopping only long enough to continue teaching their kids and attending her college classes. When homeschool hours were over for the day, the children played quietly in the bedroom so they wouldn't disturb what they called God's work. At the same time, Brenda continued to make phone calls and feed the information she was gleaning back to her Idaho team and to her co-writer, Kay, in Mexico. And with each person found, there continued to be an explosion of gratitude as they all rejoiced together.

As the days progressed, Tim, Brenda's husband, grew used to the shouts of excitement, and each time it happened, he smiled and said, "Thank you, Jesus!" But since the fax machine was in his office, he began shouting each time a signed release form came in and immediately stopped whatever he was doing and took it to Brenda. Once again, there were prayers of thanksgiving as one more name was scratched off the list.

On Wednesday and Thursday, the team worked from dawn until the wee morning hours of the next day. They spent so many hours searching for these people and trying to think of different ways to find them that they not only thought of the survivors every minute of their waking hours, but they dreamed about them, too.

The stories of how the names were found are truly amazing. Sometimes Brenda would go through thirty names that Denise and Brenda Marie had found before she finally located someone who knew the person they were searching for. The Idaho team at times googled all the neighbors. That's how they found Nancy Fitzsimmons, who knew where Wilbur LaFleur lived (see chapter 5). Nancy not only knew Wilbur, but because he couldn't be reached by phone, she ended up running over to his house more than a dozen times to try to catch him at home. His stepson, Joseph Heckler—the last person to be found—was located by finally talking to his girlfriend, Alane Vix, who knew how to reach him in Iraq!

Once Brenda even called the fire department of a certain town because Rhonda West had mentioned it in her story. "Do you know Rhonda West?" she asked. She finally found a fireman who said, "I don't know her, but I think I know her sister." And the contact was made!

As the week went on, Brenda Marie, who is very shy and would rather do the research than talk to people, began making exploratory calls. This itself was a major step out of her comfort zone. At one point she called a neighbor of Brenda Ashton. She said to the man who answered, "Hello, this is Brenda Abbott, calling on behalf of Brenda Walsh. I'm trying to locate Brenda Ashton."

The man exclaimed, "Are you crazy?" and hung up! Brenda Marie called Brenda Walsh and said, "I think you're going to have to make this call and do some explaining!"

Brenda called the man back. "Hello. Please don't hang up! This is not a crank call. This really is Brenda Walsh, and I'm trying to locate Brenda Ashton to ask her to sign a release for a book. Do you know her?"

All in all, it was a pretty incredible week. Here's what Denise said about this experience:

When we offered to help with this project, little did I know how it would affect my life. After all, our part was only to help locate the people so their stories and pictures could be in the book. I had no idea that finding these people would become very personal and that their stories would weave their way into my heart and life. When after many hours of searching we would run into a dead end, it was almost like the death of a dear friend, and then we would find someone and jubilantly celebrate. That invigorated us, and we would return to the list of people we couldn't find and try again. There were times we even used the very same search sites, and after prayer, miraculously their names would appear!

In visiting with these precious people, I heard some of their stories firsthand, and there are no words that could ever be put to paper that could truly tell the story of their terror, pain, loss, and hopelessness—or their determination to live again. Their stories inspired me to look beyond myself and reach out to help others. They taught me that there is a God who loves us very much and that in life's darkest moments, He will give us the courage we need to survive.

One lady I talked to I will never forget, and her story is not even in this book. She was a neighbor of Wilbur LaFleur, who lost his wife, Connie, in the storm. We must have spent a half hour on the phone talking as she shared her story. She apologized for crying on the shoulder of a stranger. She may never know that it was I who received the blessing that day.

And it wasn't just Denise and Brenda Marie whom God used to find all the people whose signatures were needed for the book. There was an angel from Michigan by the name of Joyce Stevenson, who

In Michigan, Joyce Stevenson joined the challenge of finding people and getting information.

helped find the people in the stories that Brenda's brother, Pastor Ken Micheff, had related to us. Four stories, in particular, were especially challenging. Two of these stories were about people Pastor Ken had not even met, making it extremely difficult to find the person the story actually happened to. How do you find people who know the people, who know the people, that the story happened to? This seemed impossible, but God had a plan for this challenge, too.

Pastor Ken told his sister that the person she should contact was Joyce Stevenson, who had been on the mission trip with him. After just a few minutes on the phone with Brenda, Joyce willingly rolled up her sleeves and asked, "What can I do?"

She started by going through all her notes from the trip. She searched for any connecting pieces that might trigger a memory. She made dozens of phone calls to people who had been on the Gulf Coast mission. "Do you remember this story? Do you remember what street you may have been working on?" She had people look at their photographs for clues. The person behind one story was found by enlarging two photographs from two different people. Someone had a picture of the house, and when it was enlarged, you could make out the house number. Another had a picture of the street sign, and when enlarged, you could read the name. When Brenda took that information to her Idaho team, they searched the Internet for every address in Mississippi until the correct town came up. They had a match!

After all the addresses were located and contacts made, the next hurdle came. These people had no way to receive the release forms and fax them back in order to meet the one-week deadline. Their computers and fax machines had been destroyed in the storm. In some cases, they had no means of transportation. Now it was God's time to send in a few more of His special angels!

Brenda next called Renee Aue-Weaver, her contact at the Morrell Foundation in Waveland. "Do you have any volunteers that you can spare to go over and get some release forms signed?"

"As a matter of fact," Renee said, "I have someone right here. Let me ask."

Within seconds Brenda was speaking with Keli Forbeck.

After Brenda started to explain who she was and what she needed, Keli interrupted. "I know exactly who you are. I just heard you preach in Fletcher, North Carolina. And I also know your family. Your brother Ken was my Bible teacher in academy, and your sister Linda was my girl's dean. I'll be more than happy to get the release forms. You just tell me what you need and I'm on my way!"

Brenda was in shock. This was no mere coincidence. There was no question in her mind but that Keli was a significant part of God's plan for this book. Keli, with her husband, Mike, made numerous trips to the homes to get the release forms signed. Just to catch the people at home was a major challenge. In some cases they waited for up to two hours in front of a house praying for the person to return. Others required numerous trips. For one person, they ended up driving to a town a half hour away and meeting her at work. For another, they were told that if they could get to the lady's house in the next fifteen minutes, she would sign. They ran to their car to make this deadline, but their car wouldn't start. They turned the key again and again. Nothing. The engine wouldn't even turn over. *What was wrong?* The car had been running perfectly all day. They knew they had only a few minutes or they would never make it. They looked at each other and decided to pray. Then, with one more turn of the key, the engine started up instantly. Just one more of God's miracles.

And that wasn't all the Forbecks did. When they heard that a few more pictures were needed, they cheerfully drove back to the homes to snap the photos. And then, if that wasn't enough, they drove a half hour to a location where they could download the pictures from their camera onto a computer so they could be emailed to Brenda. Nothing short of amazing!

Mike and Keli Forbeck with their children, Ashley and Michael. Mike and Keli went the extra mile getting release forms signed and photographs taken.

Renee, a volunteer herself at the Morrell Foundation, was deeply involved in Keli's and Mike's adventures in getting the signed release forms and pictures. She knew they were looking for Red. In fact, Brenda had called everyone she could think of to be on the lookout for him. Renee was in the process of helping a busload of spring vacation volunteers get situated when she saw Red drive up. She dropped everything and ran to him for his signature. As it turned out, Red ended up getting a signature that no one else could have gotten, because the person had worked with Red and trusted him.

And so it was, with everyone's help, that around noon on Thursday, March 9, exactly one week after the search began, Brenda called Kay with excitement ringing in her voice, "God did it! Can you believe it! God gave us every single name we needed—and so much more."

We now knew why God had impressed the publisher to make such a bold decision as to not publish the book without release signatures. In the process of finding these wonderful people, Brenda was able to talk with each person, pray with them, check out their story as we had written it, correct the spelling of their names, clarify misleading information, and, in a number of cases, add significant details that we hadn't known before. In addition, we were able to get pictures of the people and places that we weren't able to get previously!

Wow, was God good! We made many, many new friends through this process. Hundreds of people who wouldn't have known about *Between Hell and High Water* are now waiting anxiously for its release, eager to read the stories of the survivors whom they helped to locate. And we even got a few new—and we must add—incredible stories!

God knew that when we thought the book was finished—it wasn't! Now, we feel confident that the stories are ready to be told to the world. And as a bonus, we have an incredible testimony. Because of our experience finding the names that everyone knew were impossible to find, we can encourage others that no matter what happens in life—when you feel you're stuck between hell and high water—GOD IS THERE! Never forget that *with God, nothing is impossible!*

God also impressed us with His truth in Jeremiah 29:11. God has a plan for each of our lives. He knows what's best for us. Now we are even more passionate to let others know that God has a plan for them, too. It may not be what we *want* to do, but if we're willing to be willing, and willing to be obedient to His call, we will end up rejoicing—as we are doing at this very moment as we end this book. Our prayer is that this will be your experience, as well. May God richly bless you.

—Kay Kuzma and Brenda Walsh

The Brenda Walsh Story
Battered to Blessed
Brenda Walsh with Kay D. Rizzo

At 18, after a whirlwind courtship and marriage, Brenda found herself at the mercy of a deceptive, cruel husband whose rage and escalating violence threatened her very life and endangered the safety of her baby.

Battered to Blessed is Brenda's amazing journey from pain to peace and to loving again, trusting again, and living a whole new life of incredible joy in Jesus.
0-8163-2067-5   US$14.99

Also available as a 3ABN audio book: *Battered to Blessed* 6-CD set
4333003793   US$21.95

Mending Broken People
Kay Kuzma

Mending Broken People shares the miracle stories of the Three Angels Broadcasting Network (3ABN). See how God led in the establishment of this ministry, and continues to lead in lives touched and blessings given and received.
Paper, 384 pages.   0-8163-2066-7   US$19.99

The First Seven Years
Kay Kuzma, Ed.D.

The first seven years of your child's life are critical years of growth and development. Dr. Kuzma offers her considerable knowledge and expertise to parents.
Paper, 688 pages.   0-8163-2087-X   US$29.99

Micheff Sisters Cookbooks
As seen on 3ABN
Cooking With the Micheff Sisters

A vegan cookbook that proves that good taste and good health can go together. More than 100 recipes. Includes nutritional information. Color photographs.
Paper, 240 pages.   0-8163-1994-4   US$16.99

Cooking Entrees With the Micheff Sisters

The Micheff sisters bring you recipies for delicious, elegant entrees made with vegan ingredients. Put a fantastic dinner on the table tonight with a minimum of fuss and a maximum of flavor. More than 120 recipes. Includes nutritional information. Color photographs.
0-8163-2135-3   US$16.99

Order from your ABC by calling **1-800-765-6955**, or get online and shop our virtual store at <**www.AdventistBookCenter.com**>.
• Read a chapter from your favorite book
• Order online
• Sign up for email notices on new products